THE HEAVY BEAR WHO GOES WITH ME

For Kate FitzPatrick,
from both of us

The Heavy Bear
Who Goes with Me

edited by
BRENDAN KENNELLY
& NEIL ASTLEY

BLOODAXE BOOKS

ISBN: 978 1 85224 440 8

First published 2022 by
Bloodaxe Books Ltd,
Eastburn,
South Park,
Hexham,
Northumberland NE46 1BS.

www.bloodaxebooks.com
For further information about Bloodaxe titles
please visit our website and join our mailing list
or write to the above address for a catalogue.

Supported by
**ARTS COUNCIL
ENGLAND**

Printed in Great Britain by Bell & Bain Limited, Glasgow, Scotland, on
acid-free paper sourced from mills with FSC chain of custody certification.

CONTENTS

PREFACE

The Making of the Heavy Bear

I began working with Brendan Kennelly on this anthology over 25 years ago. We started talking about the idea of such a book in the spring of 1996 when I was in Dublin for Trinity College's celebrations for his 60th birthday that April, and began sharing poems by post, sending each other photocopies and logging our choices in a growing wishlist. We took our title from Delmore Schwartz's poem 'The Heavy Bear Who Goes with Me' [19], in which the poet is in conversation with himself, as Brendan describes in the essay which follows this preface, written to serve as our book's introduction.

That July he headed for his summer retreat at Collins's Cottage by the beach at Ballybunion in Co. Kerry with Kate FitzPatrick where he immersed himself in reading and re-reading the poems which had accrued from our exchanges. As the waves crashed and sizzled outside, Kate sat listening to him reading the poems aloud, always the best test of poetry with staying power. Half way through their stay he wrote to me:

> Some of the best poems in English (from England) are built on an I/You relationship – the rarest and most difficult there is (apart, perhaps, but I'm not sure, from the mad internalities). So 'Ode to a Nightingale' [152] might be put near Shelley's 'Skylark' (is it an ode too?) with its direct opening 'Hail to thee': – and if we accept this way of looking at Shakespeare, why not 'Shall I compare thee to a summer's day'? I know it's used a lot, but I've never read a really fresh essay on it, or about it.
>
> This I/You is in 'Dover Beach' [176] also – 'Come to the window'. The entire meditation of that poem is coloured by this presence, this relationship. Kavanagh's 'Spring Day' is a direct address to poets ('O come all ye youthful poets and try to be more human'), and it would altogether strengthen the sense that the anthology should have of both questioning and strengthening the humanity of the reader. I would see this as a crucial poem/ statement to poets, to young people, to all readers really. The new Penguin Selected Poems by Kavanagh has this poem on pp.90-91. Do you make music? I mean do you compose it? 'Spring Day' should be set to music. It's a singing, frontal, daring message.
>
> [21 July 1996, page numbers added by me]

11

In the event, Kavanagh's 'Spring Day' was to be supplanted by his 'Epic' [270], and Shakespeare's sonnet 18 gave way to sonnet 73 [48], while Shelley's 'Skylark' was pushed out by his 'Ode to the West Wind' [146] as the dynamic Brendan wanted the anthology to embody was fleshed out between us. We wanted to produce a reader's companion, a book to go with the reader, holding conversations with anyone who opened it. The plan was that Brendan would talk about the particular poem we'd chosen, and I would tell the reader about the poet and give some background on the poem. My note would appear first, providing biographical or historical context, but I could only write it when I had Brendan's commentary.

A week later (28 July 1996) he wrote again from Ballybunion after I'd expressed doubts about the Housman poem he wanted us to include [215], continuing to develop his thoughts about the ethos of the book:

> When you devour this, may we begin to cut and shape, include/ exclude, and get the best poems we can, with the sort of inner echoing resonance that's in both our minds. Themes like I/You, love, death, violence, England, Ireland, America, poetry, language, are already coming through. Our problem may well be to allow this anthology to achieve its proper ultimate precision, which we must try to define.
>
> I'm enjoying the reading a great deal, and loving, as I always did, that passion that can exist only when form insists on coming into being. It's impossible, then, to tell the difference between them, in fact they both seem to vanish, and what is left is poetry. I think the anthology will contain a fair amount of such poetry.
>
> I'm seeing poems in my sleep these nights, like fish on the ceiling, laughing and dancing. And me without a drop of Jameson's.
>
> I have no way of keeping a copy of this list, so here's hoping it doesn't get lost in Dublin!

The list wasn't the only thing lost on his return to Dublin. His health deteriorated and that October – when he was to have been working with actors in Newcastle on his new version of Lorca's *Blood Wedding* – he underwent a quadruple heart bypass operation, experiencing the 'I/You' visions he describes in *The Man Made of Rain* (1998). That winter *The Heavy Bear Who Goes With Me* went into the first of several hibernations.

The following summer found Brendan back in Ballybunion with Kate, getting back into reading for our *Bear* while recuperating, sharing thoughts about our 'anthology of echoes' in phone conversations, and through exchanges of letters and annotated photocopies of poems, including this comment on our still evolving list:

> When I say 'I want', 'I think' etc, on the enclosed, that's what I mean, but in the context of knowing that there are two footballers at work here. I have to say, or try to say, exactly what I envision, so that you can agree or disagree or demolish or support or whatever. In other words, there's no real cooperation without me sharing my prejudices, 'tastes' etc in the most forthright way. So the next time we meet, please don't step back a few yards and then give me a running kick in the arse. [4 July 1997]

Brendan didn't avail himself then of the famed Collins's Seaweed Baths (established 1932) a stone's throw away, but a week later he came back refreshed from his morning paddle, his standing in the sea (he couldn't swim), with these further thoughts on the book:

> I think Marvell has a poem that is a dialogue between Self and Soul. It's a good one (years since I read it, thought of it in the sea this morning, then thought of Yeats's 'A Dialogue of Self and Soul'). Then I thought of a possible architecture for the book, based loosely on themes, not obvious, but there, echoing, resonant. I'm just putting forward some possibilities to you.
>
> 1) Love / Sex / Identity / the other. This expanding theme would let poems be themselves, but also connect them, echoing to other poems, 'scattered' (but deliberately placed) throughout the book.
>
> 2) Death / Separation / Division / Isolation / Partition. The sense of failure/cynicism (as death of the sense of values)/
>
> 3) Land / Place / Territory / Country / Rivers / Mountains / Maps of the Spirit / Being lost / Being found / Visitors / the sea. Poems that deal with movement, energy. Stillness.
>
> 4) Hatred / Fierce and primitive forms of self-animation / Enemies / Disconnection / Sure ground of knowing what and when to despise / Racial intolerance / Fear of altruism / Poems that try to define egotism, its necessity and its horror.
>
> 5) Sickness and health.
>
> 6) Mindflow. Joycean/Proustean poems.
>
> 7) Family.
>
> 8) The experience of being haunted, accompanied, bruised, manipulated, bullied, inspired, pushed about, used as someone's raw material for ends not known yet sensed (the Heavy Bear, but there are some light bears also). 'My conscience or my vanity appalled.'[1]
>
> 'That goes with me' –

13

Movement, accompaniment, being pressed and haunted, discovering echoes everywhere (this must be an echoing book, not just good poems, there must be a policy of haunting or insinuating connective resonances behind the reader's eyes, so that two or three poems will flash befoe his/her eyes when they see a child at the edge of knowing something, or a broken bicycle tied to green railings, or hear a fascist murmur from a docile mouth).

I'm writing this to you, Neil, because, like yourself, I want this anthology to be risk-taking in its sureness. That sureness must have a strong yet flexible structure so that the risks will be dramatic, exciting, mind-catching.

[11 July 1997]

We wanted this anthology to embody our conviction that poetry is a force for change and that critical response is an engagement with that change in all its complexity. It is poetry as living company which enables us as readers 'to define the ripples and storms that happen in solitude and then go with us into the ordered mayhem of life'.

By the end of July 1997 our discussions and disputations had left us with a list of 167 poems. We talked at length about possible thematic arrangements drawing on the ideas he'd put forward in his letters, but none of them felt right for the whole book.

Instead we agreed that poems would be ordered chronologically according to when they were written; or if that wasn't known, then by date of first publication, which wouldn't always be in a book. That way we could set up other kinds of surprises: not following the often misleading convention of ordering poems by a writer's year of birth, or by date of first publication in book form, which can often be many years after a poem has become known to readers and to other writers. This is shown by the date given after each poem: a date in italics indicates when a poem was written; a date in roman type in square brackets when it was first published.

We wanted to show that poets regarded as belonging to particular movements or periods in poetry (often designated years or centuries later) were sometimes writing at the same time as their supposed followers or predecessors; and how in several cases poets we now regard as major figures of particular periods were unpublished, unread or unknown in their own time. And we agreed that spellings in poems from the 16th, 17th and 18th centuries should be modernised to make them more accessible to our imagined reader.

Brendan was also writing his commentaries:

14

I enclose thirty-four efforts for you to knock into shape – including the essay/commentary/introduction on Schwartz. I'm planning to hit for Dublin in a few days.
[25 August 1997]

Those were half the commentaries Brendan was able to produce. Due to the demands on his time at Trinity and elsewhere, his progress on the *Bear* was slow over the next year. It was not just that other books he was working on needed to be completed – including a collection of new and "rescued" poems with 'Begin' as its title-poem – but as time went on new ideas came to him for other books in which he was soon immersed. This was to become one of the most productive periods of his writing life. At the same time he was giving numerous readings, talks, presentations and interviews on TV and radio, and not just in Ireland. Our next meetings had to be snatched after readings he gave in Cambridge and Middlesbrough in October 1998. We agreed to start cutting poems but ended up adding more than we dropped as we tried to bring in more contemporary poets.

By the time we touched base again on the project in the summer of 2000, with Brendan back with Kate in Ballybunion trying get back into the saddle of our *Bear*, we had 170 poems, but only 70 commentaries, few of these covering the later poets. Brendan also had another collection he was trying to finish, *Glimpses*. When that was published the following year, he was already working on his versions of the Roman poet Martial, published as *Martial Art* in 2003, and I was sidetracked into working on my own anthology, *Staying Alive*. That pattern continued, ensuring that our *Heavy Bear* was going nowhere, a realisation we came to regard as inevitable as Brendan's health suffered various setbacks. But we still talked about the book as if it was going to happen someday, when we both had time to complete it.

He went on to publish seven more books, one of these – *The Essential Brendan Kennelly* – assembled with his blessing by his friends Terence Brown and Michael Longley, and launched on his 75th birthday in 2011. But when *Guff* followed in 2013, I realised that this would be his last collection. The public row over a contentious biography published earlier that year had taken its toll on his general health. He had already retired from teaching some years earlier, which relieved him of much of his Trinity workload, and he was taking on fewer public engagements, but he missed the stimulation of engaging with students. He was used to walking around Dublin day and night, talking to anyone he met, but found himself unable to walk as far. Eventually his exhaustion left him mostly marooned in new rooms in the college, where he suffered a series of falls, ending up in St James's Hospital. I saw him there at the start of his long road to recovery, which led to him later leaving his adoptive city of Dublin for his beloved native Kerry.

Within a few months of moving into a care home outside Listowel, his condition had stabilised. He was seeing family every day, and visitors could take him on outings. It was there that I met up with him next. Brendan wanted his sister Nancy to take us to some of his favourite places – places I knew from his poems – so we went on a drive around his parish, taking in Ballylongford where he was born, Lislaughtin Abbey where his mother and father were buried (and where he now lays), and the Ladies Beach at Ballybunion, where he'd begun working on our *Heavy Bear* over twenty years earlier.

He was still living with poems in the care home, reciting his own poems and those of the poets he loved to residents and visitors alike, but my sense was that he'd really benefit from the stimulation which engaging again more fully with the work of the poets he loved might provide. Inspired by our visit to Ballybunion, I decided it was time to bring 'the ould Bear', as he called it, out of hibernation, to revive it as best we could. Those wonderful, lively commentaries he'd written to share with readers were lying in a folder in a filing cabinet in my office, and they also needed to be liberated and re-united with the poems which had inspired their writing. We would cut our selection down to a hundred poems and fill in the missing commentaries. The next time I visited him – in April 2018 – I brought with me copies of some of the commentaries he'd written years earlier and explained my plan. He read the pieces and thought they were excellent commentaries on poems he knew well, but he couldn't remember writing them. 'Did I write these?' he asked me quizzically, sitting over coffee in the Listowel Arms. He even responded by reciting from memory whole chunks of the poems he'd written about in those commentaries, but didn't think he'd be able to write about the other poems now, for all that he still loved them and lived with them. Not to be deterred, I left photocopies of some of the other poems with him in the hope that his misgivings might prove to be misplaced, and that this would be something he might enjoy working on. I also gave copies of the poems to Kate, who tried to get him talking about the poems when she came down to see him, with the idea of recording what he might say about them, even if he wasn't up to writing more commentaries. But all to no avail. He still knew and loved those poems by Yeats, Kavanagh and many others we'd selected, but they would have to speak for themselves.

However, Brendan had written about many of the poets we'd wanted to include in other places, in lectures, essays and reviews as well as in the course of our correspondence. Having cut the number of poems back to 100, I set about finding comments by him from many different sources to fill in the gaps, helped by Åke Persson's edition of Brendan's selected prose, *Journey into Joy*,[2] by Åke's bibliography in Richard Pine's critical anthology *Dark Fathers into Light: Brendan Kennelly*,[3] and by John McDonagh sending me copies of reviews listed by Åke which I hoped might include Brendan's responses to individual poems. In some cases I had to change the poem we'd chosen in order to include Brendan's response to that poet's work, but since the poem now substituted was one he loved, I didn't think that mattered too much.

The main casualties in the cuts I had to make were poets from the past fifty years. Without Brendan's responses it no longer felt necessary to include a good many of those poems, nor to make the book as representative as we'd hoped it would be for the modern period. Being conceived a quarter of a century ago, I'm only too aware that our selection isn't sufficiently diverse, and that some of our choices might feel curiously old-fashioned now, among them poems which Brendan grew up with. Conversely, we did pick poets like Charlotte Mew whose work has since become much more widely appreciated.

My short introductions are intended to provide context for Brendan's commentary on the poem which follows it, but for poems lacking his response I have in some cases not written my own introductory note but borrowed one, or part of one, from another editor's Bloodaxe anthology. These are signalled with a square block ahead of the quoted commentary. It has long been my practice when commissioning editors to ask them to include such succinct

17

summaries in our books in order to give readers helpful context, so where another editor more familiar with the work of a particular poet had already written a better introductory note than I could manage, I decided to draw upon their expertise. I would like to thank these editors for unknowingly contributing to their publisher's anthology: Robyn Bolam,[4] W.N. Herbert and Matthew Hollis,[5] Edna Longley[6] and Deryn Rees-Jones.[7] Their contributions add to this book's multiplicity of voices, making it even more of a treasure trove of poems and talk about poetry. Some of my notes also adapt what I have written about the poets in other books.

I would like to thank Kate FitzPatrick, midwife to the *Bear*, who was always to have this book's dedication, for her input and assistance in so many areas, as well as Peter and Margaret Lewis for sharing their recollections of Brendan, Tracey Herd for her suggestions, and Geraldine Mangan, Brendan's ever dependable secretary at Trinity, not just for typing out his sometimes difficult to decipher handwritten commentaries for the *Bear* but also for her impeccable work in typing the manuscripts for all of his books for three decades. And I must thank Åke Persson, and the Brendan Kennelly Literary Trust, and in particular Brendan's ever helpful nieces Bridget (who proof-read the whole book) and Mary McAuliffe.

The work involved in reviving this project and producing the book took a couple more years. I had intended that we should publish it for Brendan's 85th birthday in April 2021, but a further obstacle prevented our *Heavy Bear* from making his way into the world: publication needed to be supported by bookshops across Ireland, and they were all closed due to the pandemic. So we took the decision to defer publication for another year, and in April 2022 I would drive down to Listowel again and present Brendan with his copy of the book on his birthday. I feel very sad that he never got to see the fruits of his labour of love from decades ago.

We had no idea then that these conversations would take so long to be completed, or that reading Brendan's commentaries now – after his only too recent passing – I would feel that he is still talking to me, and to everyone else, about the poems he loves. Brendan may no longer be with us in the flesh but we can still celebrate being able to hear him again, talking to us in his own highly individual and inimitable way from these pages.

NEIL ASTLEY

DELMORE SCHWARTZ (1913-66)

The Heavy Bear Who Goes with Me
'the withness of the body'

The heavy bear who goes with me,
A manifold honey to smear his face,
Clumsy and lumbering here and there,
The central ton of every place,
The hungry beating brutish one
In love with candy, anger, and sleep,
Crazy factotum, dishevelling all,
Climbs the building, kicks the football,
Boxes his brother in the hate-ridden city.

Breathing at my side, that heavy animal,
That heavy bear who sleeps with me,
Howls in his sleep for a world of sugar,
A sweetness intimate as the water's clasp,
Howls in his sleep because the tight-rope
Trembles and shows the darkness beneath,
– The strutting show-off is terrified,
Dressed in his dress-suit, bulging his pants,
Trembles to think that his quivering meat
Must finally wince to nothing at all.

That inescapable animal walks with me,
Has followed me since the black womb held,
Moves where I move, distorting my gesture,
A caricature, a swollen shadow,
A stupid clown of the spirit's motive,
Perplexes and affronts with his own darkness,
The secret life of belly and bone,
Opaque, too near, my private, yet unknown,
Stretches to embrace the very dear
With whom I would walk without him near,

Touches her grossly, although a word
Would bare my heart and make me clear,
Stumbles, flounders, and strives to be fed
Dragging me with him in his mouthing care,
Amid the hundred million of his kind,
The scrimmage of appetite everywhere.

[*In Dreams Begin Responsibilities*, 1938]

Delmore Schwartz (1913-66) was a precociously gifted but deeply troubled poet and prose writer whose work gave voice to the disillusion and disappointment of mid 20th-century America. Born in Brooklyn of Romanian Jewish immigrant parents, Delmore (as he was always known) established his reputation early with the publication of a short story, 'In Dreams Begin Responsibilities', in the first issue of *Partisan Review* in 1937. His debut book of poems and prose with the same title followed in 1938, and was praised by T.S. Eliot, Ezra Pound and William Carlos Williams. But early promise gave way to burn-out as alcohol, drugs (barbiturates), depression (bipolar) and mental instability took their toll. Twice divorced, he lost touch with friends and ended up living in a seedy New York hotel, dying there from a heart attack. His body lay unclaimed in the morgue for two days. As his biographer James Atlas later wrote: 'Over a quarter of a century, Schwartz had gone from a literary Adonis to a derelict stumbling in the street.'

An inventive self-mythologiser whose work was neglected for many years after his early death, his influence on other writers, including Robert Lowell, John Berryman, Randall Jarrell and John Ashbery, came both from his work and from the man himself. The paranoid protagonist of Saul Bellow's novel *Humboldt's Gift* (1975) is a savage portrait of Schwartz in his declining years. He features in two poems by Lowell, a dozen of Berryman's 'Dream Songs', and two songs by his one-time Syracuse student Lou Reed. Bono's song 'Acrobat' on U2's *Achtung Baby* (1991) is a later tribute.

In 'Dream Song #149' Berryman recalls 'the brightness of his promise [...] blazing with insight, warm with gossip'; while in 'Dream Song #157', he has to let him go:

Ten Songs, one solid block of agony,
I wrote for him, and then I wrote no more.
His sad ghost must aspire
free of my love to its own post, that ghost,
among its fellows, Mozart's, Bach's, Delmore's
free of its careful body [...]

His work downhill, I don't conceal from you,
ran and ran out. The brain shook as if stunned,
I hope he's over that,

flame may his glory in that other place,
for he was fond of fame, devoted to it [...][8]

BK ▪ The notion and the feeling of 'withness' are at the core of
'The Heavy Bear Who Goes with Me' and are embodied in both
the title and the phrase Schwartz places at its head: 'the withness of
the body'. Schwartz endures and communicates eloquent, sensitive,
depressed witness to the 'withness' of the heavy bear who goes
everywhere, and at all times, *with* him. This heavy bear, this gross,
lumbering, hungry, brutish, clumsy presence, this disheveller 'In
love with candy, anger, and sleep' is Schwartz's constant company,
weighing him down, inescapable, sleeping with him, moving where
he moves, breathing forever at his side, a 'Crazy factotum', a gross
caricature, a perverse parody of ordinary, orderly, decent humanity.
This gross, endless presence 'Howls in his sleep for a world of
sugar' but howls also because he's aware of 'the darkness beneath'.
Towards the end of the second stanza, the poem concentrates on
the fact that this heavy bear is 'terrified' because he knows that
'his quivering meat / Must finally wince to nothing at all'.

The bear is endlessly terrified and endlessly menacing, clownishly
distorting 'the spirit's motive', at once perplexing and 'too near'.
In the third and final stanza, this stumbling, threatening, bestial
presence 'Stretches to embrace the very dear / With whom I would
walk without him near'.

The bear violates his love.

It is here, I think, that we realise very clearly – this moment of
clarification, this Joycean epiphany has been building up through-
out the poem – that the heavy bear is Schwartz, Schwartz's body,
Schwartz's own grossness and fear which he might express, bring

out into the open since he is fully aware that 'a word / Would bare my heart and make me clear'.

Instead, he stumbles and flounders on in the eternal 'withness' of the heavy bear's company; he is dragged by the bear, conscious now most of all of the fact that this hideous withness is a universal fact, and is endlessly, relentlessly growing and expanding like an appetite, the kind of appetite that is never satisfied, the kind that grows the more it feeds. In the final line, Schwartz uses the phrase 'the scrimmage of appetite'. A scrimmage is a brawl, a row, a confused struggle. Scrimmage is also a term used in American football; it's a sequence of play which begins by placing the ball on the ground with its longest axis at right angles to the goal-line. In the first stanza, Schwartz says the bear 'kicks the football'. This commitment to brawling, skirmishing, rough tactics is another strong thread throughout the poem.

We have chosen the title of this poem as the anthology's title, for several reasons. Poems are written because of various kinds of 'withness'; the sense of mortality, failure in love, the challenge of history, the nature of consciousness, dreams, loneliness, prejudice, inexplicable hatreds, the urge to make sense of confusion, the seething need to protest against forms of injustice, to talk to somebody about things only partly grasped or understood, or not grasped or understood at all but hurtful and pressing, violating sleep, miscolouring daylight's encounters and images, the sense of suffering an appetite that can never really be fed.

Any anthology powered by curiosity, by the sense of enquiry, as this one is, must try to find poems that, though years or centuries or cultures or continents apart, are nevertheless bonded in their determination to question, to investigate the sources, nature and consequences of 'withness' in its troubling and multiple manifestations. To live with Schwartz's poem (reading is itself a form of intense, concentrated 'withness') is to undergo both a sense of oppression and of enlightenment; one soon realises that this enlightenment is born of living with the sense of oppression. This is true of many poems closely read and, more importantly, re-read; the poem's darkness spawns the mind's light. Poetry is a kind of pitiless education; but one must reach endlessly for that pitilessness because comforting lies are everywhere and endlessly available.

Schwartz deals implacably with his body in 'The Heavy Bear

Who Goes with Me'. Only once is the spirit mentioned; in the third stanza when the heavy bear is referred to as a 'stupid clown of the spirit's motive'.

Somewhere in this poem, or in the forces that generated it, is a buried and wounded spirit, a fineness of feeling, thought and expression. The insistence on the bear's awful, pressing, overwhelming physicality is clearly linked with that once-mentioned spirit and its hurt.

How much poetry is born of hurt? And what, precisely, *is* hurt? The spirit? The heart? The hope we have but can hardly bring ourselves to utter? When we call the body, or the heavy bear, 'clumsy', 'lumbering', 'gross', 'crazy', 'inescapable', 'stupid', are we also silently thinking of ideals of elegance, decorum, style, intelligence and beauty? Is there a silent battle going on, a battle which provides the birthing of the poem? How much of a poem's meaning is rooted in this silence?

It's a brief step from that rootedness to the notion that poetry is largely dialogue, even a dialogue with silence. Poems are usually talking to somebody, something, some feeling or picture, some memory, dream or idea. Yet they often sound, not like dialogues, but monologues. Schwartz doesn't speak directly to the heavy bear; he refers constantly to it in the third person, distancing himself. But the sense of pained intimate address in the poem is so powerful as to be almost overwhelming.

Many of the poems in this anthology are based on the conviction that poetry is a kind of dialogue, a way of talking *to* somebody or something other, either beyond or within the self. It is a kind of passionate, deeply private connection in a world characterised by the scrimmage of disconnection. And this connection extends beyond individual poems. Poems, far apart in time, by poets who have perhaps never read each other's work, can set up a dialogue with each other in a reader's mind, creating a climate of contrast and comparison, discussion and shared analysis. This is a calm, continuing drama of ever-deepening, enlightened connection. Poetry itself is a kind of 'withness'; it goes with us through life, not heavily but lightly, touching memory and imagination in its delicate, firm way. There are moments, though, when it is more hair-raising than the heavy bear could ever be.

Many of the poems included here are evidence of the connection made possible because the poets undertook to explore feelings, ideas, perceptions and images that tend to present themselves to the imagination working in a state of aloneness. Connection, therefore, is the fruit of this aloneness allowed to shape itself in language, nurtured by words. This argues a continuing life in the imagination which has to be sustained in its own momentum despite disabling periods brought on by lethargy, illness, lies, or even by forms of responsibility and work. Every poem is an act of faith in that imaginative momentum; every poem longs to connect with that energy whether it be pressingly immediate or blatently ignored. This is the connecting power that enables Schwartz, for example, to bring the heavy bear lumbering into our lives. Our dialogue with the gross, barging presence follows that moment of admission.

Our hope, as editors, is that we have provided an anthology of poems marked by dialogue and connection, although these poems may be, usually are, born of the awareness of mortality, failure, inadequacy, loss, absurd or gross caricatures or perversions of what we take to be reality. Why not have it out, once and for all, with the heavy bear who goes with us?

SIR THOMAS WYATT (1503–1542)

'They flee from me that sometime did me seek'

They flee from me that sometime did me seek
With naked foot stalking in my chamber.
I have seen them gentle, tame and meek
That now are wild and do not remember
That sometime they put themself in danger
To take bread at my hand; and now they range
Busily seeking with a continual change.

Thanked be fortune, it hath been otherwise
Twenty times better, but once in special,
In thin array after a pleasant guise,
When her loose gown from her shoulders did fall,
And she me caught in her arms long and small,
Therewith all sweetly did me kiss,
And softly said 'Dear heart, how like you this?'

It was no dream: I lay broad waking.
But all is turned through my gentleness
Into a strange fashion of forsaking.
And I have leave to go, of her goodness
And she also to use newfangleness.
But since that I so kindly am served
I would fain know what she hath deserved.

Sir Thomas Wyatt was a poet and diplomat in the court of Henry VIII. He was the first great English lyric poet, and introduced the sonnet, terza rima and ottava rima into English poetry, drawing on Italian models, principally the work of Petrarch. He narrowly missed execution because of his relationships with Anne Boleyn and later with his mistress Elizabeth Darnell, maid of honour to Katherine of Aragon, as well as his association with Thomas Cromwell, and was imprisoned for treason after Cromwell's execution in 1541. Like other court poets of Tudor times, he circulated his poems in manuscript among friends. His poetry wasn't published in book form until 1557. This poem may be an imitation of Ovid's *Amores* III, 7.

BK ■ Wyatt carries a nagging burden of what Delmore Schwartz called 'witness': living with the fact that he has changed, or been forced to change, from being a desirable lover to a repulsive object, in the eyes of those women who actively pursued him 'with naked foot stalking within my chamber'. To go from being sought after to being avoided is dramatically depicted over three stanzas. The poem speaker's plight is condensed into the poem's opening line:

> They flee from me that sometime did me seek

There's a collective, pluralistic feeling in this first stanza; further, there's a primitive, animalistic throb, a sense of creatures stalking their prey, even using self-endangering devices or postures to achieve their ends, their prize. But they're gone now, ranging 'wild', seeking different sexual prey.

From that pluralistic climate we turn, in the second stanza, to a very particular situation. This is intimate, sexually warm and sweet. One woman, out of all the crowd, lives in his memory. She

> all sweetly did me kiss,
> And softly said 'Dear heart, how like you this?'

But now, 'all is turned' into 'forsaking'. This desolate feeling of being forsaken fills the third and final stanza. Ironically, Wyatt says that it is his 'gentleness' which has brought this about, and has made him a victim of the search for 'newfangleness'. His gentleness puts him outside the prowling sexuality of those in search of 'continual change'; and the poem ends with the quiet irony of his private speculation concerning her who once said softly 'Dear heart, how like you this?' before forsaking him for 'newfangleness' (inconstancy). The calm, ironic wondering of the sexual outcast fills these final lines:

> But since that I so kindly am served,
> I would fain know what she hath deserved.

This poem creates a memorable portrait of the sexual pariah, the person quietly enduring sexual rejection and aloneness. It is a portrait marked by considerable self-knowledge and no self-pity.

HENRY HOWARD, EARL OF SURREY (1517–1547)

'Wyatt resteth here'

Wyatt resteth here, that quick could never rest;
Whose heavenly gifts increasèd by disdain
And virtue sank the deeper in his breast:
Such profit he by envy could obtain.

A head, where wisdom mysteries did frame;
Whose hammers beat still in that lively brain
As on a stithe, where that some work of fame
Was daily wrought to turn to Britain's gain.

A visage stern and mild; where both did grow,
Vice to condemn, in virtue to rejoice:
Amid great storms, whom grace assurèd so
To live upright and smile at fortune's choice.

A hand that taught what might be said in rhyme;
That reft Chaucer the glory of his wit;
A mark the which, unparfited for time,
Some may approach, but never none shall hit.

A tongue that served in foreign realms his king;
Whose courteous talk to virtue did enflame
Each noble heart; a worthy guide to bring
Our English youth by travail unto fame.

An eye, whose judgement none affect could blind,
Friends to allure, and foes to reconcile;
Whose piercing look did represent a mind
With virtue fraught, reposèd, void of guile.

stithe: anvil (also a forge or smithy); *unparfited for time:* unfinished for want
of time; *corse:* body

27

A heart, where dread was never so impressed
To hide the thought that might the truth advance;
In neither fortune lost nor yet repressed,
To swell in wealth, or yield unto mischance.

A valiant corse, where force and beauty met;
Happy, alas, too happy, but for foes;
Lived and ran the race that nature set;
Of manhood's shape, where she the mould did lose.

But to the heavens that simple soul is fled,
Which left with such as covet Christ to know
Witness of faith that never shall be dead;
Sent for our health, but not receivèd so.

Thus, for our guilt, this jewel have we lost.
The earth his bones, the heavens possess his ghost.

c. 1542 [1542]

Henry Howard, Earl of Surrey was elder son of the third Duke
of Norfolk. Wyatt and Surrey are often paired together as the
fathers of the English sonnet, Wyatt coming first with the Petrarchan
form and Surrey then developing what became known as the
Elizabethan or Shakespearian sonnet. Surrey also introduced blank
verse (unrhymed iambic pentameter) into English poetry in his
translations of Virgil. His tribute to Wyatt was probably his first
appearance in print, originally forming part of an eight-page
memorial pamphlet printed shortly after Wyatt's death in 1542.
    Surrey was another courtier who fell from grace in Henry's
court. Despite distinguishing himself in the king's campaigns in
France as well as in anti-invasion defences, he was out of favour
several times. In 1532 he married Lady Frances de Vere, daughter
of the Earl of Oxford, and they had five children. In 1536 he
witnessed the trial of his first cousin, Anne Boleyn; in 1537 he
was imprisoned at Windsor for striking Sir Edward Seymour; and
in 1542 he had to attend the execution of another first cousin, the

king's fifth wife, Catherine Howard. In 1543 he was imprisoned again, this time for riotous behaviour in the streets of London (eating flesh in Lent and breaking windows), but later that year served, with the Emperor Charles V, at the siege of Landrecy. Eventually the long-running family rivalry with the Seymours for the king's favours caused him to be charged with treason for allegedly plotting to have Henry's son Edward set aside when the king died and have the former heir apparent, his father the Duke of Norfolk, assume the throne. Like Wyatt, he was imprisoned in the Tower, becoming the last person to be executed on the orders of Henry VIII, in 1547, at the age of 30. His father was saved only because the king died before he could be executed. Surrey's elder son Thomas later became the fourth Duke of Norfolk, in 1554, and was beheaded in 1572 for plotting with Mary, Queen of Scots against Elizabeth.

BK ■ A tribute, to be convincing, should capture a sense of the total character of the person to whom the tribute is being paid. Some tributes degenerate into flattery and are ultimately empty, even incredible. The Earl of Surrey's tribute to Wyatt is moving because it conveys what feels like a complete portrait of the man. In this poem, Surrey presents Wyatt as a restless person finally at rest; a gifted, decent, wise and lively man. Wyatt is both stern and mild, graceful, intrepid, smiling, witty, hard-working, loyal, a courteous model for English youth, distinguished for his unifying power through the workings of a balanced mind and a truth-loving heart. And yet this man was rejected by his peers, arrested in 1541 on charges of treason and, though released soon after, was never again in favour. Wyatt died in 1542, struck down by a fever while on a diplomatic errand for the king.

Surrey's line, 'Thus, for our guilt, this jewel have we lost' gives a striking validity to his tribute to Wyatt because it means that in recognising Wyatt's intrinsic value, a strong element of self-accusation – and of accusation of an entire society – ends this poem. The honest portrayal of Wyatt's worth causes Surrey to question his own.

SIR PHILIP SIDNEY (1554-1586)

'Thou blind man's mark'

Thou blind man's mark, thou fool's self-chosen snare,
Fond fancy's scum, and dregs of scattered thought;
Band of all evils, cradle of causeless care;
Thou web of will, whose end is never wrought:
Desire! Desire! I have too dearly bought,
With price of mangled mind, thy worthless ware;
Too long, too long, asleep thou hast me brought,
Who shouldst my mind to higher things prepare.
But yet in vain thou hast my ruin sought,
In vain thou mad'st me to vain things aspire,
In vain thou kindlest all thy smoky fire,
For Virtue hath this better lesson taught:
Within myself to seek my only hire,
Desiring nought but how to kill Desire.

c. 1581 [1591]

Sir Philip Sidney was a courtier, soldier and poet, the eldest son
of Sir Henry Sidney and his wife, Lady Mary Dudley, daughter
of the Duke of Northumberland, and godson of King Philip II of
Spain. His uncle Robert Dudley, Earl of Leicester, was one of
Queen Elizabeth's most trusted advisors, while his wife Frances
was the daughter of her secretary of state, Sir Francis Walsingham.
  Sidney became the quintessential Elizabethan gentleman, an
excellent horseman who aspired to a life of heroic action but was
mostly confined to ceremonial duties. He wrote to amuse himself
and his friends, not allowing his work to be published in his life-
time, and was a patron of writers including Edmund Spenser and
Thomas Lodge. When Spenser brought him a copy of *The Faerie
Queene*, Sidney was said to have been too busy to read it at first,
but had him called back, according to John Aubrey, and 'ordered
his servant to give him many pounds in gold'.

Sidney's best-known work of poetry is his witty sonnet cycle *Astrophel and Stella*, which tells of a courtier's passion and self-denial in the cause of virtue and public service, inspired by his unrequited love for Penelope Devereux, Lady Rich (described by James I as 'a fair woman with a black soul'), whom he had first met in 1581, when his sonnet 'Thou blind man's mark' is said to have been written. Like his pastoral romance *Arcadia*, Sidney's *Astrophel and Stella* wasn't published until the 1590s. Written around the same time, his *Defence of Poesie* (also known as *An Apology for Poetry*) was a pioneering work in Elizabethan literary criticism setting out poetry's role in instilling virtue, drawing on classical and Italian writers, but not published until after his death, in 1595. A collected edition of his works followed in 1598, and was reprinted in 1599 and nine times during the 17th century.

In 1585 Sidney was appointed joint master of the ordnance, administering the Queen's military supplies ahead of her despatch of a force to support the Dutch rising against Spanish occupation. As governor of Flushing, Sidney commanded a company of cavalry in a series of actions against the Spaniards, in the last of which, on 22 September 1586, he charged three times through enemy lines, riding wounded from the battlefield with a bullet-shattered thigh. He died in Arnhem a month later from an infected wound. On his deathbed he sought again to kill desire: 'There came to my remembrance a vanity wherein I had taken delight, whereof I had not rid myself. It was the Lady Rich. But I rid myself of it, and presently my joy and comfort returned.'

BK ▪ For a man with a reputation for nobility and virtue Sir Philip Sidney is a dab hand at cursing. His ability to curse gives this poem its enraged energy, its abusive conviction. Like all poets accomplished in the art of cursing, Sidney piles it on, develops a maledictory momentum, has no mercy on the object of his wrath and finally works himself into a state of triumph over desire, the battered victim of his cursing.

I just wonder if the man doth protest too much when he asserts that he desires nothing 'but how to kill desire'. Without desire, would he have written such an impassioned poem? And is not his desire as essential a part of himself as his 'virtue'?

What would desire say if it got the opportunity to answer back?

EDMUND SPENSER (1552-1599)

'One day I wrote her name upon the strand'

One day I wrote her name upon the strand,
But came the waves and washèd it away:
Again I wrote it with a second hand,
But came the tide, and made my pains his prey.
Vain man, said she, that dost in vain assay
A mortal thing so to immortalise,
But I myself shall like to this decay,
And eke my name be wipèd out likewise.
Not so (quod I) let baser things devise
To die in dust, but you shall live by fame;
My verse your virtues rare shall eternise,
And in the heavens write your glorious name:
Where, whenas death shall all the world subdue,
Our love shall live, and later life renew.

[*Amoretti*, 1595]

Edmund Spenser was another Elizabethan courtier poet, but not of noble standing. Born in Smithfield, he was probably the son of a clothmaker. Admitted as a poor student to the University of Cambridge in 1569, his later rise to literary eminence – which enhanced his social status – would not have been possible without the learning he acquired there, particularly his knowledge of Latin and Greek classics along with the great European works of his time.

His greatest contribution to English literature was to be his allegorical epic *The Faerie Queene*. Set in the land of Faerie with a queen, Gloriana, the poem is a romance narrative cast in nine-line stanzas, Spenser's own invented form (now known as Spenserian stanzas). It presents the virtuous life as a Christian quest, and was in part a response to the conflict between Protestant England and Roman Catholic Spain, to a war between good and evil, a stance which later Irish readers might find morally ambiguous in view of his position as one of Queen Elizabeth's officials responsible for securing her rule in Ireland. Spenser was no Cromwell, but serving as secretary to Arnold Lord Grey, Lord Deputy of Ireland, he was involved in ruthless military campaigns against resistance to English occupation, and was probably present at the Siege of Smerwick in 1580 when a Papal invasion force of 600 men surrendered and were massacred on Grey's orders, the executions led by officers including Walter Ralegh. During the second half of the 1580s Spenser assisted the English governors of Munster in the colonisation of the province, receiving a large "plantation" for himself at Kilcolman near Cork, west of lands owned by Ralegh who had been similarly rewarded. Ralegh helped Spenser publish *The Faerie Queene*, travelling back to England with him in 1589 so that he could present the completed part of the work to Queen Elizabeth. The first three books of the work were printed in 1590 with a dedication to her.

Rather than seek advancement in England, Spenser chose Ireland as the land of opportunity where he could gain power and privilege. Apart from *The Shepheardes Calender* (1579), all his major work was written while living as an English "gentleman" colonist in Ireland. 'One day I wrote her name upon the strand' is LXXV in his sonnet sequence *Amoretti*, published in 1595 with his *Epithalamion*, both dedicated to his new wife, Elizabeth Boyle, sister of the Earl of Cork. Written in 1595-96, his tract *A View of the Present State of Ireland* (1633), advocates a scorched earth policy to enforce English rule, including the destruction of crops and animals and the eradication of the Irish language. In 1598 Spenser was driven from Kilcolman when the forces of Hugh O'Neill burned the castle. He returned to London in 1599, where he died, aged 46.

BK ■ Spenser is not slow to claim that his poem will 'eternise' the name of the woman to whom it's addressed. When she sees him writing her name in sand, twice, she considers him a 'vain man' trying to immortalise 'a mortal thing'. His reply is that his verse will write her name not in sand but 'in the heavens' and that when death will conquer 'all the world' the couple's love will live in poetry and 'later life renew'. Future life will be further animated by this poem. Yet I'm struck by the irony that while Spenser promises that the woman's 'glorious name' will be written 'in the heavens', he doesn't actually write her name in this sonnet. Nevertheless, in celebrating the power of poetry, this fine poem endows the woman with immortality.

CHIDIOCK TICHBORNE   (*c*.1558-1586)

Tichborne's Elegy

written with his own hand in the Tower before his execution

My prime of youth is but a frost of cares;
   My feast of joy is but a dish of pain;
My crop of corn is but a field of tares;
   And all my good is but vain hope of gain:
The day is past, and yet I saw no sun;,
And now I live, and now my life is done.

My tale was heard, and yet it was not told;
   My fruit is fallen, and yet my leaves are green;
My youth is spent, and yet I am not old;
   I saw the world, and yet I was not seen:
My thread is cut, and yet it is not spun;
And now I live, and now my life is done.

I sought my death, and found it in my womb;
   I looked for life, and saw it was a shade;
I trod the earth, and knew it was my tomb;
   And now I die, and now I was but made;
My glass is full, and now my glass is run;
And now I live, and now my life is done.

1586 [*Verses of Praise and Joy*, 1586]

Chidiock Tichborne was a Catholic conspirator against Queen Elizabeth I. His fame – or notoriety at the time – rests on this one poem written on the eve of his execution and sent to his wife in a letter. Only two other poems by him have survived, neither particularly distinguished.

Tichborne came from a landed family in Hampshire. Arrested with his father in 1583 for being in possession of 'popish relics' brought back from an unauthorised trip abroad, he was clearly under suspicion as a possible traitor. In June 1586 he agreed to take part in the Babington Plot to kill Elizabeth and give the English crown to Mary, Queen of Scots, who was next in line to the throne. The conspiracy was uncovered by Elizabeth's secretary of state and "spymaster" Sir Francis Walsingham, who was also Sir Philip Sidney's father-in-law. Chidiock (pronounced *Chidik*) Tichborne was arrested on 14 August 1586, three days after Mary herself had been captured while out riding.

On 20 September Tichborne was taken from the Tower of London to St Giles Field to be executed with Anthony Babington and five other conspirators, knowing that the stipulated punishment for high treason was to be drawn, eviscerated, hanged and quartered. When Elizabeth learned that their gruesome executions were gaining support for the Catholic cause, she ordered that the seven remaining conspirators were only to be disembowelled once they were dead. Mary was executed at Fotheringhay Castle in February 1587.

Tichborne is one of four poets in this anthology who were executed for treason, the others being Surrey, Ralegh and Southwell, while Wyatt was very lucky not to share their fate.

BK ■ It is unusual to find a poet writing an elegy for himself; elegies are usually written by others, by friends or admirers of those who've died. In writing an elegy for himself, in his late 20s, just before his execution, Chidiock Tichborne confronts his life in a brave, concise, candid way. His response recognises that he is considering and describing a life that has hardly happened, so brief does it seem.

> My youth is spent, and yet I am not old
>
> My thread is cut, and yet it is not spun
>
> And now I die, and now I was but made
>
> And now I live, and now my life is done

This repeated recognition of the sheer brevity of his existence is made without a shred of self-pity. The lines are strong and clear-cut, lucid statements of a terrible fact. The sharp images underline the desolation of Tichborne's elegy for himself.

CHRISTOPHER MARLOWE (1564–1593)

Elegia VI
(Ovid's Elegies, Book III)

Quod ab amica receptus cum ea coire non potuit, conqueritur

Either she was foul, or her attire was bad,
Or she was not the wench I wished t'have had.
Idly I lay with her, as if I loved not,
And like a burden grieved the bed that moved not.
Yet though both of us performed our true intent,
Yet I could not cast anchor where I meant.
She on my neck her ivory arms did throw,
Her arms far whiter than the Scythian snow.
And eagerly she kissed me with her tongue,
And under mine her wanton thigh she flung.
Yea, and she soothed me up, and called me 'Sir',
And used all speech that might provoke and stir.
Yet like as if cold hemlock I had drunk,
It mockèd me, hung down the head, and sunk.
Like a dull cipher or rude block I lay,
Or shade or body was I, who can say?
What will my age do, age I cannot shun,
When in my prime my force is spent and done?
I blush, that being youthful, hot and lusty,
I prove neither youth nor man, but old and rusty.
Pure rose she, like a nun to sacrifice,
Or one that with her tender brother lies.
Yet boarded I the golden Chie twice,
And Libas, and the white-cheeked Pitho thrice.
Corinna craved it in a summer's night,
And nine sweet bouts we had before daylight.
What, waste my limbs through some Thessalian charms?
May spells and drugs do silly souls such harm?

With virgin wax hath some imbasted my joints
And pierced my liver with sharp needles' points?
Charms change corn to grass and make it die.
By charms are running spring and fountains dry.
By charms mast crops from oaks, from vines grapes fall,
And fruit from trees when there's no wind at all.
Why might not then my sinews be enchanted,
And I grow faint as with some spirit haunted?
To this add shame: shame to perform it quailed me,
And was the second cause why vigour failed me.
My idle thoughts delighted her no more
Than did the robe or garment which she wore.
Yet might her touch make youthful Pylius fire
And Tithon livelier than his years require.
Even her I had and she had me in vain;
What might I crave more, if I ask again?
I think the great gods grieved they had bestowed
The benefit which lewdly I forslowed.
I wished to be received in, in I get me;
To kiss. I kiss; to lie with her she let me.
Why was I blessed? Why made king to refuse it?
Chuff-like had I not gold and could not use it?
So in a spring thrives he that told so much,
And looks upon the fruits he cannot touch.
Hath any rose so from a fresh young maid,
As she might straight have gone to church and prayed?
Well, I believe she kissed not as she should,
Nor used the sleight and cunning which she could.
Huge oaks, hard adamants might she have moved,
And with sweet words cause deaf rocks to have loved.
Worthy she was to move both gods and men,
But neither was I man, nor livèd then.
Can deaf ear take delight when Phaemius sings?
Or Thamyras in curious painted things?
What sweet thought is there but I had the same?
And one gave place still as another came.
Yet notwithstanding, like one dead it lay,

Drooping more than a rose pulled yesterday.
Now, when he should not jet, he bolts upright,
And craves his task, and seeks to be at fight.
Lie down with shame, and see thou stir no more,
Seeing thou wouldst deceive me as before.
Thou cozenest me; by thee surprised am I,
And bide sore loss with endless infamy.
Nay more, the wench did not disdain a whit
To take it in her hand and play with it.
But when she saw it would by no means stand,
But still drooped down, regarding not her hand,
'Why mockst thou me?' she cried. 'Or, being ill,
Who bade thee lie down here against thy will?
Either thou art witch, with blood of frogs new dead,
Or jaded camest thou from some other bed.'
With that, her loose gown on, from me she cast her;
In skipping out her naked feet much graced her.
And, lest her maid should know of this disgrace,
To cover it, spilt water on the place.

1580s [1580s]

Christopher Marlowe was the preeminent Elizabethan dramatist
before Shakespeare, the author of such celebrated plays as *Tambur-
laine* (the first English play in blank verse), and *Doctor Faustus*, as
well as a precociously gifted poet and translator. His bold and sensual
writing struck a new note in English poetry, and the influence of
his verse drama on Shakespeare's work cannot be underestimated,
not just its themes but the clarity of spoken language in the verse.

The son of a Canterbury shoemaker, Kit Marlowe (as he was
generally known) gained a scholarship to study at Cambridge, where
he is reputed to have been recruited as a secret agent working for
Queen Elizabeth's "spymaster" Sir Francis Walsingham (who was
also Sir Philip Sidney's father-in-law).

It was also while at Cambridge that he made the first translation
into English of Ovid's *Amores*, rendering Latin couplets in elegiac

metre (hexameter followed by unrhymed pentameter) into dramatically immediate rhyming pentameter, adapting a classical mode to an English one. Marlowe's Ovidian elegies were so transformed by his ingenuity, wit and command of language that they can be regarded as original works of English poetry. They were soon in print but attracted notoriety: one of several editions was banned and burned by episcopal order in 1599.

Ovid's Latin glosses were retained by Marlowe to introduce each of his elegies. The one for our poem, 'Elegia VI' from Book III, translates as 'He bewails the fact that, in bed with his mistress, he was unable to perform.'

Marlowe's brilliant literary career ended in 1593 at the age of 29 when he was murdered in a tavern in Deptford, supposedly over payment of a bill or 'reckoning'. There has been much speculation over the years about the nature of that 'reckoning': whether it related to his more shadowy dealings, or possible Catholic sympathies, atheism, homosexuality; or because he knew too much about Ralegh or Walsingham or members of the Privy Council. All attempts to unravel the true circumstances of his murder have been inconclusive. Like Byron, he does appear to have led a wild life. As the anonymous author, or authors, of the play *The Return from Parnassus* (1598) pronounced: 'Pity it is that wit so ill should dwell, / Wit lent from heaven, but vices sent from hell.'

BK ■ The classical allusions in these lines, far from clouding or concealing the narrator's perplexed disappointment at his (temporary?) sexual impotence, underline and intensify it, and even add a somewhat mocking note to the scene. What might have been an enjoyable, robust physical event rapidly becomes an intense, labyrinthine drama of fluent and intense self-questioning, bordering at times on narcissistic self-absorption, which culminates in the woman, properly and literally, washing this rusty, creaking old bore of a would-be lover out of her life and her bed. Still, as most men will admit at moments of honesty, it could happen to a bishop.

Marlowe's version of Ovid is a sensual delight and refreshingly funny.

SIR WALTER RALEGH (1552-1618)

The Lie

Go soul, the body's guest,
    upon a thankless arrant,
Fear not to touch the best,
    the truth shall be thy warrant:
Go, since I needs must die,
    and give the world the lie.

Say to the Court it glows
    and shines like rotten wood;
Say to the Church, it shows
    what's good, and doth no good:
If Church and Court reply,
    then give them both the lie.

Tell potentates they live
    acting by others' action,
Not loved unless they give,
    not strong but by affection:
If potentates reply,
    give potentates the lie.

Tell men of high condition,
    that manage the estate,
Their purpose is ambition,
    their practice only hate:
And if they once reply,
    then give them all the lie.

Tell them that brave it most,
    they beg for more by spending,
Who in their greatest cost
    seek nothing but commending.

And if they make reply,
  then give them all the lie.

Tell zeal it wants devotion,
  tell love it is but lust,
Tell time it is but motion,
  tell flesh it is but dust.
And wish them not reply,
  for thou must give the lie.

Tell age it daily wasteth,
  tell honour how it alters,
Tell beauty how she blasteth,
  tell favour how it falters,
And as they shall reply,
  give every one the lie.

Tell wit how much it wrangles
  in tickle points of niceness,
Tell wisdom she entangles
  herself in overwiseness.
And when they do reply,
  straight give them both the lie.

Tell physic of her boldness,
  tell skill it is prevention;
Tell charity of coldness,
  tell law it is contention,
And as they do reply,
  so give them still the lie.

Tell fortune of her blindness,
  tell nature of decay,
Tell friendship of unkindness,
  tell justice of delay.
And if they will reply,
  then give them all the lie.

Tell arts they have no soundness,
  but vary by esteeming,
Tell schools they want profoundness
  and stand too much on seeming.
If arts and schools reply,
  give arts and schools the lie.

Tell faith it's fled the city,
  tell how the country erreth,
Tell manhood shakes off pity,
  tell virtue least preferreth,
And if they do reply,
  spare not to give the lie.

So when thou hast, as I
  commanded thee, done blabbing,
Although to give the lie,
  deserves no less than stabbing,
Stab at thee he that will,
  no stab thy soul can kill.

c. 1592 [*A Poetic Rhapsody*, 2nd edition, 1608]

Sir Walter Ralegh was a soldier and adventurer, an ambitious courtier who became a favourite of Elizabeth I but had to undertake hazardous colonising expeditions to retain her support and later that of James I. He was credited at one time of having brought the potato and tobacco to England from South America, but the evidence for the first is thin and tobacco was actually brought from the Americas via Spanish colonists. As a soldier he served with the Huguenots in the religious civil wars in France, followed by brutal service for the English crown in putting down rebellions in Ireland. He was knighted in 1585 and led expeditions in 1595 and 1617 to the Orinoco River in South America in search of the fabled golden city of El Dorado. He was granted permission for his final expedition on condition that he respect a peace treaty with Spain, but a detachment of his men attacked a Spanish outpost against his orders. Ralegh was held responsible for this breach, and was beheaded at Westminster on his return to England.

He began writing poetry in his mid 20s but it took up little of his time, and publishing it was of far less concern to him than that of his voluminous *Historie of the World* written while imprisoned in the Tower from 1603 to 1616. He wrote in response to particular experiences and to his changing fortunes, influenced by the work of poets such as George Gascoigne, Surrey, Sidney and Spenser, but favoured a plainer style.

BK ■ Ralegh speaks directly to his soul, telling it not to be afraid because the truth is its 'warrant'. Twice in the opening stanza Ralegh tells his soul, 'the body's guest', to 'go', to launch itself on a thankless enterprise, to 'give the world the lie'. This note of uncompromising candour is maintained right through the poem. Ralegh instructs his soul to tell its truth to the entire world. The word 'Tell' resounds like a bell of integrity 26 times through the poem; 26 times Ralegh exhorts his soul to tell its unique truth. This truth may be fierce and hurtful and will most likely be met with 'no less than stabbing' but it is the only way, in Ralegh's eye, to 'give the world the lie'.

This is the poem of a man whose wish is that his soul survive the shining rottenness of life, its waste, greed, hypocrisy, vicious and pointless blabbing; in short, its lie, its lies. The poem has the moral ferocity of one determined to cling to his own truth. The poem's desperation is matched only by its determination.

ROBERT SOUTHWELL (1561-1595)

The Burning Babe

As I in hoary winter's night stood shivering in the snow,
Surprised I was with sudden heat which made my heart to glow;
And lifting up a fearful eye to view what fire was near,
A pretty Babe all burning bright did in the air appear;
Who, scorchèd with excessive heat, such floods of tears did shed
As though his floods should quench his flames which with his tears
  were fed.
'Alas,' quoth he, 'but newly born in fiery heats I fry,
Yet none approach to warm their hearts or feel my fire, but I!
My faultless breast the furnace is, the fuel wounding thorns,
Love is the fire, and sighs the smoke, the ashes, shame and scorns,
The fuel Justice layeth on, and Mercy blows the coals,
The metal in this furnace wrought are men's defilèd souls,
For which, as now on fire I am to work them to their good,
So will I melt into a bath to wash them in my blood.'
With this he vanished out of sight and swiftly shrunk away,
And straight I callèd unto mind that it was Christmas day.

c. 1595 [*St Peter's Complaint*, 1595]

St Robert Southwell was a devout and selfless Catholic scholar, the author of religious poetry, homilies, sermons and meditations, much of which was circulated in secret during his lifetime, with his poetry becoming popular after his death. Born in Norfolk, he was sent abroad as a youth, in 1576, to be educated in the Jesuit school at Douai, and later in Rome, where he was ordained as a Jesuit priest in 1584, returning secretly to England in 1586. Most of his poetry was written during his six years in London as an undercover missionary. Captured by the notorious priest hunter Robert Topcliffe in 1592, he was imprisoned in the Tower and tortured over a three-year period before being hanged, drawn and quartered in 1595 at the age of 33. Pope Paul VI canonised him in 1970.

His poetry asserts that beauty and truth are revealed through Christ and the Virgin Mary and that humanity must respond to divine revelation with contrition, repentance and love. Such beliefs were heretical in Elizabethan England where Catholics had to renounce their faith on pain of death.

'The Burning Babe' presents a vision of the Christ child burning like Daniel in a purgatorial fiery furnace fuelled by the 'wounding thorns' of the Crucifixion, his death thus figured simultaneously with his birth at the time of incarnation. There are also echoes of Isaiah 48:10 ('Behold, I have refined thee, but not with silver; I have chosen thee in the furnace of affliction.') and Revelation 7:14 ('These are they which came out of great tribulation, and have washed their robes, and made them white in the blood of the Lamb.').

The poem is unusual in being written in iambic heptameter – it's a fourteener in rhyming couplets – and has often been recast for singing in a ballad metre, with each line broken in two, becoming alternating lines of tetrameter and trimeter, as used by Coleridge in 'The Rime of the Ancient Mariner'.

BK ■ This poem's central image – the Christ child, burning, weeping, isolated – has a striking visionary vividness. There are 16 lines in the poem; the burning child speaks for eight of these, telling us, among other things, that love is the fire that burns him, yet, sadly, 'none approach to warm their hearts or feel my fire but I!' This combination of burning vividness and sad isolation makes the child's words poignant and memorable.

This poem, like so many others in this anthology, transmits that poignancy with special power when it is read aloud. It is then we savour the full, animated swing of the rhythm, bringing the narrative into complete life and giving a dramatic prominence to the burning child's burning words. As the child shrinks away, the rhythm and the words linger like an echo that survives the original statement, haunting the mind and heart with delicate yet stubborn insistence.

MICHAEL DRAYTON   (1563-1631)

Since There's No Help

Since there's no help, come let us kiss and part:
Nay, I have done, you get no more of me;
And I am glad, yea glad with all my heart
That thus so cleanly I myself can free.
Shake hands forever; cancel all our vows;
And when we meet at any time again,
Be it not seen in either of our brows
That we one jot of former love retain.
Now at the last gasp of love's latest breath
When, his pulse failing, passion speechless lies,
When faith is kneeling by his bed of death
And innocence is closing up his eyes –
  Now, if thou wouldst, when all have given him over,
  From Death to Life thou might'st him yet recover.

1590s? [*Idea*, 1619]

Michael Drayton was a versatile poet of humble origins who published his first book in 1590, gaining favour during the reign of Elizabeth I, and went on to become a prolific writer, publishing his last book, *The Muses Elizium*, 40 years later, in 1630, when Charles I was on the throne. Credited with introducing the Horatian ode to English poetry, Drayton reinvented himself as a poet, not always successfully, in response to changing literary fashions and fickle fortune, being dependent on unreliable patronage as well as suffering from a declining interest in historical epics and didactic verse.

Born in the village of Hartshill in Warwickshire, he was employed in his youth as a servant in the house of Thomas Goodyer of Collingham in Nottinghamshire. Drayton's penchant

46

for dedicating books to figures of high social standing to gain favour led to biographers crediting the poet himself with higher status, better education and closer friendships with gentry than he actually enjoyed. Among those dedications was that of the 1619 folio edition of his early poems, *Poems by Michael Drayton Esquyer*, to Sir Walter Aston, whom he probably served as a secretary or steward. That book included the final version of his sonnet sequence, *Idea*, which he had begun in 1594 and revised several times, and which included 'Since There's No Help'.

His most original works include *Englands Heroicall Epistles* (1597), pairs of letters exchanged between famous lovers; his well-known 'Ballad of Agincourt' ('Fair stood the wind for France'); and his monumental *Poly-Olbion* (1612), one of the longest poems in English, an account of England's history, topography and legends written in alexandrines, dedicated first to Prince Henry and later to Prince Charles.

Drayton was in the habit of erasing or changing dedications to his many works in line with what was expedient. In 'Since There's No Help' it is past love which must be erased.

BK ■ The sense of likely emotional turnabout, of possible passionate reunion following a somewhat dire statement of determination to separate, animates this intense poem with the electric possibilities of love. It is direct, dramatic and passionate; and the note of hope in the last couple of lines throws a touching, ironic aura back over the rest of the poem.

The poem's speaker is trying hard to convince himself of his intention to separate. He seems very determined to do so. But that ultimate hope of reconciliation is hinted at in the first line of the resolution to end the relationship: 'come let us kiss and part'.

WILLIAM SHAKESPEARE (1564-1616)

Sonnet 73

That time of year thou mayst in me behold,
When yellow leaves, or none, or few, do hang
Upon those boughs which shake against the cold,
Bare ruined choirs, where late the sweet birds sang.
In me thou see'st the twilight of such day,
As after sunset fadeth in the west,
Which by and by black night doth take away,
Death's second self that seals up all in rest.
In me thou see'st the glowing of such fire,
That on the ashes of his youth doth lie,
As the death-bed, whereon it must expire,
Consumed with that which it was nourished by.
    This thou perceiv'st, which makes thy love more strong,
    To love that well, which thou must leave ere long.

[*Shake-speares Sonnets*, 1609]

William Shakespeare was born and grew up in Stratford-upon-Avon, the son of Thomas Shakespeare, an alderman and glover, and Mary Arden, daughter of a landowning farmer. His education at a grammar school in Stratford gave him a grounding in the Latin classics. In 1582, aged 18, he married Anne Hathaway, who was 26 and pregnant with their first child Susanna. Little is known of him between the birth of their twins in 1585 and a jealous put-down made by a rival, better-educated playwright in 1592 ('the lost years'), by which time Shakespeare had written and staged several of his early plays and was living in London.

When the theatres were closed in 1593-94 due to the plague, he produced his long narrative poems *Venus and Adonis* and *The Rape of Lucrece*, but for many years his sonnets were read only by friends. In 1609 an edition of 154 of them was published. Stylistically they develop the Petrarchan model introduced by Wyatt and cast into rhymed quatrains by Surrey, using iambic pentameter and an ABAB CDCD EFEF GG rhyme scheme, later termed the Shakespearian sonnet. Thematically, they are very different from the sonnets of Petrarch, Dante, or even Sidney. Addressed to a dark lady, a rival poet or a fair youth, their subjects include love, ageing, beauty, time and mortality (as in the 'fair youth' sonnet 73), as well as lust, jealousy, infidelity and misogyny.

BK ■ Shakespeare's constant and sane awareness of the bond between inner and outer weathers works effectively here to shiver the reader with a sense of pure fragility and to communicate the further bond between love's intensity and the nature of transience. Shakespeare is here the object of scrutiny; he is seen, looked into, deeply perceived by the other. Three times the phrase 'in me' occurs. 'In me thou see'st.' This being seen into merely serves to deepen the vision of transience and of love at the heart of the poem which beautifully captures the fusion, the sheer oneness, of human and inhuman weathers. It's as if Shakespeare said, 'You see October in my heart with its dead and dying leaves. You see the fading twilight world vanishing into night, and the glow of the fire dying on the ashes of my youth. You see this, you know it, and it makes your love stronger.'

There are moments when Shakespeare sounds like the many voices of weather itself. He connects various kinds of external forces to his own inner condition in such a way that the voices of sun and rain, twilight, and 'black night', leaves and boughs become his agents of self-expression. Nature is privileged to be his language and his imagery. He may speak of the savage, demolishing power of time, the merciless decay of lovers' bodies, the inevitability of sundering, but he does this with a flowing ease that brings to mind a confident river making its way to the sea, certain of connection.

This sonnet, like so many of Shakespeare's, is a gem of compact revelation. It has an intense inner logic; it moves firmly towards the final rhyming couplet which succinctly states the consequence of the preceding perceptions. The ending has that quality of concise, proverbial wisdom, of concentrated knowledge that is clear, calm and indisputable.

> This thou perceiv'st, which makes thy love more strong,
> To love that well, which thou must leave ere long.

49

THOMAS NASHE (1567–1601)

'Adieu, farewell, earth's bliss'

Adieu, farewell, earth's bliss;
This world uncertain is;
Fond are life's lustful joys,
Death proves them all but toys,
None from his darts can fly;
I am sick, I must die.
    Lord, have mercy on us!

Rich men, trust not in wealth,
Gold cannot buy you health;
Physic himself must fade,
All things to end are made,
The plague full swift goes by;
I am sick, I must die.
    Lord, have mercy on us!

Beauty is but a flower
Which wrinkles will devour:
Brightness falls from the air,
Queens have died young and fair,
Dust hath closed Helen's eye.
I am sick, I must die.
    Lord, have mercy on us!

Strength stoops unto the grave,
Worms feed on Hector brave,
Swords may not fight with fate,
Earth still holds ope her gate;
Come! come! the bells do cry.
I am sick, I must die.
    Lord, have mercy on us!

Wit with his wantonness
Tasteth death's bitterness;
Hell's executioner
Hath no ears for to hear
What vain art can reply.
I am sick, I must die.
    Lord, have mercy on us!

Haste, therefore, each degree,
To welcome destiny.
Heaven is our heritage,
Earth but a player's stage;
Mount we unto the sky.
I am sick, I must die.
    Lord, have mercy on us!

1592 [*Summer's Last Will and Testament*, 1600]

Thomas Nashe was an Elizabeth writer of some notoriety known for his brilliant, vituperative prose, combative pamphleteering and salacious poetry as well as for collaborating with other dramatists.

The son of a Lowestoft parson, Nashe was admitted to St John's College, Cambridge, as a poor student; like Spenser he was a sizar, having to work for his keep. On leaving Cambridge for London (he may have been expelled), he looked for ways to earn his crust as a writer, many of which involved attacks on literary rivals or puritan critics of the bishops who employed him to mount counter-attacks on their behalf.

His most popular work at the time was a satirical pamphlet, *Pierce Penniless, His Supplication to the Divell* (1592), but his most influential was to be *The Unfortunate Traveller; or, The Life of Jacke Wilton* (1594), the first picaresque novel in English, in which Henry Howard, Earl of Surrey, figures as the roguish adventurer's travel companion. Nashe worked in some capacity with Christopher Marlowe on *Dido, Queen of Carthage* (1594), and may have written parts of *Shakespeare's Henry VI, part 1* (c. 1591), along with Marlowe and another author. With Ben Jonson he wrote a satirical play, *The Isle of Dogs* (1597), suppressed as slanderous and seditious, for which Jonson was briefly jailed while Nashe's house was raided in his absence, prompting him to extend a stay in Great Yarmouth.

'Adieu, farewell, earth's bliss' was written during the autumn of 1592 while Nashe was staying at Archbishop Whitgift's palace at Croydon, for inclusion in a play he devised for performance there, *Summer's Last Will and Testament*, which was later published in 1600. The plague of 1592 is a haunting presence in the play and this lyric has often been published under the title 'A Litany in Time of Plague'. It is quite different from the rest of Nashe's poetry, much of which quite scurrilous, and follows the paradigm of the Litany in the Church of England's *Book of Common Prayer* (1549) with its refrain of 'Good lorde deliver us'.

BK ▦ An overwhelming sense of plague-presence fills this poem. The refrain reeks of sickness and death and cries out for mercy. Line after line proclaims the pathetic brevity of all living things; and in stanza after stanza the refrain rings its confirmation of the universal fact of transience.

> Beauty is but a flower
> Which wrinkles will devour:
> Brightness falls from the air,
> Queens have died young and fair,
> Dust hath closed Helen's eye.
> I am sick, I must die.
>   Lord, have mercy on us!

Yet the final stanza exhorts all 'To welcome destiny', to 'Mount we unto the sky' because 'Heaven is our heritage'. It is a desperately brave climax to a grim and moving poem, a particularly harrowing song of unrelenting misfortune as 'The plague full swift goes by'.

THOMAS CAMPION (1567–1620)

What if a Day

What if a day, or a month, or a year,
Crown thy delights with a thousand sweet contentings?
Cannot a chance of a night or an hour
Cross thy desires with as many sad tormentings?
>   Fortune, honour, beauty, youth
>   Are but blossoms dying;
>   Wanton pleasure, doting love
>   Are but shadows flying.
>   All our joys are but toys,
>   Idle thoughts deceiving,
>   None have power of an hour
>   In their lives' bereaving.

Earth's but a point to the world, and a man
Is but a point to the world's comparèd centure;
Shall then the point of a point be so vain
As to triumph in a seely point's adventure?
>   All is hazard that we have,
>   There is nothing biding;
>   Days of pleasure are like streams
>   Through fair meadows gliding.
>   Weal and woe, time doth go,
>   Time is never turning;
>   Secret fates guide our states,
>   Both in mirth and mourning.

c. 1600? [1606]

Thomas Campion was a poet and composer whose lyric poetry
is distinguished by its mastery of rhythmic and melodic structure.
Largely forgotten for two centuries after his death, his work was
rediscovered in the late 1800s. Among later poets influenced by his

poetry were W.H. Auden, Ezra Pound, Basil Bunting and Robert Creeley. T.S. Eliot called Campion, 'except for Shakespeare...the most accomplished master of rhymed lyric of his time'. He wrote over a hundred lute songs, set by himself and by composers including John Dowland and Philip Rosseter, lutenist to King James I, and three of his masques were presented at court.

Born in London, the son of a Chancery clerk, Campion studied at Cambridge before training as a lawyer but wasn't called to the bar, instead taking a medical degree at the University of Caen and supporting himself thereafter as a physician. In 1601, Rosseter's *Book of Ayres* included 21 of Campion's lute songs. Two songbooks of his own followed, in 1613 and 1617. His neglect following his death in 1620, aged 52, was probably largely due to the repudiation of secular music during the Puritan period.

BK ■ A friend once remarked to me that he thought a lot of lyric poetry was marked by whining and moaning about the cruelty of time, the loss of love, the poor, bruised sensibility of the afflicted lyricist. I disagreed, but could, nevertheless, see what he was getting at. The raw material of beauty can be very far from beautiful; much "healthy" poetry is born of physical, emotional or spiritual sickness.

Reading 'What if a Day', one is struck by a litany of misfortunes such as 'sad tormentings', 'blossoms dying', 'shadows flying', 'Idle thoughts deceiving', 'lives' bereaving', 'All is hazard', 'nothing biding', 'weal and woe' and so on. And it's true, all true. Yet something in us doesn't want to be hammered by this apparently endless catalogue of sorrows. And it is here that the magic of poetry, or in this case, the magic of Campion's song transforms the misery-litany into a moving, memorable work. The change of rhythm after four lines of each of the two stanzas is extremely effective in altering what might have been construed as 'whining' or 'moaning' into a haunting act of expression. By 'haunting' I mean a dramatic transformation of the mind and heart which strikes one as one goes about one's daily work or strolling the streets of a village or city. Where does this haunting power, this transformation come from? It would appear to be the inexplicable power of song. Campion possesses this power in abundance. Sing the sorrow; the sorrow becomes not merely bearable, but for a while at least, beautiful.

JOHN DONNE   (1572–1631)

The Flea

Mark but this flea, and mark in this,
How little that which thou deny'st me is;
Me it sucked first, and now sucks thee,
And in this flea, our two bloods mingled be;
Confess it, this cannot be said
A sin, or shame, or loss of maidenhead,
   Yet this enjoys before it woo,
    And pampered swells with one blood made of two,
    And this, alas, is more than we would do.

Oh stay, three lives in one flea spare,
Where we almost, nay more than married are.
This flea is you and I, and this
Our marriage bed, and marriage temple is;
Though parents grudge, and you, we'are met,
And cloistered in these living walls of jet.
   Though use make you apt to kill me,
    Let not to this, self murder added be,
    And sacrilege, three sins in killing three.

Cruel and sudden, hast thou since
Purpled thy nail, in blood of innocence?
In what could this flea guilty be,
Except in that drop which it sucked from thee?
Yet thou triumph'st, and say'st that thou
Find'st not thy self, nor me the weaker now;
   'Tis true, then learn how false, fears be;
    Just so much honour, when thou yield'st to me,
    Will waste, as this flea's death took life from thee.

1590s? [*Songs and Sonnets*, 1635]

John Donne was a poet and scholar known for both his glorious love poetry and his passionately argued religious verse, although hardly any of his poetry was published in his lifetime, most of it being circulated in manuscript among his circle of friends. Donne was the foremost English metaphysical poet of the 17th century, but was not known as such at the time, nor were his contemporaries.

Born into a Roman Catholic family, the son of a wealthy merchant, Donne went up to Oxford at the age of 12 and continued his education at Cambridge, but was unable to graduate because Catholics could not swear the oath of allegiance to Queen Elizabeth. However, he must have embraced Anglicanism by 1597, when he took up a post as secretary to Sir Thomas Egerton, Lord Keeper of the Great Seal. In 1601 he married Egerton's wife's niece Anne More in secret, for which her father had him briefly imprisoned. Denied any dowry, the Donnes lived in poverty for the next ten years, dependent on relatives and patrons, but their fortunes changed in 1615 when Donne was ordained as a deacon and priest, only for Anne to die two years later after their twelfth child was stillborn. In 1621 Donne was made Dean of St Paul's Cathedral, and quickly earned a reputation – and royal approval – for his powerfully eloquent sermons.

In Donne's poetry the established conventions of 16th-century English poetry are discarded. Whether about love or God, his poems develop arguments which are taken forward by a succession of extended metaphors or 'conceits'. This inventive mode of poetry was not to gain full critical recognition until the 20th century, being scorned by earlier critics, most notably by Dr Johnson.

Dryden wrote of Donne that he 'affects the metaphysics, not only in his satires, but in his amorous verses, where nature only should reign; and perplexes the minds of the fair sex with nice speculations of philosophy, when he should engage their hearts, and entertain them with the softnesses of love'. Probably picking up on Dryden's put-down, Johnson wrote in his *Lives of the Most Eminent English Poets* (1779–81) that in the early 17th century there 'appeared a race of writers that may be termed the metaphysical poets' in whose poetry 'heterogenous ideas are yoked by violence together, nature and art are ransacked for illustrations, comparisons, and illusions', referring to the work of Donne, Abraham Cowley and John Cleveland in particular. Responding to Herbert Grierson's seminal anthology *Metaphysical Lyrics and Poems of the Seventeenth Century* (1921), T.S. Eliot disagreed: 'A thought to Donne was an experience; it modified his sensibility.'[9] Eliot's revaluation of Donne and other poets of the Baroque period in his essay 'The Metaphysical Poets' (1921) prompted a revival of interest in their work.

The image in line 4 of 'The Flea' of 'our two bloods mingled' alludes to a belief still held in Donne's time that sexual intercourse involved a mingling of bloods, a notion derived from Aristotle.

BK ■ There's a sprightly element of playful manipulation, of self-consciously clever, ludic argument in the way John Donne handled many of the conceits in his poems. The word 'conceit' has its own playful ambiguity; apart from the adroit treatment of ingenious images, it also suggests a slightly conceited imagination marked, but not tainted, by an element of superbly talented vanity. All of which takes a very modest second place to the splendid complexity and subtlety of his poems.

Fleas are agile little bloodsuckers, tiny, audacious hoppers that can cause decent folk to itch and scratch like tormented demons. Donne, or Donne's poem-speaker, uses the flea to try to get his way with a woman. This commitment to sexual conquest underlies his brilliant manipulation of the 'pampered' bloodsucker; the flea, as a result of its sucking lifestyle, has its own blood, Donne's blood and the woman's blood in its body; a minute little bloody trinity.

Equipped with this fact, Donne pushes his argument forward with impressive moral earnestness and, perhaps, an underlying sense of humour. (It's hard to continue speaking of fleas without a chuckle, however silent and private.) Marriage, murder, suicide, sacrilege, innocence, guilt, triumph, fear, honour and, of course, sexual surrender, all these pass through Donne's meditation on, and manipulation of, the flea that contains the blood of the almost-lovers.

Donne would really love to be in the flea's position; like the flea, he'd love to suck a little life from his beloved but he would not, one presumes, wish to be crushed or 'purpled' by her nails. Donne's smooth, brilliant treatment of the flea-conceit leads sweetly and inevitably to that moment when 'thou yield'st to me'. The flea may be dead but Donne's hopes are very much alive. Which is, presumably, the entire point of this poem's brilliant, convincing metaphysical argument.

BEN JONSON   (1572–1637)

On My First Son

Farewell, thou child of my right hand, and joy;
My sin was too much hope of thee, loved boy.
Seven years thou wert lent to me, and I thee pay,
Exacted by thy fate, on the just day.
O, could I lose all father, now. For why
Will man lament the state he should envy?
To have so soon 'scaped world's, and flesh's rage,
And, if no other misery, yet age?
Rest in soft peace, and, asked, say, here doth lie
Ben Jonson his best piece of poetry.
For whose sake, henceforth, all his vows be such,
As what he loves may never like too much.

1603 [*Workes*, 1616]

Ben Jonson was a dramatist, poet and critic, second only to Shake-speare as a playwright during the Stuart period. His most successful plays were satirical comedies, most notably *Volpone* (1605) and *The Alchemist* (1610). Born two months after the death of his father, a minister, he attended Westminster School until obliged to follow his stepfather's trade as a bricklayer for a time. After serving with the English forces in Flanders, he turned to the stage, acting and writing plays, establishing his name with *Every Man in His Humour* (1598), in which each of the four main characters embodied medi-cine's four "humours": choler, melancholy, phlegm and blood. That year he was also briefly imprisoned after killing a fellow actor in a duel.

He married in 1594, describing his wife Ann to William Drum-mond as 'a shrew, yet honest'. Their daughter Mary, the subject of his poem 'On My First Daughter', died at six months. His son Benjamin, commemorated in 'On My First Son', died of bubonic plague at the age of seven. A second son, also called Benjamin, died in 1635, by which time Jonson and his wife were living apart.

Jonson wrote much dramatic verse for performance in his plays as well as large body of work in heroic couplets which was to influence Alexander Pope. Often reviving classical forms, he also wrote songs and hymns in a variety of metres, including elaborate stanzaic and Pindaric odes, Italian and English sonnets, quatrains, and terza rima. His poetry is noted for its grace and clarity of diction, the hallmarks of Cavalier poetry. In contrast with Donne and the metaphysical tradition in 17th-century poetry, Jonson has been called the father of the Cavalier poets, with followers including Robert Herrick, Richard Lovelace, Sir John Suckling and Thomas Carew. His circle of admirers and friends, 'the Tribe of Ben', met regularly at taverns in London.

BK ■ Several poems in this book confront and explore the sense of loss. Ben Jonson's loss of his first son at the age of seven is presented with a kind of eloquent restraint. It involves the poet-father in some close questioning which is also, one feels, self-questioning.

> For why
> Will man lament the state he should envy?
> To have so soon scap'd world's, and flesh's rage,
> And, if no other misery, yet age?

The poem shows how an innocent's death can push an experienced, world-burdened person into a state of self-scrutiny, of questioning all that he is and has. The dead can change the living in crucial ways. Jonson's sense of loss is profound, calm and enduring. So is his poem. Jonson himself, however, says that his son, 'lent' to him and now returned in death, is 'his best piece of poetry'.

ROBERT HERRICK (1591–1674)

To the Virgins, to Make Much of Time

Gather ye rose-buds while ye may,
 Old Time is still a-flying:
And this same flower that smiles today
 Tomorrow will be dying.

The glorious lamp of heaven, the sun,
 The higher he's a-getting,
The sooner will his race be run,
 And nearer he's to setting.

That age is best which is the first,
 When youth and blood are warmer;
But being spent, the worse, and worst
 Times still succeed the former.

Then be not coy, but use your time;
 And while ye may, go marry:
For having lost but once your prime,
 You may forever tarry.

[*Hesperides*, 1648]

Robert Herrick was a country parson poet who spent most of his life in rural obscurity in Devon, far from the poets of 'Tribe of Ben' attendant on Ben Jonson whose company and admiration he enjoyed as a young man. Regarded then by many as the foremost Cavalier poet, he did not publish a book of poetry until 1648, when he was nearly 60, by which time much of his work was seen as outmoded. The poems of *Hesperides* were not reprinted for another 150 years, with Herrick's work largely forgotten for two centuries.

Born in London, the son of a goldsmith who died falling from an attic window when he was an infant, Herrick was apprenticed to his uncle at 16 as a goldsmith, but released after six years to study at Cambridge in 1613. He took holy orders in 1623, and in 1630 was given the living of Dean Prior, a remote Devon parish a day's ride from Exeter or Plymouth in either direction. There he remained until 1647, when he was expelled by the Puritans in a mass purge of clergy, returning during the Restoration and serving for another 14 years until his death in 1674.

Hesperides contained around 1400 poems of four kinds: amatory (addressed to an imagined mistress), pastoral, occasional and epigrammatic; the divine poems presumed to be dated after his move to Devon, the others while he still lived in London. The earlier poems would not have been thought old-fashioned had he published them when that body of work would have been complete, around 1630. Why he took so long to publish his meticulously organised volume of collected verse is a mystery.

He does not appear to have taken the advice of 'Gather ye rose-buds', never marrying but apparently content with the company of his pets, including a domesticated pig, and his devoted housekeeper Miss Baldwin. He was 'much beloved by the Gentry in those parts for his florid and witty discourse', according to one report.

BK ■ For Herrick, the will to live is based on his awareness of the inevitability of death. The energy and enthusiasm with which he exhorts young people to live, love and 'go marry' because 'Old Time is still a-flying' is extremely infectious. The vigour of his counsel would rouse even the most lethargic heart to action. In fact, I've heard people long past what is popularly known as their "prime" quote this poem, or part of it, to explain why, in drowsy, droopy middle-age (or even later!) they suddenly discovered a spark of youth and began to prove to themselves and to others that they were well and truly alive in the manner advocated by Herrick. His poem is as fresh and youthful as the life it exhorts us to pursue and enjoy. The sparkling, fragrant, advice of 'Gather ye rose-buds' is aimed not just at the young but at the young-at-heart.

HENRY KING (1592–1669)

The Exequy

Accept, thou shrine of my dead saint,
Instead of dirges this complaint;
And for sweet flowers to crown thy hearse
Receive a strew of weeping verse
From thy grieved friend, whom thou might'st see
Quite melted into tears for thee.

   Dear loss! since thy untimely fate,
My task hath been to meditate
On thee, on thee: thou art the book,
The library whereon I look,
Though almost blind. For thee, loved clay,
I languish out, not live the day,
Using no other exercise
But what I practise with mine eyes:
By which wet glasses I find out
How lazily time creeps about
To one that mourns: this, only this
My exercise and bus'ness is:
So I compute the weary hours
With sighs dissolved into showers.

   Nor wonder if my time go thus
Backward and most preposterous;
Thou hast benighted me; thy set
This eve of blackness did beget,
Who wast my day (though overcast
Before thou hadst thy noontide past)
And I remember must in tears
Thou scarce hadst seen so many years
As day tells hours. By thy clear sun
My love and fortune first did run;

But thou wilt never more appear
Folded within my hemisphere,
Since both thy light and motion,
Like a fled star, is fall'n and gone,
And 'twixt me and my soul's dear wish
The earth now interposed is,
Which such a strange eclipse doth make
As ne're was read in almanake.

I could allow thee for a time
To darken me and my sad clime,
Were it a month, a year, or ten,
I would thy exile live till then;
And all that space my mirth adjourn,
So thou wouldst promise to return,
And putting off thy ashy shroud
At length disperse this sorrow's cloud.

But woe is me! the longest date
Too narrow is to calculate
These empty hopes: never shall I
Be so much blest as to descry
A glimpse of thee, till that day come
Which shall the earth to cinders doom,
And a fierce fever must calcine
The body of this world like thine,
My little world! That fit of fire
Once off, our bodies shall aspire
To our souls' bliss: then we shall rise
And view ourselves with clearer eyes
In that calm region where no night
Can hide us from each other's sight.

Meantime thou hast her, earth: much good
May my harm do thee. Since it stood
With Heaven's will I might not call
Her longer mine, I give thee all

My short-lived right and interest
In her whom living I loved best:
With a most free and bounteous grief
I give thee what I could not keep.
Be kind to her, and prithee look
Thou write into thy Doomsday book
Each parcel of this rarity
Which in thy casket shrined doth lie,
See that thou make thy reck'ning straight,
And yield her back again by weight;
For thou must audit on thy trust
Each grain and atom of this dust,
As thou wilt answer Him that lent,
Not gave thee, my dear monument.

    So close the ground, and 'bout her shade
Black curtains draw: my bride is laid.

    Sleep on, my Love, in thy cold bed
Never to be disquieted!
My last good-night! Thou wilt not wake
Till I thy fate shall overtake:
Till age, or grief, or sickness must
Marry my body to that dust
It so much loves; and fill the room
My heart keeps empty in thy tomb.
Stay for me there; I will not fail
To meet thee in that hollow vale.
And think not much of my delay:
I am already on the way,
And follow thee with all the speed
Desire can make, or sorrows breed.
Each minute is a short degree
And every hour a step towards thee.
At night when I betake to rest,
Next morn I rise nearer my west
Of life, almost by eight hours sail,
Than when sleep breathed his drowsy gale.

This from the sun my bottom steers,
And my days' compass downward bears:
Nor labour I to stem the tide
Through which to thee I swiftly glide.

'Tis true, with shame and grief I yield,
Thou, like the van, first took'st the field;
And gotten hast the victory
In thus adventuring to die
Before me, whose more years might crave
A just precedence in the grave.
But hark! my pulse, like a soft drum,
Beats my approach, tells thee I come;
And slow howe'er my marches be
I shall at last sit down by thee.

The thought of this bids me go on
And wait my dissolution
With hope and comfort. Dear (forgive
The crime) I am content to live
Divided, with but half a heart,
Till we shall meet and never part.

c. 1624 [*Poems, Elegies, Paradoxes and Sonnets*, 1657]

Henry King was a poet and Anglican clergyman. Son of John King, Bishop of London, he studied at Christ Church, Oxford, and began his clerical life as a prebend in St Paul's Cathedral. In 1617 he was made Archdeacon of Colchester, and married Anne Berkeley around that time. Appointed Bishop of Chichester in 1642, his tenure was cut short the following year when the town surrendered to Cromwell's parliamentary forces, his library was seized and his estates sequestrated. He took refuge during the Interregnum at the houses of relatives and friends in Buckinghamshire, and was reinstated as Bishop of Chichester at the Restoration.

King's friends included John Donne (he was later an executor of Donne's estate), Ben Jonson and Izaak Walton, and his poetry shows the influences of the work of both Donne and Jonson. Five years after their marriage, his beloved wife Anne died, aged 23, having borne him four or five children, only two of whom survived. Written in iambic tetrameter couplets, the 'Exequy' is a highly dignified and deeply moving personal meditation on his grief at her death.

BK ■ This poem was originally entitled 'An Exequy to His Matchlesse Never To Be Forgotten Friend'. I mention this because Henry King's poem to his dead young wife ('Thou scarce hadst seen so many years / As day tells hours') is both a moving love-poem and a beautifully sculpted statement of friendship. It is a love-poem shot through with grief and a raw grief-poem touched and animated at every point, at each impassioned moment, by love. It is marked most of all by a calm, sustained dignity of thought and expression. It progresses with a grave logic, in a tone of deep loss accommodating a relentless, meditative loneliness, a determination to express that loneliness even to the earth that contains his wife's body.

> With a most free and bounteous grief,
> I give thee what I could not keep.
> Be kind to her...

King's own kindness of heart and mind, uttered with skill, candour and restraint, makes this a superb poem of love, grief, friendship, understanding, consciousness, acceptance and tough determination to rejoin his love, his friend, his wife.

> The thought of this bids me go on
> And wait my dissolution
> With hope and comfort. (Dear, forgive
> The crime) I am content to live
> Divided, but with half a heart,
> Till we meet and never part.

This is no facile optimism on King's part. Whatever hope this poem contains has been well and truly earned in the long, lonely stretches of his grief. The spiritual reality of this particular 'Exequy' is undeniable.

GEORGE HERBERT   (1593–1633)

Love (III)

Love bade me welcome. Yet my soul drew back
    Guilty of dust and sin.
But quick-eyed Love, observing me grow slack
    From my first entrance in,
Drew nearer to me, sweetly questioning,
    If I lacked any thing.

A guest, I answered, worthy to be here:
    Love said, You shall be he.
I the unkind, ungrateful? Ah my dear,
    I cannot look on thee.
Love took my hand, and smiling did reply,
    Who made the eyes but I?

Truth Lord, but I have marred them: let my shame
    Go where it doth deserve.
And know you not, says Love, who bore the blame?
    My dear, then I will serve.
You must sit down, says Love, and taste my meat:
    So I did sit and eat.

[*The Temple*, 1633]

George Herbert, scholar and priest, is known as both one of the most technically versatile 17th-century metaphysical poets as well as the writer of some of the finest devotional poetry in English. He spent the last three years of his life as rector at St Andrew's parish church in the Wiltshire village of Bemerton, where he died from consumption just before his 40th birthday.

Herbert was born into a wealthy Welsh landowning family in Montgomeryshire, the son of Richard Herbert, member of parliament, high sheriff and justice of the peace. His mother Magdalen was a patron of John Donne, who became George's godfather when his father died when he was three and a half. Raised by his mother with nine siblings, he was educated at Westminster School and Trinity College, Cambridge, where he was elected a senior fellow and was later appointed Reader in Rhetoric. His fluency in Latin and Greek earned him election to the university's politically influential post of Public Orator in 1620. Following his mother's death in 1627, he left Cambridge, and married Jane Danvers, his stepfather's cousin, in 1629. After brief attempts at a political career, he entered the priesthood instead.

Apart from a collection of verses in Latin and Greek, Herbert never published his poetry, much of which was written during his Cambridge years, with many of the later devotional lyrics added at Bemerton. Shortly before his death he sent the manuscript of his only collection, *The Temple*, to his close Cambridge friend, Nicholas Farrar, founder of the religious community at Little Gidding, asking him to publish the book if it had any worth or otherwise to burn it, describing it, according to his first biographer, Izaak Walton, as 'a picture of the many spiritual conflicts that have passed between God and my soul, before I could subject mine to the will of Jesus, my Master, in whose service I have now found perfect freedom'.

BK ■ George Herbert's lightness of touch and tone, the unobtrusive skill of his poetic architecture, his ability to handle intricate dialogue, are evident in this poem. Love questions; Herbert replies; the dialogue proceeds, deepens, clarifies finally into a firm invitation (is it so firm as to be a command?) from Love to Herbert that he 'must sit down and taste my meat'. The poem's last line, brief and decisive, is a happy conclusion to the 'welcome' of the opening line and of the dialogue that follows Levels sweet 'questioning'.

Much of this poem's strength derives from Herbert's innate dramatic instinct which is used here with considerable skill and effect. Guilt, sin, unkindness, ingratitude, waste and shame enter the dialogue with 'quick-eyed Love'. The interchange is delicately yet firmly handled; and the final line is a concise, gracious portrait of a person gratefully accepting the invitation to Love's banquet: 'So I did sit and eat.'

Herbert handles this kind of intense spiritual drama with a rare and convincing stylistic completeness.

EDMUND WALLER (1606–1687)

Go, Lovely Rose

Go, lovely Rose,
Tell her that wastes her time and me,
That now she knows
When I resemble her to thee,
How sweet and fair she seems to be.

Tell her that's young
And shuns to have her graces spied
That hadst thou sprung
In deserts, where no men abide,
Thou must have uncommended died.

Small is the worth
Of beauty from the light retired;
Bid her come forth,
Suffer herself to be desired,
And not blush so to be admired.

Then die that she
The common fate of all things rare
May read in thee;
How small a part of time they share
That are so wondrous sweet and fair.

Late 1620s? [*Poems*, 1645]

Edmund Waller was an English country gentleman, a poet and
politician of wavering allegiances, who was elected to Parliament in
his late teens. Born in Buckinghamshire, his family connections were
with leading Parliamentarians; he was second cousin to Cromwell
by marriage, but supported the Crown and was arrested in 1643
for leading a plot to seize London for Charles I. Fortunate to be

spared execution, he went into exile, and was living in Paris in 1645 when a manuscript of his work came into the hands of a London printer and was published as *Poems*. He wrote eulogies on both Charles I and Cromwell, and was allowed to return in 1651. 'Go, Lovely Rose' is an early poem, a song often set to music. He is best-known for writing highly refined heroic couplets in a regular metre, which became a model for later Augustan poets, most notably Alexander Pope and John Dryden, who wrote of his mastery of smooth verse that 'Mr Waller reformed our numbers'.

BK ■ As in Sir Walter Ralegh's poem 'The Lie' [40] the word 'Tell' is used here by Waller not with comparable frequency but with a comparable sense of urgency. Waller talks to the 'lovely Rose' and makes an ally or intermediary of it, telling it to tell the shy young woman how 'sweet and fair' he thinks she is when compared with the Rose itself; that a Rose unwitnessed is a Rose 'uncommended'; that she must come out into the light and be admired. Finally, Waller tells the Rose to die so that 'she' may realise the fate 'of all things rare'

> How small a part of time they share
> That are so wondrous sweet and fair.

Waller, from his position of authorial power, makes the Rose his go-between, telling it precisely what to say to the woman. Her voice is unheard, in fact non-existent. One wonders what she, given the opportunity, might have replied to the Rose and how the Rose might have felt when communicating her words to Waller.

It's always interesting and sometimes revealing to explore the egotism of beautiful lyric poems such as this. Could the beauty exist without the unself-questioning, somewhat self-righteous and manipulative egotism that motivated the poem? To Waller, the woman is wasting her time. Could it be that, as far as the woman is concerned, her time, far from being wasted, is hers to do what she likes with, including, perhaps the opportunity to escape the attention of someone she finds boring?

Is it fair, one wonders, to ask such questions of a poem? But if the questions suggest themselves, if they insist on the right to 'come forth', should they not be asked and, if possible, answered?

One possible answer is that asking such questions might involve writing more poems.

RICHARD CRASHAW (1612–1649)

from The Flaming Heart

Upon the book and picture of the seraphical Saint Teresa,
as she is usually expressed with a seraphin beside her

O heart, the equal poise of love's both parts,
Big alike with wounds and darts,
Live in these conquering leaves; live all the same,
And walk through all tongues one triumphant flame;
Live here, great heart, and love and die and kill,
And bleed and wound, and yield and conquer still.
Let this immortal life, where'er it comes,
Walk in a crowd of loves and martyrdoms;
Let mystic deaths wait on 't, and wise souls be
The love-slain witnesses of this life of thee.
O sweet incendiary! show here thy art,
Upon this carcass of a hard cold heart,
Let all thy scattered shafts of light, that play
Among the leaves of thy large books of day,
Combined against this breast, at once break in
And take away from me my self and sin;
This gracious robbery shall thy bounty be,
And my best fortunes such fair spoils of me.
O thou undaunted daughter of desires!
By all thy dow'r of lights and fires,
By all the eagle in thee, all the dove,
By all thy lives and deaths of love,
By thy large draughts of intellectual day,
And by thy thirsts of love more large than they,
By all thy brim-filled bowls of fierce desire,
By thy last morning's draught of liquid fire,
By the full kingdom of that final kiss
That seized thy parting soul and sealed thee his,
By all the heavens thou hast in him,
Fair sister of the seraphim!

By all of him we have in thee,
Leave nothing of my self in me:
Let me so read thy life that I
Unto all life of mine may die.

[*Carmen Deo Nostro*, 1652]

Richard Crashaw was a High Anglican cleric, son of a famous
Puritan preacher and anti-Catholic pamphleteer, who lost his post
at Peterhouse, and his curacy of St Mary the Less, Cambridge,
when Cromwell seized the largely Royalist city in 1643. After a
period of living in penury in Paris, he found employment with a
prominent cardinal in Rome in 1646, converted to Catholicism and
was later made canon of the Cathedral of Santa Casa at Loreto,
where he died of a fever within a few months of arrival.

Like Donne and other English metaphysical poets Crashaw makes
use of extended metaphors or 'conceits' in his work, drawing
analogies between the physical beauties of nature and the spiritual
significance of existence, but more in the manner of continental
Baroque poets.

While at Cambridge he met George Herbert's friend Nicholas
Ferrar, and was a frequent visitor to the religious community at
Little Gidding. He clearly saw himself as following in Herbert's
footsteps, with his first collection of poetry in English, *Steps to the
Temple* (1646), titled after Herbert's *The Temple* (1633). The writings
of the Catholic saints (Aquinas, Teresa of Ávila, John of the
Cross, Ignatius of Loyola) were particularly important for him.
His influences were both religious and secular, including not only
the Italian and Spanish mystics, whose work he read in the original,
but also the courtly love and classical traditions associated with
Petrarch and Ovid.

While deeply engaged with the writings of the mystics, his
poetry doesn't fully testify to mystical experiences of his own but
rather an emotional, sensuous devotion to figures like the Virgin
Mary in particular, as well as Teresa of Ávila and Mary Magdalene,
as embodiments of virtue, purity and salvation. His most powerful
work in his vein includes three poems written to Teresa, 'A Hymn
to the Name and Honour of the Admirable Saint Teresa', 'An

Apology for the foregoing Hymn' and 'The Flaming Heart upon the Book and Picture of the Seraphical Saint Teresa' (to give it its full title). 'The Flaming Heart' draws on St Teresa's autobiography, *Life* (1565), in which she tells how a flaming angel appeared beside her:

> His face was aflame with fire so much that he appeared to be one of the highest ranks of angels, those that we call seraphim or cherubim... In his hands, I saw a golden spear, with an iron tip at the end that appeared to be on fire. He plunged it into my heart several times, all the way to my entrails. When he drew it out, he seemed to draw them out, as well, leaving me all on fire with love for God.

BK ■ The heavy bear that goes with Crashaw is 'my self and sin'. His purpose is to rid himself of this burden by praying to Saint Teresa as he contemplates her book and picture. The imagery of books and reading is strongly present; and Crashaw's stated purpose in his concentrated reading of the saint's life is that he may die 'Unto all life' of his own. This is a prayer for martyrdom, for self-sacrifice; and it is expressed through extravagant baroque images of hearts, doves, eagles, lights, 'bowls of fierce desire' and draughts 'of liquid fire'. Self-immersion in the flaming heart will purge that self.

Reading is, like poetry, a form of 'withness'. Reading is company, an experience in special togetherness, the private, imaginative exploration of a theme or idea or world of a poem, play or novel. It can be an experiment in being lost in order to discover a truth. The purpose of Crashaw's reading of Teresa's life is to achieve self-obliteration, the ecstasy of oblivion.

> Let me so read thy life that I
> Unto all life of mine may die.

This is an extravagant, forceful poem that confronts its own heavy bear of sin and degradation and tries to free the spirit in the manner it appears to know best.

RICHARD LOVELACE   (1618–1657)

To Althea, from Prison

When Love with unconfinèd wings
    Hovers within my gates,
And my divine *Althea* brings
    To whisper at the grates;
When I lie tangled in her hair,
    And fettered to her eye,
The *Gods* that wanton in the air,
    Know no such liberty.

When flowing cups run swiftly round
    With no allaying *Thames*,
Our careless heads with roses bound,
    Our hearts with loyal flames;
When thirsty grief in wine we steep,
    When healths and draughts go free,
Fishes that tipple in the deep
    Know no such liberty.

When (like committed linnets) I
    With shriller throat shall sing
The sweetness, mercy, majesty,
    And glories of my King;
When I shall voice aloud how good
    He is, how great should be,
Enlargèd winds, that curl the flood,
    Know no such liberty.

Stone walls do not a prison make,
    Nor iron bars a cage;
Minds innocent and quiet take
    That for an hermitage.

If I have freedom in my love,
    And in my soul am free,
Angels alone that soar above,
    Enjoy such liberty.

1642

Richard Lovelace was a Cavalier poet, courtier, soldier and owner of country estates in Kent. He joined the regiment of Lord Goring in 1649 and served as a captain in the Bishops' Wars in Scotland. He was imprisoned twice, firstly in 1642 for presenting a pro-Episcopal petition to Parliament, when he wrote 'To Althea, from Prison' while being held for seven weeks in Westminster Gatehouse. After selling most of his lands, he spent several years in Holland, and in 1646 was wounded while fighting for the French against the Spaniards. In 1648-49 he was imprisoned again, this time in Peterhouse Prison, Aldgate, for nearly a year, after being arrested by Parliamentary troops as a dangerous Royalist. His support for the Royalist cause is said to have left him financially ruined, and he died in 1657, at the age of 40.

BK ■ This lyrical celebration of freedom is said to have been written in Gatehouse prison. Lovelace says that not the wanton Gods nor tippling fishes nor 'winds that curl the flood' know such liberty as he when

        Love with unconfinèd wings
    Hovers within my gates;
    And my divine *Althea* brings
        To whisper at the grates.

The last stanza is a splendid climax to this celebratory song. Only the angels enjoy the kind of liberty known to the poet, a liberty born of the fact that he has freedom in his love and is free in his soul. Althea, whispering at the grates, is the source and inspiration of this liberty, convincingly and concisely asserted by the imprisoned Lovelace:

    Stone walls do not a prison make,
        Nor iron bars a cage.

75

ANNE BRADSTREET (1612–1672)

A Letter to her Husband, Absent upon Publick Employment

My head, my heart, mine eyes, my life, nay more,
My joy, my magazine of earthly store,
If two be one, as surely thou and I,
How stayest thou there, whilst I at Ipswich lie?
So many steps, head from the heart to sever;
If but a neck, soon should we be together:
I, like the earth this season, mourn in black,
My sun is gone so far in's zodiac,
Whom whilst I 'joyed, nor storms, nor frosts I felt,
His warmth such frigid colds did cause to melt.
My chilled limbs now numbed lie forlorn;
Return, return sweet Sol from Capricorn;
In this dead time, alas, what can I more
Than view those fruits which through thy heat I bore?
Which sweet contentment yield me for a space,
True living pictures of their father's face.
O strange effect! Now thou art southward gone,
I weary grow, the tedious day so long;
But when thou northward to me shalt return,
I wish my sun may never set, but burn
Within the Cancer of my glowing breast,
The welcome house of him my dearest guest.
Where ever, ever stay, and go not thence,
Till nature's sad decree shall call thee hence;
Flesh of thy flesh, bone of thy bone,
I here, thou there, yet both but one.

Mid 1640s? [Several Poems Compiled with Great Variety of Wit and Learning, 1678]

Anne Bradstreet was the first poet from England's New England colonies to be published, and the first Puritan writer in American literature. Born Anne Dudley to a wealthy Puritan family in Northampton, England, she was well educated and married her childhood sweetheart, Simon Bradstreet, at the age of 16. In 1630 she emigrated with her husband and both their families to the New England colonies, raising eight children there and living in several different settlements in Massachusetts in the course of the next four decades: Salem, Charlestown, Boston, Cambridge, Ipswich and North Andover. Both her father and then her husband became governors of Massachusetts Bay Colony.

In Puritan society women were expected to serve God, their husbands and families, confining their work to homemaking. But Anne Bradstreet believed that her poetry could help spread what she believed was a truer version of Christianity to the English-speaking world. While her work espoused her commitment to Puritanism, she was criticised nonetheless because writing was not considered an acceptable role for women; so she had to take care not to offend the Puritan authorities more than was necessary. When her book, *The Tenth Muse, Lately Sprung Up in America* ('by a Gentlewoman of those Parts') was published in London, in 1650, by her brother-in-law, Rev. John Woodbridge, this was supposedly without her knowledge.

Most of her early work is conventional and derivative, reflecting her reading of 16th-century English poets such as Spenser and Sidney, as well as the French poet, Guillaume du Bartas (1544–90), but her later work, published after her death, is highly accomplished and more personal, drawing on her experiences as a Puritan woman, her spiritual questioning and her deep attachments to her husband and family, as in 'A Letter to Her Husband, Absent on Publick Employment', one of a number of poems written to him.

She addresses her husband in the poem by a series of metaphors linked to the signs of the zodiac: he is Sol, her Sun, away from her in 'this dead time' of winter (under Capricorn), to be welcomed back in summer within 'the Cancer of my glowing breast' when her Sun's warmth returns to the world and to her. In another striking metaphor, she refers to their children as 'those fruits which through thy heat I bore'. The 'magazine' in the line 'My joy, my magazine of earthly store' is the term then used for a store of provisions or arms.

BK ■ A personal letter can be one of the most candid forms of direct address. From Keats to Eliot, from Byron to Yeats to Philip Larkin, the letter is a mode of casual revelation of matters profound and trivial, speculative and sure. It can deal with the most complex aesthetics, the state of the weather or the price of fish. A personal letter which is also a poem tends to have a special quality of vulnerable warmth, of naked sincerity. However, the formal discipline and demanding technique necessary for the making of a poem tend to ensure that the sincerity doesn't slip into nostalgia or sentimentality. If successful, the letterpoem captures a rare purity of feeling. So it is with Anne Bradstreet writing to her husband, absent upon public employment.

This is naked writing. He is absent, away from home. She misses him deeply. She writes to express her feelings. She describes the coldness of being alone, she is compelled to 'mourn in black', her 'chilled limbs' suffer 'frigid colds', and she endures all this in what she calls the 'dead time'. Thinking of her husband brings 'warmth' into her heart; through his 'heat' she bore children, her only 'contentment' now. But without her husband she grows 'weary' and life is 'tedious'. Only when he returns will this dull, heavy, boring pain of separation be healed. The last two lines in this 26-line poem assert her vision of togetherness when husband and wife, for the time being still apart, are finally 'one'.

> Flesh of thy flesh, bone of thy bone,
> I here, thou there, yet both but one.

Anne Bradstreet wrote several such poems to her husband. This particular letterpoem, emotionally open and intense, is a good example of her ability to express her feelings of sustained, chilling loneliness at being separated from her loved one.

HENRY VAUGHAN (1621–1695)

They Are All Gone into the World of Light!

They are all gone into the world of light!
   And I alone sit ling'ring here;
Their very memory is fair and bright,
   And my sad thoughts doth clear.

It glows and glitters in my cloudy breast,
   Like stars upon some gloomy grove,
Or those faint beams in which this hill is drest,
   After the sun's remove.

I see them walking in an air of glory,
   Whose light doth trample on my days:
My days, which are at best but dull and hoary,
   Mere glimmering and decays.

O holy hope! and high humility,
   High as the heavens above!
These are your walks, and you have shewed them me
   To kindle my cold love.

Dear, beauteous Death! the jewel of the just,
   Shining nowhere, but in the dark;
What mysteries do lie beyond thy dust
   Could man outlook that mark!

He that hath found some fledged bird's nest, may know
   At first sight, if the bird be flown;
But what fair well or grove he sings in now,
   That is to him unknown.

And yet, as angels in some brighter dreams
    Call to the soul, when man doth sleep:
So some strange thoughts transcend our wonted themes
    And into glory peep.

If a star were confined into a tomb,
    Her captive flames must needs burn there;
But when the hand that locked her up, gives room,
    She'll shine through all the sphere.

O Father of eternal life, and all
    Created glories under thee!
Resume thy spirit from this world of thrall
    Into true liberty.

Either disperse these mists, which blot and fill
    My perspective still as they pass,
Or else remove me hence unto that hill,
    Where I shall need no glass.

[*Silex Scintillans*, second edition, 1655]

Henry Vaughan was an Anglo-Welsh metaphysical poet who abandoned the writing of secular poetry to become a spiritually converted devotional poet. He was born and died in the parish of Llansantffraed near Brecon in Wales, and called himself a Silurist after the original inhabitants of Breconshire, the Celtic Silures. Educated without taking a degree at Oxford, he was studying law in London when the first Civil War broke out, returning home a disappointed supporter of the Royalist cause, at some point somehow becoming a medical doctor and practising as such in Breconshire. His twin brother Thomas, a priest, philosopher and alchemist, was ejected from his living at Llansantffraed after the Royalist defeat, later dying from mercury poisoning from one of his experiments.

Inspired by the example and poetry of George Herbert, Vaughan turned his back on a world in chaos, finding refuge in an ordered private world of devotional verse imbued with the divine presence.

His seminal collection, *Silex Scintillans* (Sparks from the Flint, 1650), offers an imaginative account of his spiritual regeneration, with the divine spark, the spiritual pilgrimage and the ultimate union with God who is Light as its central metaphors. Added to the 1655 second edition, 'They Are All Gone into the World of Light!' reflects his loneliness at the death in 1653 of his first wife Catherine, who had given him a son and three daughters. He married her sister Elizabeth two years later, and wrote no poetry of any note for the next 40 years.

BK ■ The 'withness' that Henry Vaughan experiences so intensely is his sense of the vanished dead and of his own loneliness. (Loneliness is a strong, recurring theme in this book.) Memory is a help to Vaughan but it also serves to drive home to him the fact that his 'dull and hoary' days are but 'glimmerings and decays'.

At this point, he begins to have an even deeper sense of his own impoverished limitations of knowledge and perception, although there are moments when his 'strange thoughts' have the ability to glimpse, to 'peep' into glory.

A choice begins to create itself, and then to assert itself in Vaughan's mind. This choice involves achieving a perspective leading to knowledge of the dead who 'are all gone into the world of light', or else joining these dead so that in their presence his darkness will actually become light.

For Vaughan, this light is 'true liberty' with the power to release him from 'this world of thrall'. The poem's central thrust is towards this light, this liberty, this release into knowing and sharing the fate of those in 'the world of light'. To this end, Vaughan speaks directly to death,

> Dear, beauteous Death! the jewel of the just,

and finds in this direct address the courage to confront the need to choose. This is a poem of dark logic rooted in a passionate desire for light.

ANDREW MARVELL (1621–1678)

To His Coy Mistress

Had we but world enough, and time,
This coyness, Lady, were no crime.
We would sit down, and think which way
To walk, and pass our long love's day.
Thou by the Indian Ganges' side
Shouldst rubies find: I by the tide
Of Humber would complain. I would
Love you ten years before the flood:
And you should, if you please, refuse
Till the conversion of the Jews.
My vegetable love should grow
Vaster than empires, and more slow;
An hundred years should go to praise
Thine eyes, and on thy forehead gaze.
Two hundred to adore each breast:
But thirty thousand to the rest.
An age at least to every part,
And the last age should show your heart:
For, Lady, you deserve this state,
Nor would I love at lower rate.
  But at my back I always hear
Time's wingèd chariot hurrying near:
And yonder all before us lie
Deserts of vast eternity.
Thy beauty shall no more be found;
Nor, in thy marble vault, shall sound
My echoing song: then worms shall try
That long-preserved virginity:
And your quaint honour turn to dust;
And into ashes all my lust;
The grave's a fine and private place,
But none, I think, do there embrace.

Now therefore, while the youthful glue
Sits on thy skin like morning dew,
And while thy willing soul transpires
At every pore with instant fires,
Now let us sport us while we may;
And now, like amorous birds of prey,
Rather at once our time devour,
Than languish in his slow-chapped power.
Let us roll all our strength, and all
Our sweetness, up into one ball:
And tear our pleasures with rough strife,
Through the iron gates of life.
Thus, though we cannot make our sun
Stand still, yet we will make him run.

Early 1650s (?) [*Miscellaneous Poems*, 1681]

Andrew Marvell was one of the later English metaphysical poets, a politician who served as MP for Hull at various times from 1659 until his death in 1678. Born near Hull in the East Riding of Yorkshire, he attended Trinity College, Cambridge, from the age of 13, and spent some years travelling in Europe during the English Civil War. His poem 'Upon Appleton House', dedicated to Lord General Thomas Fairfax, was written during the early 1550s when he was tutor to the daughter of Cromwell's general on his estate near York. 'To His Coy Mistress' was written around that time.

In 1653 he moved to Eton to take up a post as tutor to Cromwell's ward William Dutton, and in 1657 joined John Milton, by now blind, as Latin secretary to Cromwell's Council of State. The two writers became friends, and when Milton was at risk of execution for his anti-monarchical writings following the Restoration, Marvell intervened with others to obtain a pardon, leaving Milton free to embark on the writing of his great work *Paradise Lost*.

Like Donne and other 17th-century metaphysical poets, Marvell wasn't known as a poet in his lifetime. Most of his work was only circulated in manuscript and later published posthumously, and it wasn't until the 20th century that Marvell was recognised as one of the major poets of his time. While T.S. Eliot contended that 'his best poems are not very many', his essay for 'the tercentenary of the former member for Hull' prompted a revaluation of Marvell's poetry, appearing just after his seminal essay 'The Metaphysical Poets' (1921). In Eliot's view, Marvell, 'more a man of the century than a Puritan, speaks more clearly and unequivocally with the voice of his literary age than does Milton':

> This voice speaks out uncommonly strong in the *Coy Mistress.* The theme is one of the great commonplaces of European literature. It is the theme of *O mistress mine*, of *Gather ye rosebuds*, of *Go, lovely rose*; it is in the savage austerity of Lucretius and the intense levity of Catullus. Where the wit of Marvell renews the theme is in the variety and order of the images. [...] It will hardly be denied that this poem contains wit; but it may not be evident that this wit forms the crescendo and dimuendo of a scale of great imaginative power. The wit is not only combined with, but fused into, the imagination. [...] In fact, this alliance of levity and seriousness (by which the seriousness is intensified) is a characteristic of the sort of wit we are trying to identify.[10]

Marvell's 'best poems' are a great many more in number than Eliot admits, but most date from his earlier years as a Cavalier lyricist. These were followed by eulogies for Cromwell, and then bitter satires attacking monarchy and church after the Restoration. Irish readers are unlikely to register the ironic deprecation which English critics assert is present in his equivocal encomium 'An Horatian Ode upon Cromwell's Return from Ireland'.

Line 11: 'vegetable love' means love that grows, as in the doctrine of the three souls, vegetative, sensitive and rational. Line 33: some editions have 'hue' instead of 'glue' but 'youthful glue' is consistent with the poem's manuscript as well as with its theme, as in 'Life is nothing else but as it were a glue, which in man fasteneth the soul and body together' (William Baldwin, *Moral Philosophy*, 1547).

BK ■ Coyness is a kind of shyness, a self-protective stance of cultivated modesty, knowingly and archly reticent, essentially a sort of emotional equipment used to ward off whatever or whoever the coy person considers should be so treated. Marvell speaks directly to his coy mistress in a poem falling neatly into three sections which might be headed Fantasy, Reality and Resolution or Exhortation. Attitudes to time, as in so many of the poems in this anthology, are central to each of these three themes. In the first section, the fantasy centres on the possibility, or the impossibility of time being always available, plenty time, more than enough time for the poet to do justice to the coy mistress's beauty; she, of course, may reject his praises at will because centuries are easily available, simply waiting to be used in her service. Needless to say, she richly deserves these protracted ages of deliberate and appropriate homage. Unfortunately, as we enter the second section, Reality, the real nature of time (as explored by many poets included here) begins to assert itself.

> But at my back I always hear
> Time's wingèd chariot hurrying near;
> And yonder all before us lie
> Deserts of vast eternity.

We switch suddenly from the slow, idyllic vision of the opening section to the work of what Shakespeare calls 'Devouring time'. Marvell, too, presents time's devouring force at work as he speaks of worms trying the coy mistress's 'long preserved virginity' her 'giant honour' being turned 'to dust', and his own 'lust' becoming 'ashes'. This second section ends with two memorable lines, lines that are best described as, yes, coy: 'The grave's a fine and private place, / But none, I think, do there embrace.'

Equipped with the knowledge that love is unlikely ('I think') between corpses, Marvell goes on to give us his own robust version of 'Gather ye rosebuds while ye may' when he says 'Now let us sport us while we may'. Coyness, blandness, feigned indifference are swept aside and Marvell and his mistress become, in his ebullient exhortation, 'amorous birds of prey' determined to 'devour' time rather than 'languish' in it. The poem roughens up, develops muscle and intention. The lovers will

> tear our pleasures with rough strife,
> Through the iron gates of life:
> Thus, though we cannot make our sun
> Stand still, yet we will make him run.

The change in the poem from blandness to intensity, from coyness that is 'no crime' to passion that is no joke, is fluent, firm and exhilarating. The poem's toughening, joyous character is strengthened by Marvell's skilled, unobtrusive handling of the octosyllabic couplet as he presents us with fantasy, reality and resolution. This poem feels like an emotional journey of different stages and character. When we reach the end of that journey we realise how thought-provoking and refreshing it has been.

JOHN MILTON   (1606–1687)

from **Paradise Lost**
(Book 1, lines 27-75)

Say first, for Heaven hides nothing from thy view
Nor the deep tract of Hell, say first what cause
Moved our grandparents in that happy state,
Favoured of Heaven so highly, to fall off
From their Creator, and transgress his Will
For one restraint, lords of the world besides?
Who first seduced them to that foul revolt?
The infernal Serpent; he it was, whose guile
Stirred up with envy and revenge, deceived
The Mother of Mankind, what time his pride
Had cast him out from Heaven, with all his host
Of rebel angels, by whose aid aspiring
To set himself in glory above his peers,
He trusted to have equalled the most High,
If he opposed; and with ambitious aim
Against the throne and monarchy of God
Raised impious war in Heaven and battle proud
With vain attempt. Him the Almighty Power
Hurled headlong flaming from the ethereal sky
With hideous ruin and combustion down
To bottomless perdition, there to dwell
In adamantine chains and penal fire,
Who durst defy the Omnipotent to arms.
Nine times the space that measures day and night
To mortal men, he with his horrid crew
Lay vanquished, rowling in the fiery gulf
Confounded though immortal. But his doom
Reserved him to more wrath; for now the thought
Both of lost happiness and lasting pain
Torments him; round he throws his baleful eyes
That witnessed huge affliction and dismay

Mixed with obdurate pride and steadfast hate:
At once as far as angels ken he views
The dismal situation waste and wilde,
A dungeon horrible, on all sides round
As one great furnace flamed, yet from those flames
No light, but rather darkness visible
Served only to discover sights of woe,
Regions of sorrow, doleful shades, where peace
And rest can never dwell, hope never comes
That comes to all; but torture without end
Still urges, and a fiery deluge, fed
With ever-burning sulphur unconsumed:
Such place eternal justice had prepared
For those rebellious, here their prison ordained
In utter darkness, and their portion set
As far removed from God and light of Heaven
As from the centre thrice to the utmost pole.
O how unlike the place from whence they fell!

1658-64 [1667/1674]

John Milton was an English poet and polemicist who worked as a civil servant for the Commonwealth of England under Cromwell. Writing at a time of religious flux and political upheaval, he cast his epic poem *Paradise Lost* in blank verse – in unrhymed iambic pentameter – to 'justify the ways of God to men'. First published in 1667, the poem retells the biblical story of the Fall of Man: the temptation of Adam and Eve by the fallen angel Satan and their expulsion from the Garden of Eden. The shorter *Paradise Regained* – on Satan's temptation of Christ – followed in 1671. His other great works included sonnets and longer pastoral elegies.

Most of Milton's poetry doesn't use rhyme. And not only did he *not* rhyme *Paradise Lost*, but in its preface he was quite definite – in the 1660s – about this 'troublesome and modern bondage of rhyming'. He pointed out that rhyme 'was no necessary Adjunct or true Ornament of Poem or good Verse...' and went so far as to call it 'trivial' – 'the Invention of a barbarous Age, to set off wretched matter and lame Meeter'.

BK ■ Milton invokes the aid of the Holy Spirit in Book One of *Paradise Lost* to help him pursue 'Things unattempted yet in Prose or Rhime'. He is keenly aware of the huge problems confronting him as he undertakes his great epic; some of these problems have to do with the nature of his own inner life as man and poet. He prays for help:

> What in me is dark
> Illumine, what is low, raise and support.

Such help is essential if he is to achieve his aim, which is 'to justify the ways of God to men'.

Milton deliberately hands his poem over to the Holy Spirit. Twice in the first two lines of this extract from Book One his request to the Holy Spirit is 'Say first [...] say first'.

Milton wishes heaven to be on his side, to be his oracle, his inspiration, yet it could be argued that his poem achieves some of its most sublime moments when it confronts and portrays Hell, Lucifer and the hordes of fallen angels, thrown out of Heaven because they assisted Lucifer in his plans

> equalled the most High,
> If he opposed; and with ambitious aim
> Against the throne and monarchy of God
> Raised impious war in Heaven and battle proud
> With vain attempt.

Hell is Lucifer's reward and Milton's harrowing picture of Hell is one of the most thunderously eloquent successes in English poetry. To read it closely and repeatedly is to experience some, at least, of the horror confronting Lucifer's eyes and mind when he faces the thought both 'of lost happiness and lasting pain' and 'torture without end' in a prison of 'utter darkness'.

There are many portrayals of Hell in literature. Milton's is one of the most unforgettable because of its searing images and shockingly precise words which, once allowed into memory, continue to echo down the years, deepening always in ferocity and power like a nightmare that cannot be shaken off. And yet, even in the depths of his savagely imagined Hell, Milton achieves a bleak, desolate beauty; it travels with one, haunting one's heart, mind and imagination, through one's life.

THOMAS TRAHERNE (1636–1674)

Dreams

'Tis strange! I saw the skies,
I saw the hills before mine eyes,
The sparrow fly,
The lands that did about me lie,
The real sun, that heavenly eye!
Can closèd eyes even in the darkest night
See through their lids, and be informed with sight?

The people were to me
As true as those by day I see,
As true the air;
The earth as sweet, as fresh, as fair
As that which did by day repair
Unto my waking sense! Can all the sky,
Can all the world, within my brain-pan lie?

What sacred secret's this
Which seems to intimate my bliss?
What is there in
The narrow confines of my skin,
That is alive, and feels within
When I am dead? Can magnitude possess
An active memory, yet not be less?

May all that I can see
Awake, by night within me be?
My childhood knew
No difference, but all was true,
As real all as what I view;
The world itself was there; 'twas wondrous strange,
That heaven and earth should so their place exchange.

Till that which vulgar sense
Doth falsely call experience,
    Distinguished things:
The ribands, and the gaudy wings
Of birds, the virtues and the sins,
That represented were in dreams by night
As really my senses did delight,

    Or grieve, as those I saw
By day; things terrible did awe
    My soul with fear;
The apparitions seemed as near
As things could be, and things they were;
Yet were they all by fancy in me wrought,
And all their being founded in a thought.

    O what a thing is thought!
Which seems a dream, yea, seemeth nought,
    Yet doth the mind
Affect as much as what we find
Most near and true! Sure men are blind,
And can't the forcible reality
Of things that secret are within them see.

    Thought! Surely thoughts are true;
They please as much as things can do;
    Nay, things are dead,
And in themselves are severèd
From souls; nor can they fill the head
Without our thoughts. Thoughts are the real things
From whence all joy, from whence all sorrow springs.

Thomas Traherne was an Anglican clergyman whose poetry
wasn't known or published until the 20th century. Born the son of
a Hereford shoemaker, he must have proved himself an outstanding
scholar at Hereford Cathedral School to have been admitted to
Brasenose College, Oxford, where he is said to have spent eight

years, taking holy orders in 1656 and being appointed rector of Credenhill near Hereford the following year. In 1667 he took up the post of private chaplain to Sir Orlando Bridgeman, Lord Keeper of the Great Seal, at Teddington, Middlesex. The year before his death his only publication, *Roman Forgeries* (1673), an anti-Catholic prose polemic, was published anonymously. His modest literary reputation was based on his prose works, three of which were published posthumously, most notably a work of theological and ethic discourse entitled *Christian Ethicks: Or, Divine Morality. Opening the Way to Blessedness, By the Rules of Vertue and Reason*, prepared by Traherne before his death and published in 1675.

He is now recognised as the last great mystical English poet of the 17th century, but only due to a chance discovery of two of his manuscripts at a London bookstall in the winter of 1896-97, one of poetry, and the other titled the 'Centuries' consisting of short reflections on religion interspersed with some poems. Believed at first to be lost works by Henry Vaughan, they were identified as Traherne's by the bookseller and literary scholar, Bertram Dobell, who published the verse as *The Poetical Works of Thomas Traherne* in 1903, followed by the prose poems in a book he titled *Centuries of Meditations*, in 1908. Other Traherne manuscripts were discovered much later, including one found on fire on a rubbish dump in Lancashire, around 1967, by a man looking for spare parts for his car, the poems from which were later published as *Commentaries of Heaven: The Poems* (1989), as well as an unfinished 1800-line epic poem called 'The Ceremonial Line' found in the Folger Library in Washington, DC, in 1996, and a number of prose works identified in the Archbishop of Canterbury's library at Lambeth Palace, in 1997. It is unlikely that Traherne's entire *oeuvre* will ever be published, with a number of works likely to remain lost.

BK ■ This is a meditation on dreams, and as Traherne probes and ponders his opening statement that "'Tis strange!' he methodically thinks himself into the conclusion that

Thoughts are the real things
From whence all joy, from whence all sorrow springs.

One of the abiding ironies of dreams is that when we talk about them we tend to, we *have* to, use a rational, or acceptably reasonable language; the language of reason tries to unravel the secrets and mysteries of a state beyond reason. Is this inherently futile, ludicrous? Can language, as we believe we know it, explain or make available the amazing otherness of the life of dreams?

Traherne, in this beautifully shaped poem, as flawlessly formed as a perfect argument, delves into the vision, the truth, the apparitions, the purely vital convincingness of dreams, their complete reality, that is, when one is going through them, but changed to 'dreams' when one awakens and begins to talk about them in what we may call daylight language. At this point, we are back in our familiar world, and daylanguage speaks of nightreality. Worlds apart. But we must explain ourselves to ourselves and to each other. And when we use our daylanguage we do so with an air of truthtelling, of mystery explaining, that seems to derive its authority from the fact that we are now, once again, the controlling, articulate beings of daylight who can explain dreams and poems to each other and sincerely believe we 'know' them.

Never having heard of Jung, Freud and their gifted millions of dream-explaining disciples, Traherne explores dreams with an innocence now lost to almost everybody except dreamers. Or rather, Traherne asks questions with a vigorous, childlike wonder:

> Can closèd eyes even in the darkest night
> See through their lids, and be informed with sight?

>   Can all the sky,
> Can all the world, within my brain-pan lie?

>   May all that I can see
> Awake, by night within me be?

Much of the appeal of this poem lies in the intrepid vigour of its questioning spirit, in its attempt to get at the differences between dreamlife and mindlife, nightlife in sleep and daylife in waking. Ultimately, a poem such as this is the result of the skilled combination of these lives; it could not exist without being dream-haunted and mind-managed. The world of poetry is often poised between different worlds and tingles with life both familiar and strange.

JOHN DRYDEN (1636–1674)

from Absalom and Achitophel

This plot, which failed for want of common sense,
Had yet a deep and dangerous consequence:
For, as when raging fevers boil the blood,
The standing lake soon floats into a flood;
And every hostile humour, which before
Slept quiet in its channels, bubbles o'er:
So, several factions from this first ferment,
Work up to foam, and threat the government.
Some by their friends, more by themselves thought wise,
Opposed the power, to which they could not rise.
Some had in courts been great, and thrown from thence,
Like fiends, were hardened in impenitence.
Some by their monarch's fatal mercy grown,
From pardoned rebels, kinsmen to the throne;
Were raised in power and public office high;
Strong bands, if bands ungrateful men could tie.
    Of these the false *Achitophel* was first:
A name to all succeeding ages curst.
For close designs, and crooked counsels fit;
Sagacious, bold, and turbulent of wit:
Restless, unfixed in principles and place;
In power unpleased, impatient of disgrace.
A fiery soul, which working out its way,
Fretted the pigmy-body to decay:
And o'er informed the tenement of clay.
A daring pilot in extremity;
Pleased with the danger, when the waves went high
He sought the storms; but for a calm unfit,
Would steer too nigh the sands, to boast his wit.
Great wits are sure to madness near allied;
And thin partitions do their bounds divide:

Else, why should he, with wealth and honour blest,
Refuse his age the needful hours of rest?
Punish a body which he could not please;
Bankrupt of life, yet prodigal of ease?
And all to leave, what with his toil he won
To that unfeathered, two-legged thing, a son:
Got, while his soul did huddled notions try;
And born a shapeless lump, like anarchy.
In friendship false, implacable in hate:
Resolved to ruin or to rule the state.
To compass this the triple bond he broke;
The pillars of the public safety shook:
And fitted *Israel* for a foreign yoke.
Then, seized with fear, yet still affecting fame,
Usurped a patriot's all-atoning name.
So easy still it proves in factious times,
With public zeal to cancel private crimes:
How safe is treason, and how sacred ill,
Where none can sin against the people's will:
Where crowds can wink; and no offence be known,
Since in another's guilt they find their own.
Yet, fame deserved, no enemy can grudge;
The statesman we abhor, but praise the judge.

[1681]   *(lines 134–87)*

John Dryden was the dominant poet and literary critic of Restoration England. His 'Absalom and Achitophel' (1681) is an allegory of political events of the time drawn from Biblical story of Absalom's rebellion against King David aided by Achitophel. Dryden's 'false Achitophel' is the opportunist Earl of Shaftesbury (1621-83), who supported Monmouth's claim to the throne to prevent the succession of the future Catholic King James II after the death of Charles II.

'Dryden's genius is to me essentially satirical,' Brendan wrote in a letter, suggesting we include 'one his savage portraits', also to show 'the genius of the couplet – one of the truly powerful instruments in English poetry'. This was the extract we chose for his unwritten commentary.

JOHN OLDHAM (1653–1683)

from The third satire of Juvenal, imitated

The poet brings in a friend of his, giving him an account
why he removes from London to live in the country.

'I live in London? What should I do there?
I cannot lie, nor flatter, nor forswear:
I can't commend a book, or piece of wit
(Though a lord were the author) dully writ:
I'm no Sir Sidrophel to read the stars,
And cast nativities for longing heirs,
When fathers shall drop off: no Gadbury
To tell the minute when the King shall die,
And you know what – come in: nor can I steer,
And tack about my conscience, whensoe'er
To a new point, I see religion veer.
Let others pimp to courtier's lechery,
I'll draw no city cuckold's curse on me:
Nor would I do it, though to be made great,
And raised to be chief Minister of State.
Therefore I think it fit to rid the town
Of one that is an useless member grown.
   'Besides, who has pretence to favour now,
But he, who hidden villainy does know,
Whose breast does with some burning secret glow?
By none thou shalt preferred, or valued be,
That trusts thee with an honest secrecy:
He only may to great men's friendship reach,
Who great men, when he pleases, can impeach.
Let others thus aspire to dignity;
For me, I'd not their envied grandeur buy
For all the Exchange is worth, that Paul's will cost,
Or was of late in the Scotch voyage lost.
What would it boot, if I, to gain my end,
Forego my quiet, and my ease of mind,

95

Still feared, at last betrayed by my great friend?
    'Another cause, which I must boldly own,
And not the least, for which I quit the town,
Is to behold it made the common-shore
Where France does all her filth and ordure pour:
What spark of true old English rage can bear
Those, who were slaves at home, to lord it here?
We've all our fashions, language, compliments,
Our music, dances, curing, cooking thence;
And we shall have their poisoning too ere long,
If still in the improvement we go on.
What wouldst thou say, great Harry, shouldst thou view
Thy gaudy fluttering race of English now,
Their tawdry clothes, pulvilios, essences,
Their Chedreux perruques, and those vanities,
Which thou, and they of old did so despise?
What wouldst thou say to see th'infected town
With the foul spawn of foreigners o'errun?
Hither from Paris, and all parts they come,
The spew, and vomit of their gaols at home:
To court they flock, and to St James his Square,
And wriggle into great men's service there:
Footboys at first, till they, from wiping shoes,
Grow by degrees the masters of the house:
Ready of wit, hardened of impudence,
Able with ease to put down either Haines,
Both the King's player, and King's evidence;
Flippant of talk, and voluble of tongue,
With words at will, no lawyer better hung:
Softer than flattering court-parasite,
Or city trader, when he means to cheat,
No calling or profession comes amiss:
A needy monsieur can be what he please,
Groom, page, valet, quack, operator, fencer,
Perfumer, pimp, jack-pudding, juggler, dancer:
Give but the word, the cur will fetch and bring,
Come over to the Emperor, or King:

Or, if you please, fly o'er the pyramid,
Which Jordan and the rest in vain have tried.

'Can I have patience, and endure to see
The paltry foreign wretch take place of me,
Whom the same wind and vessel brought ashore,
That brought prohibited goods, and dildoes o'er?
Then, pray, what mighty privilege is there
For me, that at my birth drew English air?
And where's the benefit to have my veins
Run British blood, if there's no difference
'Twixt me and him, the statute freedom gave,
And made a subject of a true-born slave?

'But nothing shocks, and is more loathed by me,
Than the vile rascal's fulsome flattery:
By help of this false magnifying glass,
A louse or flea shall for a camel pass:
Produce an hideous wight, more ugly far
Than those ill shapes which in old hangings are,
He'll make him straight a beau garçon appear:
Commend his voice and singing, though he bray
Worse than Sir Martin Marr-all in the play:
And, if he rhyme, shall praise for standard wit,
More scurvy sense than Prynne, and Vicars writ.

'And here's the mischief, though we say the same,
He is believed, and we are thought to sham:
Do you but smile, immediately the beast
Laughs out aloud, though he ne'er heard the jest:
Pretend you're sad, he's presently in tears,
Yet grieves no more than marble, when it wears
Sorrow in metaphor: but speak of heat,
'O God! how sultry 'tis!' he'll cry, and sweat
In depth of winter: straight, if you complain
Of cold, the weather-glass is sunk again:
Then he'll call for his frieze campaign, and swear
'Tis beyond eighty, he's in Greenland here.
Thus he shifts scenes, and oft'ner in a day
Can change his face, than actors at a play:

There's nought so mean can 'scape the flatt'ring sot,
Not his Lord's snuff-box, nor his powder-spot:
If he but spit, or pick his teeth, he'll cry,
'How everything becomes you! let me die.
Your lordship does it most judiciously!'
And swear 'tis fashionable if he sneeze,
Extremely taking, and it needs must please.
    'Besides, there's nothing sacred, nothing free
From the hot satyr's rampant lechery:
Nor wife, nor virgin-daughter can escape,
Scarce thou thyself, or son avoid a rape:
All must go padlocked: if nought else there be,
Suspect thy very stables' chastity.
By this the vermin into secrets creep,
Thus families in awe they strive to keep.
What living for an Englishman is there,
Where such as these get head, and domineer,
Whose use and custom 'tis, never to share
A friend, but love to reign without dispute,
Without a rival, full and absolute?
Soon as the insect gets his Honour's ear,
And flyblows some of 's poisonous malice there,
Straight I'm turned off, kicked out of doors, discarded,
And all my former service disregarded.

May 1682 [1683]

John Oldham was a poet of great promise who died at the age of
30 having only just established his reputation as a notable satirist.
Years later his imitations of classical satire were to provide a model
for Alexander Pope and other Augustan poets. Dryden's famous
elegy on John Oldham was one of many tributes to the 'Marcellus
of our tongue':

> Farewel, too little and too lately known,
> Whom I began to think and call my own;
> For sure our souls were nearly ally'd; and thine
> Cast in the sam Poetick mould with mine.

Born at Shipton Moyne near Tetbury in Gloucestershire, John Oldham was nine years old when his Nonconformist father was ejected from his rectory by the church authorities following the Restoration. After studying at Oxford, he became a schoolmaster in Croydon and later a private tutor. He gained some recognition with the publication in 1681 of his *Satyrs upon the Jesuits*, which drew upon the invective of the Latin poet Juvenal. His *Poems and Translations* followed in July 1682, including his imitations of Juvenal and the French poet Nicolas Boileau. That December he died at the house of his patron Willam Pierrepont at Holme Pierrepont, Nottinghamshire.

Much of this poem (including this extract, lines 54-185) is "spoken" by an invented friend, Timon, who is shown to be as self-interested as the courtiers and other villainous city dwellers he rounds upon, his retreat being more to do with his own situation than the good of society. Oldham the poet shares Timon's distaste for a morally corrupt society, but shows himself to be much more of an outsider. Oldham's version of Juvenal can be compared with Samuel Johnson's 'London' [107-13], another imitation of the third satire.

BK ■ The title says that the poem is 'imitated' but there's nothing imitative about Oldham's friend's rage and disgust at what he sees happening in his beloved London. Earlier on in this poem, a line not included in the extract given here, says '"Tis my resolve to quit the nauseous town.' Our chosen extract gives some of Oldham's 'good old' friend Timon's enraged reasons for quitting London where 'knavery' is 'the only thriving trade' and where he is compelled to see his 'slender fortune' dwindle every day.

This picture of London is devastating. It is a metropolis of lies, vanity, treachery, deceit, 'hidden villainy', blackmail, envy, betrayal and endlessly versatile forms of corruption. No real friendship is possible there. Only moral poison and pollution prevail. In this venomous atmosphere, Timon picks out one special source of poison, the human 'filth and ordure' pouring into London from France. Of the 128 lines included in this extract, 97 are given over to the detailed, savage depiction of the French in London. We see Timon's 'true old English rage' flaring up as he contemplates the vile shenanigans of those 'who were slaves at home' in France, yet manage 'to lord it here' in London. These people, 'the spew and vomit' of French jails, are actually welcomed to London by the 'gaudy fluttering race of English now'. Timon depicts the effects of French deceit at work on English gullibility, 'the foul spawn of foreigners' overrunning genuine 'British blood'. This Englishman feels displaced, 'discarded' by the 'paltry foreign wretch' whose 'fulsome flattery' wins the day. The versatility of French flattery, its ready, fraudulent approvals and reassurances, its eagerly compliant distortions, its creepy capacity to agree with the beliefs and opinions of those being flattered, result in the fact that 'He is believed and we are thought a sham'.

On top of all this,

> there's nothing sacred, nothing free
> From the hot satyr's rampant lechery:
> Nor wife, nor virgin-daughter can escape,
> Scarce thou thyself, or son avoid a rape:
> All must go padlocked: if nought else there be,
> Suspect thy very stables' chastity.
> By this the vermin into secrets creep,
> Thus families in awe they strive to keep.
> What living for an Englishman is there,
> Where such as these get head, and domineer [...]

In London, his home, Timon is an outcast. All his 'former service' is 'disregarded'. He is 'turned off, kicked out of doors, discarded'. It is time to leave.

There are moments in Oldham's ruthlessly generalised picture of the French in London when one feels the presence of a paranoid, chauvinistic pulse, a flag-waving, jingoistic fury. Yet within the scene of generalised condemnation there are brutally particular details which help to give this extract a fascinating power. London has inspired many splendid poems. Oldham's hard-hitting 'imitation' of Juvenal is impressive in its pitiless, searingly abusive way. Such savage candour is rare enough in poetry. We should remember, though, that it is a 'dear old friend' who is speaking, not the poet himself. The abuse is all the more effective for this deft use of Timon's voice. It is Timon who is leaving London. This sad fact makes his and the poem's rage completely authentic.

JONATHAN SWIFT (1667–1745)

A Description of a City Shower
(In Imitation of Virgil's Georgics)

Careful observers may foretell the hour
(By sure prognostics) when to dread a shower:
While rain depends, the pensive cat gives o'er
Her frolics, and pursues her tail no more.
Returning home at night, you'll find the sink
Strike your offended sense with double stink.
If you be wise, then go not far to dine,
You spend in coach-hire more than save in wine.
A coming shower your shooting corns presage,
Old achès throb, your hollow tooth will rage.
Sauntering in coffee-house is *Dulman* seen;
He damns the climate and complains of spleen.

   Meanwhile the South, rising with dabbled wings,
A sable cloud athwart the welkin flings,
That swilled more liquor than it could contain,
And, like a drunkard, gives it up again.
Brisk *Susan* whips her linen from the rope,
While the first drizzling shower is born aslope,
Such is that sprinkling which some careless quean
Flirts on you from her mop, but not so clean.
You fly, invoke the gods; then turning, stop
To rail; she singing, still whirls on her mop.
Not yet, the dust had shunned the unequal strife,
But aided by the wind, fought still for life;
And wafted with its foe by violent gust,
'Twas doubtful which was rain, and which was dust.
Ah! where must needy poet seek for aid,
When dust and rain at once his coat invade;
Sole coat, where dust cemented by the rain,
Erects the nap, and leaves a cloudy stain.

101

Now in contiguous drops the flood comes down,
Threatening with deluge this *devoted* town.
To shops in crowds the daggled females fly,
Pretend to cheapen goods, but nothing buy.
The Templer spruce, while every spout's abroach,
Stays till 'tis fair, yet seems to call a coach.
The tucked-up sempstress walks with hasty strides,
While streams run down her oiled umbrella's sides.
Here various kinds by various fortunes led,
Commence acquaintance underneath a shed.
Triumphant Tories, and desponding Whigs,
Forget their feuds, and join to save their wigs.
Boxed in a chair the beau impatient sits,
While spouts run clattering o'er the roof by fits;
And ever and anon with frightful din
The leather sounds, he trembles from within.
So when *Troy* chair-men bore the wooden steed,
Pregnant with *Greeks* impatient to be freed
(Those bully *Greeks*, who, as the moderns do,
Instead of paying chair-men, run them through.)
Laocoön struck the outside with his spear,
And each imprisoned hero quaked for fear.

Now from all parts the swelling kennels flow,
And bear their trophies with them as they go:
Filth of all hues and odours seem to tell
What streets they sailed from, by the sight and smell.
They, as each torrent drives, with rapid force,
From *Smithfield*, or *St Pulchre's* shape their course,
And in huge confluent joined at *Snow-Hill Ridge*,
Fall from the conduit prone to *Holborn-Bridge*.
Sweepings from butchers' stalls, dung, guts, and blood,
Drowned puppies, stinking sprats, all drenched in mud,
Dead cats, and turnip-tops come tumbling down the flood.

1710 [First published in *The Tatler*, October 1710]

depends: is imminent; *sink:* sewer; *quean;* slut; *devoted:* doomed; *kennels:* gutters

Jonathan Swift was the foremost prose satirist in English, an Anglo-Irish cleric who published his work under pseudonyms, most famously Lemuel Gulliver. Born in Dublin, he became a renowned pamphleteer, 'a Whig in politics and Tory in religion', switching his support to the 'Triumphant Tories' in 1710 – when this poem was written in London – partly because the Whigs had not given the Irish clergy the same remuneration granted to their brethren in England. He held a variety of positions in Ireland and England before becoming Dean of St Patrick's Cathedral in Dublin. His great renown as a prose writer has overshadowed his poetry which shows comparable virtuosity and wit. 'A Description of a City Shower' is a burlesque imitation of Virgil's *Georgics* in which both London society and romanticised nature poetry bear the full brunt of his mockery. In the last three lines he has a dig at poets – including Dryden – who were too fond of ending a triplet with an alexandrine. In 18th-century English 'aches' was pronounced *aitches*.

BK ■ Beginning with signs such as a cat pursuing its tail no more, and ending with a deluge of stinking 'dung, guts, and blood', Swift's 'A Description of a City Shower' is a fluently dramatic poem which, among other things, is a nose-twitching portrayal of London dirt flowing with apparently unstoppable concentration. The couplet is here joyously used by Swift to capture that drama starting with 'sure prognostics' and culminating in a jumbled pile of 'Drowned puppies, stinking sprats [...] Dead cats, and turnip-tops, come tumbling down the flood'. We all know what it means to sense an imminent downpour. In this poem, Brisk Susan whipping 'her linen from the rope' is a good example of such apprehension. There are others, too, such as 'the templer spruce', 'the tucked-up sempstress', 'Triumphant Tories and desponding Whigs', 'the beau impatient'. Swift introduces 'bully Greeks' from mythology to extend and deepen the drama before 'Filths of all hues and odour' are released to bring the poem to a reeking climax.

Shakespeare fuses inner and outer weathers perfectly in Sonnet 73, 'That time of year...' [48-49]. Swift concentrates more on the outer weather, the London rain itself, to great effect. His poem has an almost apocalyptic feeling; heaven's rage seems increasingly evident; one is glad to be able to read 'A Description of a City Shower' with a roof over one's head.

ALEXANDER POPE (1688-1744)

Epistle to Miss Blount, On Her Leaving the Town, After the Coronation

As some fond virgin, whom her mother's care
Drags from the town to wholesome country air,
Just when she learns to roll a melting eye,
And hear a spark, yet think no danger nigh;
From the dear man unwillingly she must sever,
Yet takes one kiss before she parts for ever:
Thus from the world fair *Zephalinda* flew,
Saw others happy, and with sighs withdrew;
Not that their pleasures caused her discontent,
She sighed not that They stayed, but that She went.

She went, to plain-work, and to purling brooks,
Old-fashioned halls, dull aunts, and croaking rooks,
She went from Opera, park, assembly, play,
To morning walks, and prayers three hours a day;
To pass her time 'twixt reading and Bohea,
To muse, and spill her solitary tea,
Or o'er cold coffee trifle with the spoon,
Count the slow clock, and dine exact at noon;
Divert her eyes with pictures in the fire,
Hum half a tune, tell stories to the squire;
Up to her godly garret after seven,
There starve and pray, for that's the way to heaven.

Some Squire, perhaps, you take delight to rack;
Whose game is Whisk, whose treat a toast in sack,
Who visits with a gun, presents you birds,
Then gives a smacking buss, and cries – No words!
Or with his hound comes hollowing from the stable,
Makes love with nods, and knees beneath a table;
Whose laughs are hearty, though his jests are coarse,
And loves you best of all things – but his horse.
In some fair evening, on your elbow laid,

Your dream of triumphs in the rural shade;
In pensive thought recall the fancied scene,
See Coronations rise on every green;
Before you pass the imaginary sights
Of Lords, and Earls, and Dukes, and gartered Knights;
While the spread fan o'ershades your closing eyes;
Then give one flirt, and all the vision flies.
Thus vanish sceptres, coronets, and balls,
And leave you in lone woods, or empty walls.
    So when your slave, at some dear, idle time,
(Not plagued with headaches, or the want of rhyme)
Stands in the streets, abstracted from the crew,
And while he seems to study, thinks of you:
Just when his fancy points your sprightly eyes,
Or sees the blush of soft *Parthenia* rise,
Gay pats my shoulder, and you vanish quite;
Streets, chairs, and coxcombs rush upon my sight;
Vexed to be still in town, I knit my brow,
Look sour, and hum a tune – as you may now.

1714 [*Works*, 1717]

Bohea: tea; *whisk:* whist; *flirt:* sudden movement of a fan; *chairs:* sedan-chairs

Alexander Pope succeeded John Dryden as the foremost poet and satirist of his time, turning his master's heroic couplet to comic and philosophical purposes in some of the major longer poems of the Augustan period, including *An Essay on Criticism*, *The Rape of the Lock*, *The Dunciad* and *An Essay on Man*. Written on the occasion of the coronation of George I, Pope's epistle is addressed not to his lifelong friend Martha Blount (to whom he bequeathed most of his estate), but to the earlier recipient of his attentions, her sister Teresa, regaled as 'fair Zephalinda' or 'soft Parthenia' in the poem.
    Born in London, son of a wholesale linen draper, Pope came from a Catholic family, and so was unable to attend university. Educated by Catholic priests and in Catholic schools, he taught himself Latin, Greek, French and Italian, later publishing 18th-century English versions of Homer's *Iliad* and *Odyssey*. Always in poor health, he moved out of London after the Jacobite rebellion to a villa by the

Thames in Twickenham where he could occupy himself with picturesque-style landscape gardening.

BK ■ Pope's London as depicted here is quite the opposite of Swift's stinking version in 'A Description of a City Shower' [101]. It's revealing also to compare Pope's Epistle to his much-missed Miss Blount with Anne Bradstreet's letter to her much-missed husband [76].

Pope is a superb stylist, supremely confident in his use of the couplet. His control of content, movement and tone is difficult to equal; and the sheer precision of his phrasing is a marvel.

Bradstreet's tone is ardently direct; Pope's is both oblique and frontal. Miss Blount is referred to as 'she' for the first 22 lines; then Pope switches to 'you'. Similarly, in the final section he refers to himself at first as 'your slave' and 'he'; only once, throughout the entire poem, in the penultimate line, does the word 'I' appear. This reticence, this witholding of egotistical involvement in a letter to a friend or would-be lover (was there at least 'one kiss' between them?), gives the poem a character at once gentle and sharp, removed and engaged.

This is very much a city person's poem. Miss Blount's removal to the countryside means that she's leaving 'Opera, park, assembly, play' for 'dull aunts', 'croaking rooks', and some blustering Squire who 'Makes love with nods, and knees beneath a table'. Poor Miss Blount has to forsake 'sceptres, coronets, and balls' for the company of this lumpish rustic

> Whose laughs are hearty, though his jests are coarse,
> And loves you best of all things – but his horse.

The sexual currents in the Epistle are genuine but not very developed. Nor, one feels, were they meant to be. Pope deals in suggestion and intimation; he hints at, rather than states, his emotional condition. Yet the last two lines, coming from such a convinced urbanite, are as close as Pope appears willing or able to go in saying what he feels for the removed, rusticated Miss Blount:

> Vexed to be still in town, I knit my brow,
> Look sour, and hum a tune – as you may now.

It's an interesting final image: a brow-contorted, sour-faced, humming couple. Perhaps. He misses her. Does she miss him?

SAMUEL JOHNSON (1709–1784)

from London: A Poem
In Imitation of the Third Satire of Juvenal

Since worth, he cries, in these degenerate days
Wants even the cheap reward of empty praise;
In those cursed walls, devote to vice and gain,
Since unrewarded science toils in vain;
Since hope but sooths to double my distress,
And every moment leaves my little less;
While yet my steady steps no staff sustains,
And life still vigorous revels in my veins;
Grant me, kind Heaven, to find some happier place,
Where honesty and sense are no disgrace;
Some pleasing bank where verdant osiers play,
Some peaceful vale with nature's paintings gay;
Where once the harrassed Briton found repose,
And safe in poverty defied his foes;
Some secret cell, ye powers, indulgent give.
Let —— live here, for —— has learned to live.
Here let those reign, whom pensions can incite
To vote a patriot black, a courtier white;
Explain their country's dear-bought rights away,
And plead for pirates in the face of day;
With slavish tenets taint our poisoned youth,
And lend a lie the confidence of truth.

Let such raise palaces, and manors buy,
Collect a tax, or farm a lottery,
With warbling eunuchs fill a licensed stage,
And lull to servitude a thoughtless age.

Heroes, proceed! What bounds your pride shall hold?
What check restrain your thirst for power and gold?

Behold rebellious virtue quite o'erthrown,
Behold our fame, our wealth, our lives your own.

To such, a groaning nation's spoils are given,
When public crimes inflame the wrath of Heaven:
But what, my friend, what hope remains for me,
Who start at theft, and blush at perjury?
Who scarce forbear, though Britain's court he sing,
To pluck a titled poet's borrowed wing;
A statesman's logic, unconvinced can hear,
And dare to slumber o'er the *Gazetteer*;
Despise a fool in half his pension drest,
And strive in vain to laugh at Clodio's jest.

Others with softer smiles, and subtler art,
Can sap the principles, or taint the heart;
With more address a lover's note convey,
Or bribe a virgin's innocence away.
Well may they rise, while I, whose rustic tongue
Ne'er knew to puzzle right, or varnish wrong,
Spurned as a geggar, dreaded as a spy,
Live unregarded, unlamented die.

For what but social guilt the friend endears?
Who shares Orgilio's crimes, his fortune shares.
But thou, should tempting villainy present
All Marlborough hoarded, or all Villiers spent;
Turn from the glittering bribe thy scornful eye,
Nor sell for gold, what gold could never buy,
The peaceful slumber, self-approving day,
Unsullied fame, and conscience ever gay.

The cheated nation's happy favourites, see!
Mark whom the great caress, who frown on me!
London! the needy villain's general home,
The common sewer of Paris and of Rome;
With eager thirst, by folly or by fate,

Sucks in the dregs of each corrupted state.
Forgive my transports on a theme like this,
I cannot bear a French metropolis.

Illustrious Edward! from the realms of day,
The land of heroes and of saints survey;
Nor hope the British lineaments to trace,
The rustic grandeur, or the surly grace;
But lost in thoughtless ease, and empty show,
Behold the warrior dwindled to a beau;
Sense, freedom, piety, refined away,
Of France the mimic, and of Spain the prey.

All that at home no more can beg or steal,
Or like a gibbet better than a wheel;
Hissed from the stage, or hooted from the court,
Their air, their dress, their politics import;
Obsequious, artful, voluble and gay,
On Britain's fond credulity they prey.
No gainful trade their industry can escape,
They sing, they dance, clean shoes, or cure a clap;
All sciences a fasting monsieur knows,
And bid him go to Hell, to Hell he goes.

Ah! what avails it, that, from slavery far,
I drew the breath of life in English air;
Was early taught a Briton's right to prize,
And lisp the tale of Henry's victories;
If the gulled conqueror receives the chain,
And flattery prevails when arms are vain?

Studious to please, and ready to submit,
The supple Gaul was born a parasite:
Still to his interest true, where'er he goes,
Wit, bravery, worth, his lavish tongue bestows;
In every face a thousand graces shine,
From every tongue flows harmony divine.

These arts in vain our rugged natives try,
Strain out with faltering diffidence a lie,
And get a kick for awkward flattery.

Besides, with justice, this discerning age
Admires their wonderous talents for the stage:
Well may they venture on the mimic's art,
Who play from morn to night a borrowed part;
Practised their master's notions to embrace,
Repeat his maxims, and reflect his face;
With every wild absurdity comply,
And view each object with another's eye;
To shake with laughter ere the jest they hear,
To pour at will the counterfeited tear;
And as their patron hints the cold or heat,
To shake in dog-days, in December sweat.

How, when competitors like these contend,
Can surly virtue hope to fix a friend?
Slaves that with serious impudence beguile,
And lie without a blush, without a smile;
Exalt each trifle, every vice adore,
Your taste in snuff, your judgement in a whore;
Can Balbo's eloquence applaud, and swear
He gropes his breeches with a monarch's Air.

For arts like these preferred, admired, carest,
They first invade your table, then your breast;
Explore your secrets with insidious art,
Watch the weak hour, and ransack all the heart;
Then soon your ill-placed confidence repay,
Commence your lords, and govern or betray.
By numbers here from shame or censure free,
All crimes are safe, but hated poverty.
This, only this, the rigid law pursues,
This, only this, provokes the snarling muse;
The sober trader at a tattered cloak,

Wakes from his dream, and labours for a joke;
With brisker air the silken courtiers gaze,
And turn the varied taunt a thousand ways.
Of all the griefs that harrass the distressed,
Sure the most bitter is a scornful jest;
Fate never wounds more deep the generous heart,
Than when a blockhead's insult points the dart.

1738 [1738] *(lines 35-169)*

Samuel Johnson – usually known as Dr Johnson – was the quint-essential English man of letters: poet, essayist, scholar, literary critic, biographer and lexicographer. His most influential works included the poems *London* (1738) and *The Vanity of Human Wishes* (1749), among 'the greatest verse satires of the English or any other language' according to T.S. Eliot, as well as *A Dictionary of the English Language* (1755), and the collection of critical biographies now called *Lives of the Poets* (1779-81). James Boswell published his *Life of Samuel Johnson* in 1791.

Born in Lichfield, the son of a bookseller, Johnson studied for just over a year at Pembroke College, Oxford, but lacked the funds to continue. Returning to Lichfield, he became a schoolteacher for a period before heading for London, where he began a long association as a writer for *The Gentleman's Magazine* in 1738.

Just as Alexander Pope wrote imitations of Horace through which to attack political corruption of his own time, so Johnson used Juvenal to lambast the state of London, beset by vice and poverty, imitating the same Third Satire of Juvenal which John Oldham took on 50 years earlier [95-100]. As Johnson wrote, 'part of the beauty of the performance (if any beauty be allowed it) consisting in adapting Juvenal's sentiments to modern facts and persons'. Johnson's protagonist Thales is his version of Juvenal's Umbricius who leaves Rome for Cumae to escape the dangers of the capital city, and may be based on his friend the poet Richard Savage.

BK ■ Johnson's version of Juvenal's third satire is more sophisticated and urbane than that of Oldham. While it lacks Oldham's raw, abusive power, it has a lighter and at times more penetrating touch.

And Johnson's concern with the identity of London, indeed with the broader problem of English identity, is all the more impressive because of this light touch. He tells us how, when he learns that his friend Thales is leaving London where 'malice, rapine, accident, conspire', they stand together on the banks of the Thames and then 'kneel, and kiss the consecrated earth'. In doing so, they 'call Britannia's glories back to view'.

This genuine, silent love of London and England is now compelled to see 'English honour' become 'a standing jest'. The origins, nature and consequences of that sad transformation preoccupy Johnson in this strong, accomplished poem.

Thales speaks eloquently of the forces which he believes are undermining London. Phrases pile up like evidence of some terrible disease: 'degenerate days', 'slavish tenets', 'poisoned youth', 'thirst for power and gold'. A transfer of power is taking place. This is at the root of the threat, as Thales sees it, to English identity. He speaks directly to the new, greedy, invading 'heroes'.

> Behold rebellious virtue quite overthrown,
> Behold our fame, our wealth, our lives your own.

In this context of lost power, esteem and wealth, Thales sums up his own sad condition, why he is compelled to leave London.

> Spurned as a beggar, dreaded as a spy,
> Live unregarded, unlamented die.

In two powerful lines, Thales gives us a devastating picture of his city.

> London! the needy villain's general home,
> The common sewer of Paris and of Rome.

London now seems happy to suck in 'the dregs of each corrupted state'. It has become 'Of France the mimic, and of Spain the prey'.

Like Oldham, Johnson goes on to list the reasons for the poem's vision of London as 'a French metropolis'. With more concentrated power than Oldham, Johnson paints a picture of 'The supple Gaul [who] was born a parasite'. The parasitic genius of this Gaul is concisely portrayed.

> Obsequious, artful, voluble and gay,
> On Britain's fond credulity they prey.

112

No gainful trade their industry can escape,
They sing, they dance, clean shoes, or cure a clap;
All sciences a fasting monsieur knows,
And bid him go to Hell, to Hell he goes.

Of the many features of this parasitic genius presented by Thales, the most striking is the Gaul's flamboyant, agile, hypocritical theatricality. A new political reality is being created by the apparently endless resources of 'the mimic's art'. London has become a stage and French actors are the dominant figures. They win the day, and the night, playing, as they do, 'a borrowed part'.

Practised their master's notions to embrace,
Repeat his maxims, and reflect his face;
With every wild absurdity comply,
And view each object with another's eye;
To shake with laughter ere the jest they hear,
To pour at will the counterfeited tear;
And as their patron hints the cold or heat,
To shake in dog-days, in December sweat.

What Johnson brings out, through Thales, is the conniving, penetrating, insidious power of this parasitic genius, the conquering ability of those who 'with serious impudence beguile, / And eye without a blush, without a smile'.

It is from this metropolis of polished liars that Thales is determined to escape. He is resolved

To breathe in distant fields a purer air,
And fixed on Cambria's solitary shore,
Give to St David one true Briton more.

The more one reads this poem the more one appreciates how passionately Johnson is concerned with his city's identity. With impressive skill (his handling of the couplet is unfailingly effective) he paints a picture of a poxy, deluded, hypocritical metropolis which deepens in horrific ugliness with each reading of the poem. It makes one ask the question: what do contemporary poets of London think of their city now? It would be revealing to compare their responses with those of Oldham, Johnson, Blake and others.

THOMAS GRAY (1716–1771)

Elegy Written in a Country Churchyard

The curfew tolls the knell of parting day,
The lowing herd wind slowly o'er the lea,
The plowman homeward plods his weary way,
And leaves the world to darkness and to me.

Now fades the glimmering landscape on the sight,
And all the air a solemn stillness holds,
Save where the beetle wheels his droning flight,
And drowsy tinklings lull the distant folds;

Save that from yonder ivy-mantled tower
The moping owl does to the moon complain
Of such, as wandering near her secret bower,
Molest her ancient solitary reign.

Beneath those rugged elms, that yew tree's shade,
Where heaves the turf in many a mouldering heap,
Each in his narrow cell for ever laid,
The rude forefathers of the hamlet sleep.

The breezy call of incense-breathing morn,
The swallow twittering from the straw-built shed,
The cock's shrill clarion or the echoing horn,
No more shall rouse them from their lowly bed.

For them no more the blazing hearth shall burn,
Or busy housewife ply her evening care:
No children run to lisp their sire's return,
Or climb his knees the envied kiss to share.

Oft did the harvest to their sickle yield,
Their furrow oft the stubborn glebe has broke;
How jocund did they drive their team afield!
How bowed the woods beneath their sturdy stroke!

Let not Ambition mock their useful toil,
Their homely joys, and destiny obscure;
Nor Grandeur hear, with a disdainful smile
The short and simple annals of the poor.

The boast of heraldry, the pomp of power,
And all that beauty, all that wealth e'er gave,
Awaits alike the inevitable hour.
The paths of glory lead but to the grave.

Nor you, ye Proud, impute to these the fault,
If Memory o'er their tomb no trophies raise,
Where through the long-drawn aisle and fretted vault
The pealing anthem swells the note of praise.

Can storied urn or animated bust
Back to its mansion call the fleeting breath?
Can Honour's voice provoke the silent dust,
Or Flattery soothe the dull cold ear of Death?

Perhaps in this neglected spot is laid
Some heart once pregnant with celestial fire;
Hands that the rod of empire might have swayed,
Or waked to ecstasy the living lyre.

But Knowledge to their eyes her ample page
Rich with the spoils of time did ne'er unroll;
Chill Penury repressed their noble rage,
And froze the genial current of the soul.

Full many a gem of purest ray serene,
The dark unfathomed caves of ocean bear:
Full many a flower is born to blush unseen,
And waste its sweetness on the desert air.

Some village-Hampden, that with dauntless breast
The little tyrant of his fields withstood;
Some mute inglorious Milton here may rest,
Some Cromwell guiltless of his country's blood.

The applause of listening senates to command,
The threats of pain and ruin to despise,
To scatter plenty o'er a smiling land,
And read their history in a nation's eyes,

Their lot forbade: nor circumscribed alone
Their growing virtues, but their crimes confined;
Forbad to wade through slaughter to a throne,
And shut the gates of mercy on mankind,

The struggling pangs of conscious truth to hide,
To quench the blushes of ingenuous shame,
Or heap the shrine of Luxury and Pride
With incense kindled at the Muse's flame.

Far from the madding crowd's ignoble strife,
Their sober wishes never learned to stray;
Along the cool sequestered vale of life
They kept the noiseless tenor of their way.

Yet even these bones from insult to protect,
Some frail memorial still erected nigh,
With uncouth rhymes and shapeless sculpture decked,
Implores the passing tribute of a sigh.

Their name, their years, spelt by the unlettered muse,
The place of fame and elegy supply:
And many a holy text around she strews,
That teach the rustic moralist to die.

For who to dumb Forgetfulness a prey,
This pleasing anxious being e'er resigned,
Left the warm precincts of the cheerful day,
Nor cast one longing, ling'ring look behind?

On some fond breast the parting soul relies,
Some pious drops the closing eye requires;
Even from the tomb the voice of Nature cries,
Even in our ashes live their wonted fires.

For thee, who mindful of the unhonoured Dead
Dost in these lines their artless tale relate;
If chance, by lonely Contemplation led,
Some kindred spirit shall inquire thy fate,

Haply some hoary-headed swain may say,
'Oft have we seen him at the peep of dawn
Brushing with hasty steps the dews away
To meet the sun upon the upland lawn.

'There at the foot of yonder nodding beech
That wreathes its old fantastic roots so high,
His listless length at noontide would he stretch,
And pore upon the brook that babbles by.

'Hard by yon wood, now smiling as in scorn,
Muttering his wayward fancies he would rove,
Now drooping, woeful wan, like one forlorn,
Or crazed with care, or crossed in hopeless love.

'One morn I missed him on the customed hill,
Along the heath and near his favourite tree;
Another came; nor yet beside the rill,
Nor up the lawn, nor at the wood was he;

'The next with dirges due in sad array
Slow through the church-way path we saw him borne.
Approach and read (for thou canst read) the lay,
Graved on the stone beneath yon aged thorn.'

    THE EPITAPH
Here rests his head upon the lap of Earth
A youth to Fortune and to Fame unknown.

117

Fair Science frowned not on his humble birth,
And Melancholy marked him for her own.

Large was his bounty, and his soul sincere,
Heaven did a recompense as largely send:
He gave to Misery all he had, a tear,
He gained from Heaven ('twas all he wished) a friend.

No farther seek his merits to disclose,
Or draw his frailties from their dread abode,
(There they alike in trembling hope repose)
The bosom of his Father and his God.

1742-50 [1751]

Thomas Gray was an English poet and scholar whose odes and elegies made him popular with 18th-century readers, despite publishing very little in his lifetime. In 1757 he declined the much derided post of Poet Laureate, preferring to remain in the seclusion of Pembroke College, Cambridge, immersed in his studies of Celtic and Scandinavian antiquities. His poetry's combination of classical control with a romantic feeling for nature was to influence Wordsworth and Coleridge, while Vasily Zhukovsky's Russian translation of the 'Elegy', published in 1802, became a model for early 19th-century Russian poets, including the young Pushkin.

Born in London, the only survivor of twelve children born to parents working in the millinery trade, he was sent to Eton in 1725 at the age of eight. He is said to have begun writing the 'Elegy' in 1742 in the graveyard of St Giles' Church in Stoke Poges, Buckinghamshire, where his mother was buried and where he himself would be laid to rest.

BK ■ Like so many poems in this anthology, 'Elegy Written in a Country Churchyard' is set in darkness. The beast thrives there. The poem is a lament for the dead 'rude forefathers of the hamlet', but it is also a cry against the injustice of poverty, the stifling of potential, the denial of education and knowledge to these dead workers. Inevitably, this leads to a contrast between the worlds of rich and poor; 'the boast of heraldry, the pomp of power', as well as 'Ambition' and 'Grandeur', are contrasted with 'the unhonoured dead' resting at last in 'their lowly bed'.

Gray tries to get to grips with the nature of poverty in this famous 'Elegy'. He asserts that, at a certain level, those socially deprived people had 'their crimes confined' by this very deprivation, that they were never in a position

> to wade through slaughter to a throne
> And shut the gates of mercy on mankind.

Gray argues that poverty prevents murder and callousness from happening. It doesn't, not even in picturesque rural settings. Yet Gray is a persuasive writer and his powers of persuasion are strengthened by his ability to write lines that have achieved the authority of proverbial wisdom. Lines like 'The short and simple annals of the poor', 'The paths of glory lead but to the grave', 'Far from the madding crowd's ignoble strife', and 'Some mute inglorious Milton here may rest' have achieved a kind of indisputable authority. Indeed, entire stanzas from this poem are often quoted with that same indisputable air.

> Full many a gem of purest ray serene,
> The dark unfathomed caves of ocean bear:
> Full many a flower is born to blush unseen,
> And waste its sweetness on the desert air.

Looked at closely, these proverbial lines may be disputed; they cannot, however, be disproved. And neither can the central, humane thrust of the poem be disproved or ignored. This concerns the dignity of the dead, the deprived, the forgotten, the hard-working people who in all ages have had to suffer the injustice of being denied opportunities to educate and better themselves. What we get from Gray is a proverbial lament for these people and a passionate, beautifully structured and eloquent protest against a system that compels a human 'flower' to 'waste its sweetness on the desert air'. That is the fine, fierce light that shines through Gray's words when the weary ploughman 'leaves the world to darkness and to me'. Once again, the darkness has spoken. The prowling-place of the heavy bear has, as always, its own potent voice.

CHRISTOPHER SMART (1722–1771)

from Jubilate Agno

For I will consider my Cat Jeoffry.

For he is the servant of the Living God, duly and daily serving him.

For at the first glance of the glory of God in the East he worships
in his way.

For is this done by wreathing his body seven times round with
elegant quickness.

For then he leaps up to catch the musk, which is the blessing of
God upon his prayer.

For he rolls upon prank to work it in.

For having done duty and received blessing he begins to consider
himself.

For this he performs in ten degrees.

For first he looks upon his forepaws to see if they are clean.

For secondly he kicks up behind to clear away there.

For thirdly he works it upon stretch with the forepaws extended.

For fourthly he sharpens his paws by wood.

For fifthly he washes himself.

For sixthly he rolls upon wash.

For seventhly he fleas himself, that he may not be interrupted upon
the beat.

For eighthly he rubs himself against a post.

For ninthly he looks up for his instructions.

For tenthly he goes in quest of food.

For having considered God and himself he will consider his
neighbour.

For if he meets another cat he will kiss her in kindness.

For when he takes his prey he plays with it to give it a chance.

For one mouse in seven escapes by his dallying.

For when his day's work is done his business more properly begins.

For he keeps the Lord's watch in the night against the adversary.

For he counteracts the powers of darkness by his electrical skin
and glaring eyes.

For he counteracts the Devil, who is death, by brisking about the life.

For in his morning orisons he loves the sun and the sun loves him.

For he is of the tribe of Tiger.

For the Cherub Cat is a term of the Angel Tiger.

For he has the subtlety and hissing of a serpent, which in goodness he suppresses.

For he will not do destruction, if he is well-fed, neither will he spit without provocation.

For he purrs in thankfulness, when God tells him he's a good Cat.

For he is an instrument for the children to learn benevolence upon.

For every house is incomplete without him and a blessing is lacking in the spirit.

For the Lord commanded Moses concerning the cats at the departure of the Children of Israel from Egypt.

For every family had one cat at least in the bag.

For the English Cats are the best in Europe.

For he is the cleanest in the use of his forepaws of any quadruped.

For the dexterity of his defence is an instance of the love of God to him exceedingly.

For he is the quickest to his mark of any creature.

For he is tenacious of his point.

For he is a mixture of gravity and waggery.

For he knows that God is his Saviour.

For there is nothing sweeter than his peace when at rest.

For there is nothing brisker than his life when in motion.

For he is of the Lord's poor and so indeed is he called by benevolence perpetually—Poor Jeoffry! poor Jeoffry! the rat has bit thy throat.

For I bless the name of the Lord Jesus that Jeoffry is better.

For the divine spirit comes about his body to sustain it in complete cat.

For his tongue is exceeding pure so that it has in purity what it wants in music.

For he is docile and can learn certain things.

For he can set up with gravity which is patience upon approbation.

For he can fetch and carry, which is patience in employment.

For he can jump over a stick, which is patience upon proof positive.

For he can spraggle upon waggle at the word of command.

For he can jump from an eminence into his master's bosom.

For he can catch the cork and toss it again.

For he is hated by the hypocrite and miser.

For the former is afraid of detection.

For the latter refuses the charge.

For he camels his back to bear the first notion of business.

For he is good to think on, if a man would express himself neatly.

For he made a great figure in Egypt for his signal services.

For he killed the Ichneumon-rat, very pernicious by land.

For his ears are so acute that they sting again.

For from this proceeds the passing quickness of his attention.

For by stroking of him I have found out electricity.

For I perceived God's light about him both wax and fire.

For the Electrical fire is the spiritual substance which God sends
   from heaven to sustain the bodies both of man and beast.

For God has blessed him in the variety of his movements.

For, though he cannot fly, he is an excellent clamberer.

For his motions upon the face of the earth are more than any other
   quadruped.

For he can tread to all the measures upon the music.

For he can swim for life.

For he can creep.

1759-63 [1939]

Christopher Smart was an English religious poet mainly known
during his lifetime for one poem, *A Song to David* (1763), regarded
by W.B. Yeats as the inaugural poem of the Romantic period. This
was written during a prolonged period of mental instability involving
religious mania when Smart was confined to mental institutions in
London from 1757. As Dr Johnson related: 'My poor friend Smart
shewed the disturbance of his mind, by falling upon his knees,
and saying his prayers in the street, or in any other unusual place.
[...] I did not think he ought to be shut up. His infirmities were
not noxious to society.' As his health improved, he was allowed to

dig in the garden, was given access to books and newspapers, and permitted to keep a cat.

During his 'well-nigh sev'n years' of confinement Smart also composed *Jubilate Agno*, another long work in the mode of the Psalms, but not publicly known until the surviving fragments of the manuscript – about a third of the original – were discovered in a private library nearly two hundred years later by W.T. Stead, an American diplomat and Anglican churchman. This friend of T.S. Eliot published what remained of *Jubilate Agno* in 1939 under the title *Rejoice in the Lamb: A Song from Bedlam*, with the section beginning 'For I will consider my Cat Jeoffry' soon becoming celebrated as a separate, much anthologised poem in its own right.

Smart was born in Shipbourne in Kent's Medway valley, son of a steward on the Fairlawne estate remembered as his Arcadia in poems including *Jubilate Agno*. But when he was eleven, his father died and his mother took their children back to the family home in Durham. The boy was looked after by Lord Barnard at Raby Castle and sent to Durham School. Distinguishing himself in Classics, he went up to Cambridge at the age of 17, where he gained a fellowship at Pembroke Hall which would have supported him during the following years had he not been drawn to the wild life of a gallant in London. There he soon found himself married with two daughters, struggling to establish himself as a poet while earning a living by writing for journals and for popular entertainments staged by his publisher under the title *Mrs Midnight's Oratory*, with Smart taking the stage in the title role of hostess on some occasions.

The manuscript of *Jubilate Agno* breaks off with his release from confinement in 1763, but the years which followed saw little respite from his troubles. None of the poetry he published was well received. Unstable, drinking heavily, spending freely, deserted by his wife, Smart was finally arrested in 1770 and committed to the debtor's prison where he died a year later.

BK ■ In the first line of this poem Christopher Smart tells us he will 'consider' his cat, Jeoffry. This act of sustained 'considering' results in a jubilant poem which shares with Jeoffry a quality of pure vitality. Smart observes his cat with loving eye, observes him steadily and at length, noting every movement of that 'Angel Tiger' body as he 'washes himself', 'kicks up behind to clear away there', 'sharpens his paws by wood', kisses another cat 'in kindness', 'fleas himself', 'rubs himself against a post', is loved by people and God, and is hated only 'by the hypocrite and miser'.

This pure animal vitality is seen by Smart as being essentially spiritual. Jeoffry 'is the servant of the Living God' whom 'he worships in his way'. While Smart considers Jeoffry, the cat considers God, himself and his neighbour, keeping 'the Lord's watch in the night against the adversary'. God is not slow to tell Jeoffry 'he's a good Cat' , and Jeoffry in his turn knows that 'God is his Saviour'. Smart goes so far as to say of Jeoffry that 'every house is incomplete without him and a blessing is lacking in the spirit'. The reality of 'spirit' is of the utmost importance to Smart. In 1757 he was admitted to a hospital for the mentally ill; in his illness he prayed compulsively in public, a fact that prompted Dr Johnson to say 'I'd as lief pray with Kit Smart as anyone else'. Sane or insane, Smart was a spiritual being.

This poem to a cat has a quality of intense and loving prayer, the prayer of gratitude from a man who sees in the cat a manifestation of life at its most agile, vigilant, playful, grave, waggish, sweet, brisk, purring in thankfulness 'when God tells him he's a good Cat'. As Smart considers Jeoffry, 'the divine spirit comes about his body to sustain it in complete cat'.

Complete cat. Complete praise. Rarely has a creature been celebrated with such loving gusto as Jeoffry. This poem is taken from *Jubilate Agno*, or *Rejoice in the Lamb*, a work described by Smart as 'my Magnificat', celebrating the beauty and mystery of Creation. Jeoffry, treading 'to all the measures upon the music', is a vital part of God's work. This cat may be considered as a model for poets and writers intent on improving their art: 'For he is good to think on, if a man would express himself neatly.'

One doesn't have to be a cat-lover to love this poem. Nearly every line begins with 'For', a ritualistic, rhetorical, antiphonal device imported from Hebrew poetry which works very well in creating an atmosphere of wave-like, surging praise to Jeoffry.

It's clear that Jeoffry deserves every word of praise that falls on his handsome head, his accomplished body.

> For he can swim for life.
> For he can creep.

OLIVER GOLDSMITH (*c*.1730–1774)

from The Deserted Village

Sweet smiling village, loveliest of the lawn,
Thy sports are fled, and all thy charms withdrawn;
Amidst thy bowers the tyrant's hand is seen,
And desolation saddens all thy green:
One only master grasps the whole domain,
And half a tillage stints thy smiling plain;
No more thy glassy brook reflects the day,
But choked with sedges, works its weedy way.
Along thy glades, a solitary guest,
The hollow sounding bittern guards its nest;
Amidst thy desert walks the lapwing flies,
And tires their echoes with unvaried cries.
Sunk are thy bowers in shapeless ruin all,
And the long grass o'ertops the mouldering wall,
And trembling, shrinking from the spoiler's hand,
Far, far away thy children leave the land.

Ill fares the land, to hastening ills a prey,
Where wealth accumulates, and men decay;
Princes and lords may flourish, or may fade;
A breath can make them, as a breath has made.
But a bold peasantry, their country's pride,
When once destroyed, can never be supplied.

A time there was, ere England's griefs began,
When every rood of ground maintained its man;
For him light labour spread her wholesome store,
Just gave what life required, but gave no more.
His best companions, innocence and health;
And his best riches, ignorance of wealth.

But times are altered; trade's unfeeling train
Usurp the land and dispossess the swain;
Along the lawn, where scattered hamlets rose,
Unwieldy wealth, and cumbrous pomp repose,
And every want to opulence allied,
And every pang that folly pays to pride.
These gentle hours that plenty bade to bloom,
Those calm desires that asked but little room,
Those healthful sports that graced the peaceful scene,
Lived in each look, and brightened all the green;
These far departing seek a kinder shore,
And rural mirth and manners are no more.

Sweet Auburn! parent of the blissful hour,
Thy glades forlorn confess the tyrant's power.
Here as I take my solitary rounds,
Amidst thy tangling walks, and ruined grounds,
And, many a year elapsed, return to view
Where once the cottage stood, the hawthorn grew,
Here, as with doubtful, pensive steps I range,
Trace every scene, and wonder at the change,
Remembrance wakes with all her busy train,
Swells at my breast, and turns the past to pain. […]

Ye friends to truth, ye statesmen who survey
The rich man's joys increase, the poor's decay,
'Tis yours to judge, how wide the limits stand
Between a splendid and an happy land.
Proud swells the tide with loads of freighted ore,
And shouting Folly hails them from her shore;
Hoards, even beyond the miser's wish abound,
And rich men flock from all the world around.
Yet count our gains. This wealth is but a name
That leaves our useful products still the same.
Not so the loss. The man of wealth and pride,
Takes up a space that many poor supplied;
Space for his lake, his park's extended bounds,

Space for his horses, equipage, and hounds;
The robe that wraps his limbs in silken sloth,
Has robbed the neighbouring fields of half their growth;
His seat, where solitary sports are seen,
Indignant spurns the cottage from the green;
Around the world each needful product flies,
For all the luxuries the world supplies.
While thus the land adorned for pleasure all
In barren splendour feebly waits the fall. [...]

Thus fares the land, by luxury betrayed,
In nature's simplest charms at first arrayed,
But verging to decline, its splendours rise,
Its vistas strike, its palaces surprise;
While scourged by famine from the smiling land,
The mournful peasant leads his humble band;
And while he sinks without one arm to save,
The country blooms – a garden, and a grave.

Where then, ah, where shall poverty reside,
To scape the pressure of contiguous pride;
If to some common's fenceless limits strayed,
He drives his flock to pick the scanty blade,
Those fenceless fields the sons of wealth divide,
Even the bare-worn common is denied. [...]

Oh luxury! Thou curst by heaven's decree,
How ill exchanged are things like these for thee!
How do thy potions with insidious joy,
Diffuse their pleasures only to destroy!
Kingdoms by thee, to sickly greatness grown,
Boast of a florid vigour not their own.
At every draught more large and large they grow,
A bloated mass of rank unwieldy woe;
Till sapped their strength, and every part unsound,
Down, down they sink, and spread a ruin round.

Even now the devastation is begun,
And half the business of destruction done;
Even now, methinks, as pondering here I stand,
I see the rural virtues leave the land. [...]

[1770]

Oliver Goldsmith, playwright, poet, novelist and essayist, is best-known for his novel, *The Vicar of Wakefield* (1766), and his play, *She Stoops to Conquer* (1773). Son of a clergyman, he grew up in an Anglo-Irish Protestant household, spending much of his childhood in Lissoy, Co. Westmeath. His poem 'The Deserted Village' is a lament for the loss of a whole way of life. Its fictional village of Auburn may be based on Lissoy, but the picture is a composite one, drawn from his experience of both Ireland and England.

According to Terry Gifford (*Green Voices*, 1995), Goldsmith wrote 'The Deserted Village' to engage with the pressures of his own particular place and time: 'Enclosure of the commons and the consequent depopulation of the villages was taking place in England as well as Ireland in the mid-18th century. [...] There is a new callousness behind the new commercial approach to agriculture [...] the supplanting of village values by the culture of exploitation.'[12]

In the course of many years teaching as well as living at Trinity College, Brendan Kennelly always would ask visitors to meet him 'between the two lads out the front', referring to Foley's statues of Goldsmith and Edmund Burke on either side of Front Gate which figure in his visionary poem *The Man Made of Rain* ('the statues are there to prove whatever / statues prove, how cold is Oliver Goldsmith / this morning, how cold is Edmund Burke, / how cold is the man made of rain?'). Gesturing to Goldsmith – cast in bronze with book in hand – he once told me with some relish how this esteemed graduate of the university had been a lazy student who'd spent much of his time there at card games, in singing and playing the flute, and was expelled for joining rioters storming a prison. Coming from Kerry, stricken like much of Ireland by historic famine, poverty and exploitation by land owners, Brendan also identified strongly with the sentiments expressed in 'The Deserted Village', making a strong case for its inclusion here along with other poems on the people and the land by poets such as Thomas Gray.

WILLIAM COWPER (1731–1800)

The Poplar Field

The poplars are felled, farewell to the shade
And the whispering sound of the cool colonnade,
The winds play no longer and sing in the leaves,
Nor Ouse on his bosom their image receives.

Twelve years have elapsed since I last took a view
Of my favourite field, and the bank where they grew,
And now in the grass behold they are laid,
And the tree is my seat that once lent me a shade.

The blackbird has fled to another retreat
Where the hazels afford him a screen from the heat,
And the scene where his melody charmed me before,
Resounds with his sweet-flowing ditty no more.

My fugitive years are all hasting away,
And I must e're long lie as lowly as they,
With a turf on my breast and a stone on my head,
E're another such grove shall arise in its stead.

'Tis a sight to engage me, if anything can
To muse on the perishing pleasures of Man;
Though his life be a dream, his enjoyments, I see,
Have a Being less durable even than he.

1784 [First published in *Gentleman's Magazine*, 1785]

William Cowper (pronounced *Cooper*) was an English poet who spent much of his life trying to cope with recurrent bouts of depression, helped by a wide circle of friends who cared for his welfare, including Mary Unwin, the widow of a clergyman friend.

In 1767 they settled at Olney in Buckinghamshire, where he wrote 'The Poplar Field' (in 1784) and his long poem *The Task* (1785), before moving to nearby Weston Underwood in 1786. After Mary's death in 1794, he became a physical and mental invalid, writing 'The Castaway' shortly before his death in 1800. Cowper addressed simple human and rural themes in his poetry, his sympathetic feeling for nature presaging the Romanticism of the next century.

Like much of John Clare's work [163], Cowper's 'The Poplar Field' is a poem responding in part to the destruction of the English landscape caused by landowners using the Enclosure Acts to force the rural poor off their small holdings in order to farm more profitably by dividing the land into larger fields enclosed by fences, hedges and ditches, felling trees, damming rivers and destroying habitats of animals, birds and insects. The jaunty metre Cowper employs in 'The Poplar Field' seems ill-suited at first to a poem about lost years and environmental vandalism. Anapaestic tetrameter is more often used for comic effect (as in Dr Seuss's poems), but where used irregularly – as it is here by Cowper – it becomes disconcerting, and can be employed for serious effect, as it is also in Edgar Allan Poe's 'Annabel Lee' – as well as in Eminem's song 'The Way I Am', apart from its chorus (most rap songs use irregular tetrameter).

In *The Song of the Earth* (2000), Jonathan Bate describes how Jane Austen and William Cowper were both sceptical of the "improving" activities of the new landowners. In *The Task* – Austen's favourite poem – Cowper attacks 'Capability' Brown for 'altering houses and landscapes that had for generations been integrated with their local environment', while in *Mansfield Park* (1814) Fanny Price quotes Cowper on hearing 'that an avenue of trees must come down in the name of Mr Rushworth's improvement of his estate, a result of his faddish obsession with the landscape designs of Humphrey Repton'. Bate points out that the line she quotes – 'Ye fallen avenues, once more I mourn your fate unmerited' – is from a passage in Cowper's poem 'concerning Sir John Throckmorton's enclosure and improvement of his estate at Weston Underwood [...] "The Poplar-Field", one of Cowper's best-known lyrics [...] was a further lament occasioned by the gentleman improver's changes to his local environment'.[11]

WILLIAM BLAKE (1757–1827)

The Tyger

Tyger Tyger, burning bright,
In the forests of the night:
What immortal hand or eye,
Could frame thy fearful symmetry?

In what distant deeps or skies.
Burnt the fire of thine eyes?
On what wings dare he aspire?
What the hand, dare seize the fire?

And what shoulder, & what art,
Could twist the sinews of thy heart?
And when thy heart began to beat,
What dread hand? & what dread feet?

What the hammer? what the chain,
In what furnace was thy brain?
What the anvil? what dread grasp,
Dare its deadly terrors clasp!

When the stars threw down their spears
And watered heaven with their tears:
Did he smile his work to see?
Did he who made the Lamb make thee?

Tyger Tyger burning bright,
In the forests of the night:
What immortal hand or eye,
Dare frame thy fearful symmetry?

[*Songs of Experience*, 1794]

William **Blake** was a visionary English poet, artist and engraver whose genius was unrecognised in his lifetime. Considered mad by most of his contemporaries, he is said to have experienced visions from an early age. These became – along with the Bible – the chief source of inspiration for his poetry and art.

Born in Soho, London, son of a hosier, Blake left school at ten, was taught at home by his mother and then apprenticed to an engraver for seven years, becoming a professional engraver at the age of 21. He made his living from producing engravings for books by other artists and writers, learning and developing techniques he would use for his own work, including relief etching. This was the method he devised for publishing his greatest work in poetry and art: drawing his texts and designs in reverse onto copper plates, he etched over the lines and then printed them, colouring them by hand and stitching them into sugar-paper wrappers.

There were rarely more than a dozen copies of each edition offered for sale, but he printed off more copies on demand. Such was *Songs of Innocence* (1789), including 19 poems on 26 prints, followed by works including *The Marriage of Heaven and Hell* (1790-93) before the two-part *Songs of Innocence and of Experience* (1794), the second part of which included both 'The Tyger' and 'London' among its 26 lyrics.

Blake died in near poverty at the age of 69 in 1827. It wasn't until the publication of Alexander Gilchrist's *Life of William Blake* in 1863, two years after Gilchrist's death, that Blake's reputation was finally recognised. Today he is regarded as the most original poet and artist of the Romantic period, a major influence on later Modernist figures, from W.B. Yeats in poetry to Paul Nash in art, as well as on writers including Aldous Huxley and Philip Pullman.

Brendan Kennelly's early reading of William Blake exerted a profound influence on his own poetry and on his thinking about history, politics and religion. Blake's dictum 'True progress is only possible between opposites' became one of his literary touchstones, informing his belief that Ireland's difficulties were rooted in the failure of 'closed minds' to embrace that which is other and opposite, as he does throughout his work, most notably in giving a voice to repellent figures – such as Cromwell and Judas – and in his dramatisation of opposites in his versions of *Antigone*, *Medea* and *The Trojan Women*.

BK ■ William Blake asks questions few poets begin to dream of asking. He has a cosmic sense of curiosity, a spirit of inquiry that takes him into the farthest reaches of the imagination. He is, to use his own phrase, a mental traveller, committed to exploring the heights and depths of the human mind. He is the most passionately questioning of poets; and in 'The Tyger', a poem of six stanzas, there are 14 questions. Blake hammers the air and the language with questions about the Tyger. The first and last questions are identical, with one crucial difference. The opening question

> What immortal hand or eye
> <u>Could</u> frame thy fearful symmetry?

becomes

> What immortal hand or eye
> <u>Dare</u> frame thy fearful symmetry?

(underlining is mine).

The change from 'Could' to 'Dare' is brought about by the twelve intervening questions. This change relates to the difference between capacity and audacity, ability and daring.

> What creative force would <u>dare</u> frame the Tyger?

This is yet another poem of direct address; the fierce intimacy of its questioning spirit brings physical, industrial and cosmic imagery before the reader's eyes. These swift, driving images sweep us along through the Tyger's body, the banging, fiery world of industry, the world of stars and space, into the very mind and eyes of the Tyger's creator. Even here the questions persist in their unstoppable energy:

> Did he smile his work to see?
> Did he who made the Lamb make thee?

Blake's own phrase 'fearful symmetry' best describes this poem which, because of its primeval energy, has a purely explosive quality inseparable from its elemental music and its hammering interrogative rhythms that now sound like the regular beating of an anvil and now like the whispering stirrings in the dense 'forests of the night'.

'The Tyger' is not a poem that offers answers. But its questions continue to echo and resound in one's mind long after many answers and explanations are forgotten.

SAMUEL TAYLOR COLERIDGE (1772–1834)

Kubla Khan

Or a Vision in a Dream. A Fragment

In Xanadu did Kubla Khan
A stately pleasure dome decree:
Where Alph, the sacred river, ran
Through caverns measureless to man
   Down to a sunless sea.
So twice five miles of fertile ground
With walls and towers were girdled round:
And there were gardens bright with sinuous rills,
Where blossomed many an incense-bearing tree;
And here were forests ancient as the hills,
Enfolding sunny spots of greenery.

But oh! that deep romantic chasm which slanted
Down the green hill athwart a cedarn cover!
A savage place! as holy and enchanted
As e'er beneath a waning moon was haunted
By woman wailing for her demon lover!
And from this chasm, with ceaseless turmoil seething,
As if this earth in fast thick pants were breathing,
A mighty fountain momently was forced:
Amid whose swift half-intermitted burst
Huge fragments vaulted like rebounding hail,
Or chaffy grain beneath the thresher's flail:
And 'mid these dancing rocks at once and ever
It flung up momently the sacred river.
Five miles meandering with a mazy motion
Through wood and dale the sacred river ran,
Then reached the caverns measureless to man,
And sank in tumult to a lifeless ocean:
And 'mid this tumult Kubla heard from far
Ancestral voices prophesying war!

The shadow of the dome of pleasure
Floated midway on the waves;
Where was heard the mingled measure
From the fountain and the caves.
It was a miracle of rare device,
A sunny pleasure-dome with caves of ice!

A damsel with a dulcimer
In a vision once I saw;
It was an Abyssinian maid,
And on her dulcimer she played,
Singing of Mount Abora.
Could I revive within me
Her symphony and song,
To such a deep delight 'twould win me,
That with music loud and long,
I would build that dome in air,
That sunny dome! those caves of ice!
And all who heard should see them there,
And all should cry, Beware! Beware!
His flashing eyes, his floating hair!
Weave a circle round him thrice,
And close your eyes with holy dread,
For he on honey-dew hath fed,
And drunk the milk of Paradise.

1797 [1816]

Samuel Taylor Coleridge, poet and philosopher, launched the
English Romantic movement with his friend William Wordsworth
with their joint publication of *Lyrical Ballads* in 1798. 'Kubla
Khan' was probably written in October 1797 when Coleridge was
living at Nether Stowey in Somerset, from where he went on long
walks in the Quantock Hills with William and Dorothy Wordsworth,
which included discussions on their plans to publish *Lyrical Ballads*
the following year. Coleridge was a Devonshire man, son of the

vicar of St Mary's Church, Ottery St Mary, who died when the boy was eight, whereupon he was packed off to school for the rest of his youth to Christ's Hospital, going up to Jesus College, Cambridge, in 1791. At Cambridge he met the poet, Robert Southey, with whom he conceived an ill-fated plan to establish an idealistic community (Pantisocracy) on the banks of the Susquehanna River in Pennsylvania. This was also to include the three Fricker sisters, two of whom, Sarah and Edith, married Coleridge and Southey in Bristol in 1795. Coleridge later abandoned Sara after the birth of their fourth child.

Coleridge's literary reputation rests on poems such as the fragment 'Kubla Khan', 'Frost at Midnight', and the two ballads, 'Christobel' and 'The Rime of the Ancient Mariner', as well as his *Biographia Literaria* (1817), the seminal text of literary criticism from the English Romantic period.

The story behind the writing of 'Kubla Khan' has become part of literary myth, how the poem came to him in a dream but as he was writing it down he was interrupted by a 'person from Porlock' calling on him to discuss a business matter. On picking up his pen afterwards to complete the transcription, he found he'd forgotten the rest of this long poem: 'This fragment with a good deal more, not recoverable, composed, in a sort of Reverie brought on by two grains of Opium taken to check a dysentry, at a Farm House between Porlock & Linton, a quarter of a mile from Culbone Church.' In a later preface to the published poem he claimed to have been fallen asleep while reading about Kubla Khan in *Purchas his Pilgrimes* (1625), a compilation of travel writings by Samuel Purchas, whose account includes this description: 'In Xaindu did Cublai Can build a stately palace, encompassing sixteen miles of plaine ground with a wall, wherein are fertile meddowes, pleasant springs, delightful streams, and all sorts of beasts of chase and game, and in the middest thereof a sumptuous house of pleasure.'

BK ■ Coleridge wrote this poem after taking opium and reading a book, or part of it, dealing with Kubla Khan's 'stately pleasure-dome'. Coleridge is said to have fallen asleep while reading the book, *Purchas his Pilgrimes*, and when he awoke he began to write down what he'd seen in his sleep. Interrupted by 'a person from Porlock', he was unable to continue the poem in any substantial way when he returned to it. So what we have is a fragment of a dream, one of the most vivid and visionary fragments in English poetry.

Yet 'Kubla Khan' has a strange feeling of completeness about it. The famous, unforgettable images speak of pleasure, holiness, boundary-breaking fluency, 'caves of ice', fertile enclosures, bright gardens, a sunless sea, ancient forests, green sunlit places, 'a deep romantic chasm', 'a mighty fountain' that throws up 'dancing rocks' and 'the sacred river' that sinks amid tumult into 'a lifeless ocean'. There follows a vision in which Coleridge sees 'A damsel with a dulcimer', playing and singing so inspiringly that, Coleridge tells us, if he could only revive within himself 'Her symphony and song', he would be capable of building that pleasure-dome which Kubla Khan had ordered to be built. Coleridge would become the very architect of pleasure; he would take the place of Kubla Khan. Further, all who would look at him

> should cry, Beware! Beware!
> His flashing eyes, his floating hair!
> Weave a circle round him thrice,
> And close your eyes with holy dread,
> For he on honey-dew hath fed,
> And drunk the milk of Paradise.

The lines 'Could I revive within me / Her symphony and song' is the plight of the poet who was interrupted by that person from Porlock. This is how Coleridge must have felt after that interruption: frustrated, deprived, thwarted, imaginatively disabled, grasping for what he'd seen in his dream. It is something of an irony that one of the most ecstatically visionary poems in English, or any language, should be seen by its author as a 'psychological curiosity'. Its climax has a luminous intensity, the vision of one who, favoured by heaven and fed on honey-dew and 'the milk of Paradise', becomes a figure inspiring 'holy dread'. These images, captured in precise, rhythmical language, put Coleridge in the company of the world's glowing visionaries, saints, mystics and artists (Charles Lamb described Coleridge as 'an archangel slightly damaged') who glimpsed eternity and communicated to us something of what they saw. What we see, or are capable of seeing, is how we surrender to re-reading.

WILLIAM WORDSWORTH (1770–1850)

Composed upon Westminster Bridge, September 3, 1802

Earth has not anything to show more fair:
Dull would he be of soul who could pass by
A sight so touching in its majesty:
This City now doth, like a garment, wear
The beauty of the morning; silent, bare,
Ships, towers, domes, theatres, and temples lie
Open unto the fields, and to the sky;
All bright and glittering in the smokeless air.
Never did sun more beautifully steep
In his first splendour, valley, rock, or hill;
Ne'er saw I, never felt, a calm so deep!
The river glideth at his own sweet will:
Dear God! the very houses seem asleep;
And all that mighty heart is lying still!

1802 [*Poems, in Two Volumes*, 1807]

William Wordsworth launched the English Romantic movement
with Samuel Taylor Coleridge with their joint publication of *Lyrical
Ballads* in 1798. Born in Cockermouth, he spent most of his life
in England's Lake District, whose landscape deeply affected his
imagination, making him feel profoundly connected with the forces
of nature and inspiring much of his poetry. Wordsworth's most
productive years were at Dove Cottage (1799-1808), celebrated in
his poem 'Home at Grasmere' and chronicled by his sister Dorothy
in her *Grasmere Journals*, which include many evocative descriptions
of nature. He often used her journal as a starting-point for poems,
including 'I wandered lonely as a Cloud' (1804), whose description
of daffodils was inspired by her account of a walk they had taken
two years earlier. In the case of this poem, a Petrarchan sonnet, he
seems to have drawn upon her description of an earlier 'beautiful

morning' in London in July 1802: 'The City, St Pauls, with the river & a multitude of little boats, made a most beautiful sight as we crossed Westminster Bridge. The houses were not over-hung by their cloud of smoke & they were spread out endlessly, yet the sun shone so brightly with such a pure light that there was even something like the purity of one of nature's own grand spectacles.'

Wordsworth had already written the first version of his great auto-biographical poem *The Prelude* while on a walking tour of Germany in 1799. In the later 1805 version he puts forward his idea of 'spots of time' revisited in poetry, experiences through which he could trace his own development, as a man and as a poet, and which continued to resonate with new meanings many years after the events themselves: 'There are in our existence spots of time, / Which with distinct pre-eminence retain / A renovating Virtue, whence [...] our minds / Are nourished and invisibly repaired' (XI, 258-78).

BK ■ It's a bright, clear, clean September morning in London nearly two hundred years ago. Wordsworth is standing on Westminster Bridge, looking at the city which poets such as Swift and Pope had already written about in their individual ways. From the bright autumnal heights of the majestic Bridge, Wordsworth sees a city of surpassing beauty; there's nothing fairer on earth; and the beauty of the morning lies lightly on London's shoulders. The poet is privileged to see particular objects such as ships, towers, domes, theatres, temples and fields. Fields. There's still a feeling of the countryside in London in 1802. And the air is 'smokeless'. There's a suggestion of Edenic beauty in the phrase, 'first splendour', as the sun embraces the city. It is a moment of peace, of deep 'calm', of sleepy tranquillity enveloping 'the very houses'. Wordsworth is an appreciative witness of the stillness of 'that mighty heart'.

Today, that same mighty heart is a very different place after two hundred years of 'progress'. It's difficult to imagine words like 'calm', 'still', 'silent', 'smokeless' being applied to almost any city. In cities as far apart as Athens and Dublin the pollution has to be inhaled to be believed.

Yet there are moments, even now, when a city's beauty becomes visible. Very early some bright morning one can still see the hand-some character of London or Athens or Dublin. Very early. As early as that morning in September 1802, when Wordsworth stood on Westminster Bridge and looked about him.

LORD BYRON (1788–1824)

Darkness

I had a dream, which was not all a dream.
The bright sun was extinguished, and the stars
Did wander darkling in the eternal space,
Rayless, and pathless, and the icy earth
Swung blind and blackening in the moonless air;
Morn came and went – and came, and brought no day,
And men forgot their passions in the dread
Of this their desolation; and all hearts
Were chilled into a selfish prayer for light:
And they did live by watchfires – and the thrones,
The palaces of crowned kings – the huts,
The habitations of all things which dwell,
Were burnt for beacons; cities were consumed,
And men were gathered round their blazing homes
To look once more into each other's face;
Happy were those who dwelt within the eye
Of the volcanos, and their mountain-torch:
A fearful hope was all the world contained;
Forests were set on fire – but hour by hour
They fell and faded – and the crackling trunks
Extinguished with a crash – and all was black.
The brows of men by the despairing light
Wore an unearthly aspect, as by fits
The flashes fell upon them; some lay down
And hid their eyes and wept; and some did rest
Their chins upon their clenched hands, and smiled;
And others hurried to and fro, and fed
Their funeral piles with fuel, and looked up
With mad disquietude on the dull sky,
The pall of a past world; and then again
With curses cast them down upon the dust,

And gnashed their teeth and howled: the wild birds shrieked
And, terrified, did flutter on the ground,
And flap their useless wings; the wildest brutes
Came tame and tremulous; and vipers crawled
And twined themselves among the multitude,
Hissing, but stingless – they were slain for food.
And War, which for a moment was no more,
Did glut himself again: a meal was bought
With blood, and each sate sullenly apart
Gorging himself in gloom: no love was left;
All earth was but one thought – and that was death
Immediate and inglorious; and the pang
Of famine fed upon all entrails – men
Died, and their bones were tombless as their flesh;
The meagre by the meagre were devoured,
Even dogs assailed their masters, all save one,
And he was faithful to a corse, and kept
The birds and beasts and famished men at bay,
Till hunger clung them, or the dropping dead
Lured their lank jaws; himself sought out no food,
But with a piteous and perpetual moan,
And a quick desolate cry, licking the hand
Which answered not with a caress – he died.
The crowd was famished by degrees; but two
Of an enormous city did survive,
And they were enemies: they met beside
The dying embers of an altar-place
Where had been heaped a mass of holy things
For an unholy usage; they raked up,
And shivering scraped with their cold skeleton hands
The feeble ashes, and their feeble breath
Blew for a little life, and made a flame
Which was a mockery; then they lifted up
Their eyes as it grew lighter, and beheld
Each other's aspects – saw, and shrieked, and died –
Even of their mutual hideousness they died,
Unknowing who he was upon whose brow

Famine had written Fiend. The world was void,
The populous and the powerful was a lump,
Seasonless, herbless, treeless, manless, lifeless –
A lump of death – a chaos of hard clay.
The rivers, lakes and ocean all stood still,
And nothing stirred within their silent depths;
Ships sailorless lay rotting on the sea,
And their masts fell down piecemeal: as they dropped
They slept on the abyss without a surge –
The waves were dead; the tides were in their grave,
The moon, their mistress, had expired before;
The winds were withered in the stagnant air,
And the clouds perished; Darkness had no need
Of aid from them – She was the Universe.

Diodati, July 1816 [*The Prisoner of Chillon and Other Poems*, 1816]

George Gordon, Lord Byron was a highly influential figure in Romanticism as well as a controversial satirist whose poetry and personality cult captured the imagination of Europe. Famously described by Lady Caroline Lamb as 'mad, bad, and dangerous to know', this Anglo-Scottish poet died of fever while engaged in the Greek struggle for independence from the Turks.

Byron wrote 'Darkness' in Switzerland in the cold, rainy summer of 1816, 'the year without a summer' as it became known, when his storytelling challenge to guests at Lake Geneva inspired the writing of two seminal Gothic novels, Mary Shelley's *Frankenstein* (1818) and John Polidori's *The Vampyre* (1819). In his persuasive account of 'Darkness' in *The Song of the Earth* (2000), Jonathan Bate 'unlocks the impulse behind the poem': Byron's experience of the worst summer on record, which was followed by poor harvests, 'a hemispheric subsistence crisis, basic food shortage and concordant public disorder'. Bate quotes contemporary reports of 'a consistently dense haze permanently on the horizon', 'smoking vapour' and the darkening of the sun which 'led to fears of apocalypse – the exact situation of Byron's poem'.

He locates the cause in the eruption of Tamboro volcano in Indonesia in 1815, 'which killed some 80,000 people on the islands of Sumbawa and Lombok. It was the greatest eruption since 1500. The dust blasted into the stratosphere reduced the transparency of the atmosphere, filtered out the sun and consequently lowered surface temperatures. The effect lasted for three years, straining the growth-capacity of life across the planet. Beginning in 1816, crop failure led to food riots in nearly every country in Europe. [...]

'Byron does not set culture apart from nature. [...] The poem darkly narrates a history in which war temporarily ceases as human-kind pulls together in the face of inclement weather but is then renewed on a global scale as a result of the famine consequent on the absence of sunlight. The global struggle for subsistence leads ultimately to the extinction of mankind. In 1815, Byron and his public witnessed the cessation of a European, indeed worldwide, war which had lasted for more than twenty years; in 1816, they endured a year without a summer. The poem is as contemporary as it is apocalyptic. [...] But contemporary as it was, the poem remains powerfully prophetic [...] the vision of a world seasonless, herbless, treeless, the rivers, lakes and oceans silent. [...] When we read 'Darkness' now, Byron may be reclaimed as a prophet of – to adopt Bruno Latour's word – ecocide.' [13]

BK ■ 'Darkness' must surely be one of the darkest poems in the language. In expressing its vision of absolute darkness it is implacable, merciless, terrifying. As one reads and re-reads the poem, one becomes aware of the spreading power of the opening line which seems, as it were, to colonise all the lines that follow: 'I had a dream, which was not all a dream.'

This leaves the reader poised, or perhaps shattered, between the dream world and what is called the real world. It leaves the poem in the same position. Therefore, everything in the poem may be part of our dream world, waiting to haunt us. Or it may be part of our real world, waiting to engage us, swallow us, annihilate us. Written in the early part of the 19th century, 'Darkness' expresses horrors and fears that occupy a special, hideous place in 21st-century consciousness shaped to a considerable extent by the dread of nuclear bombs and warfare. Darkness is waiting to envelop the world. It is we – and we alone – who have created and developed the means to establish that universal darkness. 'She was the Universe' are the four, final words of Byron's poem. It is an almost unbearable thought.

The imagery that leads to this final thought is striking and clear. We enter a world, a dream which is not completely a dream, where the sun is 'extinguished' and the 'icy earth' swings 'blind and blackening in the moonless air'. Byron gives us a world without light, apart from the brief fires created from the broken 'palaces of crowned kings'. Nothing can halt the advance of the ferocious darkness, not even the forests that are set on fire. In a short time, Byron tells us, 'all was black'. The darkness of despair hits men and birds and 'wildest brutes'. War and famine are an essential part of this darkness.

> All earth was but one thought – and that was death

In this scene of total despair, there seems to be one moment of hope. A dog will not eat its dead master, but keeps watch over the corpse until it, too, dies of hunger. Then there are two survivors, men who are enemies of each other. They build a feeble fire and by its light they see each other –

> saw, and shrieked, and died –
> Even of their mutual hideousness they died,
> Unknowing who he was upon whose brow
> Famine had written Fiend.

The closing lines present the world as 'A lump of death' in which seas, rivers and lakes are a mass of black stagnation. It is a scene of unqualified desolation and despair.

> The waves were dead; the tides were in their grave,
> The moon, their mistress, had expired before;
> The winds were withered in the stagnant air,
> And the clouds perished; Darkness had no need
> Of aid from them – She was the Universe.

Now and then, the term 'Romantic poet' is used in a pejorative sense, suggesting a writer given over to wilting dreams and vaporous aspirations. 'Darkness', written by one of the great Romantics, shows the fierce grip Byron had on reality. Reading it now, after a century of wars, famines, pandemics, concentration camps, final solutions, ethnic purges and crimes almost beyond imagining, one discerns in it a bleakly prophetic note, a warning given to us in the shape of a dream 'which was not all a dream'. It is as if Byron were telling us that we can choose to try to make a world of darkness or of light, or at least a world in which light can fight darkness, just as it does in our own hearts.

To allow this poem to sink into the depths of our consciousness is to become rather afraid, even somewhat terrified. But that fear and terror are also the source of whatever effort we make not to create a world in which only darkness rules, a world that is 'A lump of death, a chaos of hard clay'. Is there any darkness to equal the darkness generated by our own organised, educated, justified and 'sophisticated' stupidity?

Like many good poems, 'Darkness' leaves us with a question, or questions.

What sort of world do we want?

How are we going to make it?

Poems such as 'Darkness' can help us to decide, one way or the other. Poetry, as Ibsen said, is a court of judgement on the soul. Every intelligent reader is on trial.

PERCY BYSSHE SHELLEY (1792–1822)

Ode to the West Wind

I

O wild West Wind, thou breath of Autumn's being,
Thou, from whose unseen presence the leaves dead
Are driven, like ghosts from an enchanter fleeing,

Yellow, and black, and pale, and hectic red,
Pestilence-stricken multitudes: O thou,
Who chariotest to their dark wintry bed

The wingéd seeds, where they lie cold and low,
Each like a corpse within its grave, until
Thine azure sister of the Spring shall blow

Her clarion o'er the dreaming earth, and fill
(Driving sweet buds like flocks to feed in air)
With living hues and odours plain and hill:

Wild Spirit, which art moving everywhere;
Destroyer and preserver; hear, oh hear!

II

Thou on whose stream, mid the steep sky's commotion,
Loose clouds like earth's decaying leaves are shed,
Shook from the tangled boughs of Heaven and Ocean,

Angels of rain and lightning: there are spread
On the blue surface of thine aery surge,
Like the bright hair uplifted from the head

Of some fierce Maenad, even from the dim verge
Of the horizon to the zenith's height,
The locks of the approaching storm. Thou dirge

Of the dying year, to which this closing night
Will be the dome of a vast sepulchre,
Vaulted with all thy congregated might

Of vapours, from whose solid atmosphere
Black rain, and fire, and hail will burst: oh, hear!

III

Thou who didst waken from his summer dreams
The blue Mediterranean, where he lay,
Lulled by the coil of his crystalline streams,

Beside a pumice isle in Baiae's bay,
And saw in sleep old palaces and towers
Quivering within the wave's intenser day,

All overgrown with azure moss and flowers
So sweet, the sense faints picturing them! Thou
For whose path the Atlantic's level powers

Cleave themselves into chasms, while far below
The sea-blooms and the oozy woods which wear
The sapless foliage of the ocean, know

Thy voice, and suddenly grow gray with fear,
And tremble and despoil themselves: oh, hear!

IV

If I were a dead leaf thou mightest bear;
If I were a swift cloud to fly with thee;
A wave to pant beneath thy power, and share

The impulse of thy strength, only less free
Than thou, O uncontrollable! If even
I were as in my boyhood, and could be

The comrade of thy wanderings over Heaven,
As then, when to outstrip thy skiey speed
Scarce seemed a vision; I would ne'er have striven

As thus with thee in prayer in my sore need.
Oh, lift me as a wave, a leaf, a cloud!
I fall upon the thorns of life! I bleed!

A heavy weight of hours has chained and bowed
One too like thee: tameless, and swift, and proud.

        V

Make me thy lyre, even as the forest is:
What if my leaves are falling like its own!
The tumult of thy mighty harmonies

Will take from both a deep, autumnal tone,
Sweet though in sadness. Be thou, Spirit fierce,
My spirit! Be thou me, impetuous one!

Drive my dead thoughts over the universe
Like withered leaves to quicken a new birth!
And, by the incantation of this verse,

Scatter, as from an unextinguished hearth
Ashes and sparks, my words among mankind!
Be through my lips to unawakened earth

The trumpet of a prophecy! O Wind,
If Winter comes, can Spring be far behind?

1819 [*Prometheus Unbound with Other Poems*, 1820]

Percy Bysshe Shelley was one of the foremost English Romantic poets, a radical thinker and campaigner for social justice, but his poetry wasn't accorded much critical or popular recognition in his lifetime, while his most outspoken political poetry was deemed too dangerous to be published until after his death, most notably *The Masque of Anarchy*, 'England in 1819' and 'Song to the Men of England', all written after the Peterloo Massacre in August 1819.

Born in Sussex, son of a wealthy MP and landowner mother, he had a comfortable upbringing, apart from his time at Eton. He went up to Oxford in 1810 but was sent down the following year for publishing a pamphlet, *The Necessity of Atheism*. His family disowned him when he eloped to Scotland with Harriet Westbrook, the 16-year-old schoolfriend of one of his sisters.

In 1812 he travelled to Ireland to campaign for Catholic emancipation and repeal of the union with England, an eventful visit which Brendan Kennelly describes in his poem 'Shelley in Dublin' (1974). Two years later he eloped with Mary Wollstonecraft Godwin. During the summer of 1816 they travelled around Europe, staying with Byron in Switzerland where Mary began her novel *Frankenstein* and Byron wrote 'Darkness' [140]. They married later that year after Harriet Shelley had drowned herself. His need to escape from both the English climate and his creditors led to them living in Italy, where Shelley found himself less engaged with the political issues of the time and more able to create visionary poetry embodying his ideals, including his blank verse drama *Prometheus Unbound*, as well as his 'Ode to the West Wind', of which he wrote:

> This poem was conceived and chiefly written in a wood that skirts the Arno, near Florence, and on a day when that tempestuous wind, whose temperature is at once mild and animating, was collecting the vapours which pour down the autumnal rains. They began, as I foresaw, at sunset with a violent tempest of hail and rain, attended by that magnificent thunder and lightning peculiar to the Cisalpine regions.

He invited John Keats to join them in Pisa, but Keats only made it as far as Rome. On hearing the news of Keats's death in 1821, he wrote his elegy 'Adonais'. Shelley himself died in 1822, drowned when his boat sank during a storm off the Italian coast.

BK ■ Shelley sees his ode as a 'prayer in my sore need' the purpose of which is that the fierce spirit of the west wind should be his spirit; further, that the wind and he become one.

> Be thou me, impetuous one!

This poemprayer for a being of elemental impetuosity is in five 14-line sections. An ode is a poem meant to be sung, has a tone of direct address, and enjoys an exalted style. 'Ode to the West Wind' has a majestic architecture and is intensly logical. It is untamed but not undisciplined. As with other poems in this anthology it uses weather to express emotions. It moves through different stages to a climax of renewal following Shelley's admission that time has 'chained and bowed' him. Shelley's love of freedom wins through and the west wind, with which he finally wishes to be identified, becomes his ally and his hope, his working colleague to 'quicken a new birth' for mankind. The cosmic nobility of Shelley's thought is lucidly and honestly presented here.

Each of the first three sections of the poem ends with the plea 'O, hear!' It's as if Shelley felt his isolation so deeply that he prays to the wind to pay attention to him, to hear his voice. In the first section, the wind is a 'Wild Spirit...moving everywhere' and is also both 'Destroyer and preserver'. The imagery bears out the wind's opposing roles, scattering the dead leaves, planting the 'winged seeds'; the certainty of death and the promise of growth occur simultaneously.

In the second section, the wind is the 'dirge of the dying year'. There is an 'approaching storm' and, in a prophetic outburst, we see that the 'closing night'

> Will be the dome of a vast sepulchre,
> Vaulted with all thy congregated might
>
> Of vapours, from whose solid atmosphere
> Black rain, and fire, and hail will burst: O hear!

This explosive climax to the second section ends with the plea 'O hear! and leads into the sensual, drowsy 'summer dreams' , 'blue Mediterranean', 'crystalline streams', 'sea-blooms', 'oozy woods' and 'sapless foliage' of the third section which nevertheless, despite the sleepy sensuality of its atmosphere, ends 'grey with fear' on hearing the west wind's 'voice'. And again, the last two words are 'O hear!' The repetition of this plea stresses Shelley's need for connection with the west wind and what it means to him.

Not until the fourth section does the word 'I' appear. Picking up the imagery of leaf, cloud and wave in sections one, two and three, Shelley now speaks directly to the wind and admits his weakness and frailties with complete candour:

> I fall upon the thorns of life! I bleed!

Yet this moment of admitting weakness and inadequacy is also the moment when Shelley recognises that he is 'too like' the wild west wind. Like the wind, Shelley is, or once was, 'tameless and swift and proud'. These are key words in any attempt to understand Shelley's character as a poet. Tameless. Swift. Proud.

This is the moment, spilling over into the beginning of the fifth and final section, when Shelley pleads with the wind, or prays to it, to make him its 'lyre, even as the forest is'. He wants the wind's spirit to be his, the wind to be himself, so that his 'dead thoughts' will be driven 'over the universe...to quicken a new birth'; that his fiery words will be scattered 'among mankind'; and that this spirit, this windmanspirit, will be 'The trumpet of a prophecy...to un-awakened earth'. The famous final lines form the natural conclusion of that surge of hope raised in the heart of the 'chained and bowed' man who sought renewal from the wind:

> O wind,
> If Winter comes, can Spring be far behind?

The first adjective Shelley applies to the west wind, in the first few words of the poem, is 'wild'. When he describes himself in the fourth section, the first word that comes to his mind is 'tameless'. Is it any wonder that the wild force of nature and the tameless spirit of the man should, in his prayer, come together as one? Shelley's wildness is of the spirit, the freedom-loving heart of the man. One crucial aspect of his genius is his ability to communicate this fierce love of freedom in a uniquely stylish manner. Shelley's wildness is inseparable from his style. The soaring, elemental energy of this poem is disciplined, structured and directed in a gracious, elegant manner. Shelley utters his spirit (this is one of his favourite words) with an uninhibited fullness, an unbridled passion. One senses his moral determination to do justice to his wildness, his uncurbed love of freedom. But his technical mastery is such that his poem is devoid of any trace of shapeless, spewing confessionalism. He achieves complete expression of his deepest feelings with a grace that imparts a sense of restraint and order to the emotional torrent driving the poem onwards to its timeless conclusion. Like the wild west wind itself, Shelley's Ode is still 'moving' and wholly alive.

JOHN KEATS (1795–1821)

Ode to a Nightingale

My heart aches, and a drowsy numbness pains
  My sense, as though of hemlock I had drunk,
Or emptied some dull opiate to the drains
  One minute past, and Lethe-wards had sunk:
'Tis not through envy of thy happy lot,
  But being too happy in thine happiness –
    That thou, light-wingèd Dryad of the trees,
      In some melodious plot
  Of beechen green, and shadows numberless,
    Singest of summer in full-throated ease.

O, for a draught of vintage! that hath been
  Cooled a long age in the deep-delvèd earth,
Tasting of Flora and the country green,
  Dance, and Provençal song, and sunburnt mirth!
O for a beaker full of the warm South,
  Full of the true, the blushful Hippocrene,
    With beaded bubbles winking at the brim,
      And purple-stainèd mouth;
  That I might drink, and leave the world unseen,
    And with thee fade away into the forest dim:

Fade far away, dissolve, and quite forget
  What thou among the leaves hast never known,
The weariness, the fever, and the fret
  Here, where men sit and hear each other groan;
Where palsy shakes a few, sad, last gray hairs,
  Where youth grows pale, and spectre-thin, and dies;
    Where but to think is to be full of sorrow
      And leaden-eyed despairs,
  Where Beauty cannot keep her lustrous eyes,
    Or new Love pine at them beyond tomorrow.

Away! away! for I will fly to thee,
  Not charioted by Bacchus and his pards,
But on the viewless wings of Poesy,
  Though the dull brain perplexes and retards:
Already with thee! tender is the night,
  And haply the Queen-Moon is on her throne,
    Clustered around by all her starry Fays;
      But here there is no light,
  Save what from heaven is with the breezes blown
    Through verdurous glooms and winding mossy ways.

I cannot see what flowers are at my feet,
  Nor what soft incense hangs upon the boughs,
But, in embalmèd darkness, guess each sweet
  Wherewith the seasonable month endows
The grass, the thicket, and the fruit-tree wild;
  White hawthorn, and the pastoral eglantine;
    Fast fading violets covered up in leaves;
      And mid-May's eldest child,
  The coming musk-rose, full of dewy wine,
    The murmurous haunt of flies on summer eves.

Darkling I listen; and, for many a time
  I have been half in love with easeful Death,
Called him soft names in many a musèd rhyme,
  To take into the air my quiet breath;
Now more than ever seems it rich to die,
  To cease upon the midnight with no pain,
    While thou art pouring forth thy soul abroad
      In such an ecstasy!
  Still wouldst thou sing, and I have ears in vain –
    To thy high requiem become a sod.

Thou wast not born for death, immortal Bird!
  No hungry generations tread thee down;
The voice I hear this passing night was heard
  In ancient days by emperor and clown:

Perhaps the self-same song that found a path
   Through the sad heart of Ruth, when, sick for home,
      She stood in tears amid the alien corn;
         The same that oft-times hath
   Charmed magic casements, opening on the foam
      Of perilous seas, in faery lands forlorn.

Forlorn! the very word is like a bell
   To toll me back from thee to my sole self!
Adieu! the fancy cannot cheat so well
   As she is famed to do, deceiving elf.
Adieu! adieu! thy plaintive anthem fades
   Past the near meadows, over the still stream,
      Up the hill-side; and now 'tis buried deep
         In the next valley-glades:
   Was it a vision, or a waking dream?
      Fled is that music: – Do I wake or sleep?

May 1819 [1820]

John Keats was born in London, the son of a livery stable manager, and had little formal education. Little wonder that this upstart self-taught Cockney genius received little recognition during his short life. Like William Blake, he was ridiculed by most of the critics.

Keats was apprenticed to a surgeon in his teens before working as a junior house surgeon at Guy's and St Thomas' hospitals. His first mature poems date from 1816, and nearly all his great poems were written in the course of a year, from 21 September 1818 to 21 September 1819, during which he also nursed his brother Tom, who died from tuberculosis in December 1818. He himself became increasingly ill throughout 1819.

His 'Ode to a Nightingale' dates from May 1819, but according to his friend Charles Brown, Keats drafted the poem sitting under the plum tree at the garden at Wentworth Place in Hampstead (his beloved Fanny Brawne lived next door in the other half of this double house). The theme, woodland setting and verbal echoes of the nightingale's song were inspired by his reading of *The Flower and the Leaf*, a medieval allegorical poem (then wrongly attributed to Chaucer) in a modern translation by Dryden, while the wine and Bacchus themes came from Robert Burton's *Anatomy of Melancholy*. By the time the Ode was published, in July 1820, in the volume *Lamia, Isabella, The Eve of St Agnes, and other poems*, Leigh Hunt had arranged for him to be looked after at his house. Following doctor's orders to go south for his health, he sailed for Italy with his friend Joseph Severn in September, reaching Rome in November, and died there, from tuberculosis, in February 1821.

BK ■ Keats speaks directly to the nightingale as he listens to the bird 'pouring forth thy soul abroad / In such an ecstasy!' Listening plays an important part in this poem: 'Darkling I listen'. As Keats listens to the nightingale singing 'of summer in full-throated ease', he longs to leave the world 'where men sit and hear each other groan', and he wishes to 'fade away into the forest dim' in the nightingale's ecstatic company. To achieve this he yearns, first, 'for a draught of vintage', a strong intoxicating stimulant, but then he opts for an even more potent means of joining the nightingale, that is, 'on the viewless wings of poesy', the only wings that can begin to compare with the nightingale's wings. And poetry's wings do, in fact, enable Keats to come near the singing bird, albeit in a state of darkness: 'here there is no light'.

In this darkness, Keats is content to 'guess' and to 'listen'. He is happy to be in a state of uncertainty, of doubt. He once described himself as one 'straining at particles of light in the midst of a great darkness'. This happy ability to breathe the air of dark uncertainty is one of the sources of Keats's strength as a lyric poet. In a letter to his brothers, George and Tom Keats, in December 1817, he wrote:

> it struck me what quality went to form a man of achievement, especially in literature, and which Shakespeare possessed so enormously – I mean *Negative Capability*, that is, when a man is capable of being in uncertainties, mysteries, doubts, without any irritable reaching after fact and reason – Coleridge, for instance, would let go by a fine isolated verisimilitude caught from the Penetralium of mystery, from being incapable of remaining content with half-knowledge. This pursued through volumes would perhaps take us no further than this, that with a great poet the sense of Beauty overcomes every other consideration, or rather obliterates all consideration.

Keats 'cannot see' where he is, so he is content to 'listen' and to 'guess'. The song of the unseen nightingale fills him with such a joyous awareness, standing as he is, in the speculative darkness, that he acknowledges how often during his life he has 'been half in love with easeful Death' and that now, more than ever, listening to the nightingale, it seems 'rich to die, / To cease upon the midnight with no pain'. At one level, 'Ode to a Nightingale' is a poem so deeply and intensely aware of pain and suffering that the reader is quick to appreciate why Keats' desire to 'fade away', to 'dissolve', to 'forget' this world

> Where palsy shakes a few, sad, last gray hairs,
>> Where youth grows pale, and spectre-thin, and dies,
>>> Where but to think is to be full of sorrow
>>>> And leaden-eyed despairs,

and to be in the company of the bird whose song embodies that 'sense of Beauty (which) overcomes every other consideration, or rather obliterates all consideration'.

Keats lived with a constant awareness of death. He died at the age of 26. A very ill young man, he had a profound appreciation of passionate, ecstatic life, the kind of life he discerns in the nightingale's song, and into which he seems to 'dissolve'. This capacity for emotional and imaginative dissolution into objects and creatures is for Keats a crucial way of experiencing reality. 'Nothing ever becomes real till it is experienced – Even a Proverb is no proverb to you till your Life has illustrated it,' he says in a letter to his brother George and his sister Georgiana, begun on 14th February and finished on 3rd May 1819. (It's a long letter!) In the same letter he says 'I wonder how people exist with all their worries'.

Keats, a most human and generous-spirited poet, endures a sundering of that brief ecstatic unity with the nightingale's song when the word 'forlorn' ends the penultimate stanza of the poem. 'Forlorn' means abandoned, desperate, hopeless, forsaken. The stanza considers and celebrates the power of the song of the 'immortal Bird'; how it was heard 'In ancient days by emperor and clown'; how it touched 'the sad heart of Ruth' and

> Charmed magic casements, opening on the foam
>> Of perilous seas, in faery lands forlorn.

One can feel the terrible sadness in Keats's heart when that word 'forlorn' wrenches him away from the nightingale's presence and returns him to the casual desolation of his 'sole self'.

Near the beginning of the poem, Keats wished to 'fade away into the forest dim' with the nightingale, but now it is the nightingale that fades away from him.

> thy plaintive anthem fades
> Past the near meadows, over the still stream,
> Up the hill-side; and now 'tis buried deep
> In the next valley-glades:

The last two lines of the poem take the form of two questions. The first question probes the very nature of the experience that Keats has just been through; the second explores his personal condition now, in this final shocking moment when he realises that the magical music has 'fled', the song is silent, the ecstasy spent.

> Was it a vision, or a waking dream?
> Fled is that music: – Do I wake or sleep?

'Do you not see how necessary a World of Pains and troubles is to school an Intelligence and make it a Soul? A Place where the heart must feel and suffer in a thousand diverse ways! Not merely is the Heart a Hornbook, It is the Minds Bible, it is the Minds experience, it is the teat from which the Mind or intelligence sucks its identity.'

These words are from the letter, already mentioned, to George and Georgiana Keats, in 1819. Much of Keats's achievement in 'Ode to a Nightingale' is due to the undaunted way in which he uses the troubles of his heart to become his mind's bible throughout the poem. As a result of this integrity, he pursues his relationship with the nightingale, with the song of the nightingale, to that moment of lonely sundering when all that remains are painful questions about his experience, his identity, his state of being. This brave and beautiful poem is handsomely structured and impeccably argued: its logic is inseparable from its passion; its spiritual vitality cannot be divorced from its superb, unobtrusive technique. When Ezra Pound, sensing fatigue in some areas of modern poetry, called on poets to 'Make it new', he might simply have told them to spend some time, a lot of time, reading and re-reading 'Ode to a Nightingale'. It is as 'new' today as when it was first written.

THOMAS HOOD (1799–1845)

I Remember, I Remember

I remember, I remember,
The house where I was born,
The little window where the sun
Came peeping in at morn;
He never came a wink too soon,
Nor brought too long a day,
But now I often wish the night
Had borne my breath away!

I remember, I remember,
The roses, red and white,
The violets, and the lily-cups,
Those flowers made of light!
The lilacs where the robin built,
And where my brother set
The laburnum on his birthday, –
The tree is living yet!

I remember, I remember,
Where I was used to swing,
And thought the air must rush as fresh
To swallows on the wing;
My spirit flew in feathers then,
That is so heavy now,
And summer pools could hardly cool
The fever on my brow!

I remember, I remember,
The fir trees dark and high;
I used to think their slender tops
Were close against the sky:

It was a childish ignorance,
But now 'tis little joy
To know I'm farther off from heaven
Than when I was a boy.

[*Friendship's Offering: A Literary Album*, 1826]

Thomas Hood was a poet, journalist and popular humorist best known in his lifetime for sinister light verse (such as 'Miss Kilmansegg and her Precious Leg') as well as for social protest poetry exposing the plight of the poor, most notably 'Song of the Shirt' (published in *Punch* in 1843), 'The Lay of the Labourer' (1844) and 'The Bridge of Sighs' (1844). Born the son of a London bookseller, he trained as an engraver for a period, later illustrating his own works. He suffered from ill health for much of his life and was helped by the Royal Literary Fund and with a Civil List Pension.

BK ■ Memory can be sad or joyous, inspiring or depressing, willingly induced or inexplicably suffered. It is a constant, fertile source of poetry. For Thomas Hood, memory makes his spirit, that was once so light it 'flew in feathers', a heavy burden darkening his life. What Hood remembers tends to be light and joyous; but that lightness and joy only serve, sadly, to emphasise his present, heavy joylessness. So, as he remembers the house where he was born, the morning sun, roses, violets, lilacs 'where the robin built', his brother's birthday, a special laburnum tree which is 'living yet', the place where he used to swing, swallows flying through summer, and fir trees that seemed 'close against the sky' – as he remembers these moments and images, and compares them with his present life, he's driven to the sad conclusion that

> 'tis little joy
> To know I'm farther off from Heaven
> Than when I was a boy.

For Hood, memories of the past become knowledge of the present. This punishing transformation from memory to knowledge saves this poem from sentimentality and its cosy, cruel power of self-deception. 'I Remember, I Remember' is true to experience: an authentic poem.

ALFRED, LORD TENNYSON (1809–1891)

Tithonus

The woods decay, the woods decay and fall,
The vapours weep their burthen to the ground,
Man comes and tills the field and lies beneath,
And after many a summer dies the swan.
Me only cruel immortality
Consumes: I wither slowly in thine arms,
Here at the quiet limit of the world,
A white-haired shadow roaming like a dream
The ever-silent spaces of the East,
Far-folded mists, and gleaming halls of morn.

    Alas! for this gray shadow, once a man –
So glorious in his beauty and thy choice,
Who madest him thy chosen, that he seemed
To his great heart none other than a God!
I asked thee, 'Give me immortality.'
Then didst thou grant mine asking with a smile,
Like wealthy men, who care not how they give.
But thy strong Hours indignant worked their wills,
And beat me down and marred and wasted me,
And though they could not end me, left me maimed
To dwell in presence of immortal youth,
Immortal age beside immortal youth,
And all I was, in ashes. Can thy love,
Thy beauty, make amends, though even now,
Close over us, the silver star, thy guide,
Shines in those tremulous eyes that fill with tears
To hear me? Let me go: take back thy gift:
Why should a man desire in any way
To vary from the kindly race of men
Or pass beyond the goal of ordinance
Where all should pause, as is most meet for all?

A soft air fans the cloud apart; there comes
A glimpse of that dark world where I was born.
Once more the old mysterious glimmer steals
From thy pure brows, and from thy shoulders pure,
And bosom beating with a heart renewed.
Thy cheek begins to redden through the gloom,
Thy sweet eyes brighten slowly close to mine,
Ere yet they blind the stars, and the wild team
Which love thee, yearning for thy yoke, arise,
And shake the darkness from their loosened manes,
And beat the twilight into flakes of fire.

Lo! ever thus thou growest beautiful
In silence, then before thine answer given
Departest, and thy tears are on my cheek.

Why wilt thou ever scare me with thy tears,
And make me tremble lest a saying learnt,
In days far-off, on that dark earth, be true?
'The Gods themselves cannot recall their gifts.'

Ay me! ay me! with what another heart
In days far-off, and with what other eyes
I used to watch – if I be he that watched –
The lucid outline forming round thee; saw
The dim curls kindle into sunny rings;
Changed with thy mystic change, and felt my blood
Glow with the glow that slowly crimsoned all
Thy presence and thy portals, while I lay,
Mouth, forehead, eyelids, growing dewy-warm
With kisses balmier than half-opening buds
Of April, and could hear the lips that kissed
Whispering I knew not what of wild and sweet,
Like that strange song I heard Apollo sing,
While Ilion like a mist rose into towers.

Yet hold me not for ever in thine East:
How can my nature longer mix with thine?

Coldly thy rosy shadows bathe me, cold
Are all thy lights, and cold my wrinkled feet
Upon thy glimmering thresholds, when the steam
Floats up from those dim fields about the homes
Of happy men that have the power to die,
And grassy barrows of the happier dead.
Release me, and restore me to the ground;
Thou seëst all things, thou wilt see my grave:
Thou wilt renew thy beauty morn by morn;
I earth in earth forget these empty courts,
And thee returning on thy silver wheels.

1833, revised 1859 [First published in *The Cornhill Magazine*, February 1860]

Alfred, Lord Tennyson was the leading poet of the Victorian era. Son of a Lincolnshire rector, he was a precociously talented writer in his youth, achieving great versatility in his mature work. In 1827 he went up to Cambridge where he met Arthur Hallam, who was to become his dearest friend and suitor to his sister Emily. Deeply shocked by Hallam's sudden death in Vienna in 1833, he began writing a series of elegies eventually published in 1850 as *In Memoriam*, an extended meditation on life and death in 131 sections, earning him the friendship of Queen Victoria and helping bring about his appointment as Poet Laureate. He was given a peerage in 1884.

Originally a shorter poem titled 'Tithon' and not completed until 1859, Tennyson's dramatic monologue 'Tithonus' was conceived as a companion (or 'pendent') to two other poems on mortality written in the immediate aftermath of Hallam's death, 'Ulysses' (on the need for courage of life) and 'Tiresias' (the courage of self-sacrifice). The poem's speaker is Tithonus, prince of Troy, son of a king and a water nymph, who was abducted to be her consort by Eos, goddess of the dawn, and made immortal but without being granted eternal youth, destined to live forever as a 'white-haired shadow'.

Tennyson was writing at a time when Christian faith and traditional assumptions about the nature of man were being questioned in the light of advances in science and wider circulation of liberal ideas. 'Tithonus' was published by Thackeray in *The Cornhill Magazine* just three months after Darwin published his *Origin of Species*.

JOHN CLARE (1793–1864)

I Am

I am: yet what I am, none cares or knows,
  My friends forsake me like a memory lost,
I am the self-consumer of my woes –
  They rise and vanish in oblivion's host,
Like shadows in love's frenzied, stifled throes –
And yet I am, and live – like vapours tossed

Into the nothingness of scorn and noise,
  Into the living sea of waking dreams
Where there is neither sense of life or joys
  But the vast shipwreck of my life's esteems;
Even the dearest that I love the best
Are strange – nay, rather, stranger than the rest.

I long for scenes, where man hath never trod,
  A place where woman never smiled or wept –
There to abide with my Creator, God,
  And sleep as I in childhood sweetly slept,
Untroubling, and untroubled where I lie,
The grass below – above, the vaulted sky.

c. 1844-45 [First published in the *Bedford Times*, 1848]

John Clare was born in Northamptonshire, where he worked as
an agricultural labourer. Celebrated during the 1820s by literary
London as 'the peasant poet', he published four books of poetry
between 1820 and 1835. Clare felt alienated by a series of losses: of
his first love; of his native village of Helpston after moving three
miles away; and of a childhood landscape changed after landowners
enclosed the common lands after a local Enclosure Act was passed in
1809. He suffered from severe depression, and in 1837 was certified

insane, spending most of the rest of his life in asylums, where he continued to write. 'I Am' was written in Northampton General Lunatic Asylum. His work was neglected for over a century, and Clare has only recently received full recognition as one of the great English poets of the Romantic period. Many of his poems bear witness to how the English countryside was carved up in the early part of the 19th century, and to the effects of this on the wildlife, land and people. In *The Song of the Earth* (2000), Jonathan Bate calls Clare 'the most authentically "working-class" of all major English poets [...] He viewed "the rights of man" and the "rights of nature" as co-extensive and co-dependent.' [14]

BK ■ 'I am' says John Clare. It's amazing how the simplest words and phrases, such as 'I am', have such huge reverberations and consequences. 'To be or not to be.' 'Before Abraham was, I am.' John Clare knows one thing for sure: he is. Even as he lives forsaken by his friends, living 'like vapours tossed /Into the nothingness of scorn and noise', hurt to the core that even those dearest to him are not only strange but 'stranger than the rest' to him, he still clings to the central reality embodied in these two simple words: 'I am.' The sense of existence comes face to face with the pressures of the sense of insanity. The hope of coherence confronts the threat of disintegration. The capacity to connect is in the bleak presence of disconnection and isolation.

The consciousness of going mad is a worse suffering than actually being mad. This poem reveals a strong, sensitive intelligence threatened from all sides by a world 'Where there is neither sense of life or joys / But the vast shipwreck of my life's esteems'.

John Clare does not break up in this poem. The poem's sturdy structure is a kind of eloquent testimony to the poet's strength of will and mind at a time of stress. It is only logical that the final stanza should be an expression of longing for places far removed from men and women, a longing to be with God, and to find the kind of peaceful sleep he knew in childhood, 'Untroubling and untroubled'.

This is yet another poem about darkness, the darkness of a man's heart and mind. It is troubled, candid, lucid and heroic, a poem in which Clare climbs, in the words of E.E. Cummings, to 'the pinnacle of am'. From that human pinnacle of being, the vision is almost unbearably desolate.

ROBERT BROWNING (1812–1889)

My Last Duchess. 1842

Ferrara

That's my last Duchess painted on the wall,
Looking as if she were alive. I call
That piece a wonder, now: Frà Pandolf's hands
Worked busily a day, and there she stands.
Will't please you sit and look at her? I said
'Frà Pandolf' by design, for never read
Strangers like you that pictured countenance,
The depth and passion of its earnest glance,
But to myself they turned (since none puts by
The curtain I have drawn for you, but I)
And seemed as they would ask me, if they durst,
How such a glance came there; so, not the first
Are you to turn and ask thus. Sir, 'twas not
Her husband's presence only, called that spot
Of joy into the Duchess' cheek: perhaps
Frà Pandolf chanced to say, 'Her mantle laps
Over my lady's wrist too much,' or 'Paint
Must never hope to reproduce the faint
Half-flush that dies along her throat': such stuff
Was courtesy, she thought, and cause enough
For calling up that spot of joy. She had
A heart – how shall I say? – too soon made glad,
Too easily impressed; she liked whate'er
She looked on, and her looks went everywhere.
Sir, 'twas all one! My favour at her breast,
The dropping of the daylight in the West,
The bough of cherries some officious fool
Broke in the orchard for her, the white mule
She rode with round the terrace – all and each
Would draw from her alike the approving speech,

Or blush, at least. She thanked men – good! but thanked
Somehow – I know not how – as if she ranked
My gift of a nine-hundred-years-old name
With anybody's gift. Who'd stoop to blame
This sort of trifling? Even had you skill
In speech – (which I have not) – to make your will
Quite clear to such an one, and say, 'Just this
Or that in you disgusts me; here you miss,
Or there exceed the mark' – and if she let
Herself be lessoned so, nor plainly set
Her wits to yours, forsooth, and made excuse,
– E'en then would be some stooping; and I choose
Never to stoop. Oh, sir, she smiled, no doubt,
Whene'er I passed her; but who passed without
Much the same smile? This grew; I gave commands;
Then all smiles stopped together. There she stands
As if alive. Will't please you rise? We'll meet
The company below, then. I repeat,
The Count your master's known munificence
Is ample warrant that no just pretence
Of mine for dowry will be disallowed;
Though his fair daughter's self, as I avowed
At starting, is my object. Nay, we'll go
Together down, sir. Notice Neptune, though,
Taming a sea-horse, thought a rarity,
Which Claus of Innsbruck cast in bronze for me!

[*Dramatic Lyrics*, 1842]

Robert Browning had to wait until late in life to be recognised
as a major poet of the Victorian period by his contemporaries.
Born the son of a banker, he was largely educated in his father's
extensive library, apart from a short period studying Greek at the
University of London. A gifted linguist, he had learned Latin,
Greek, French and Italian by the age of 14. He continued to live
with his parents until his mid 30s, eventually leaving in 1846 to
marry Elizabeth Barrett and elope with her to Italy. The Brownings

lived mainly in Florence, Robert only returning to England after Elizabeth's death, in 1861.

His early publications – funded by his father – met with little success. He was wise not to persist with the writing of inert verse plays but these nevertheless helped hone his skills in characterisation and dramatic lyrics. He only achieved great renown with *The Ring and the Book*, a narrative poem in 12 books published in 1868-69 in four volumes telling the story of a murder trial in Rome in 1698. He is best-known now for his psychologically astute dramatic monologues. Poems like 'My Last Duchess' (first published under the title 'Italy'), 'Bishop Blougram's Apology', 'Andrea del Sarto' and 'Fra Lippo Lippi' have had a lasting effect on later writers, including 20th-century Spanish poets, after Robert Langbaum's analysis of Browning's poetry in his critical study *The Poetry of Experience* (1957) was taken up by Jaime Gil de Biedma (1929-90) in essays on the fictional self in poetry which had a significant influence on the work of Spain's anti-modernist 'Poetry of Experience' generation.

BK ■ The reticent, monstrously possessive, urbane, egotistical, lofty, and perhaps murderous tone of the speaker in this poem is best grasped by re-reading the piece many times, at different times. The first word of the title is 'My'; the poem's final word is 'me'. These words confirm the poem's character as a kind of circle of egotism with the speaker at the centre. The poem has an actual historical background. The Duke of Ferrara, Alfonso II d'Este, was born in the North of Italy in 1533. At the age of 25, in 1558, he married the 14-year-old daughter of the Duke of Florence. She died in April 1561 in suspicious circumstances. Shortly afterwards, her husband, the speaker in Browning's poem, set out to marry the Count of Tyrol's niece. The Count's court was in Innsbruck, Austria.

Much of what a reader gets out of a monologue depends on his or her ability to hear the speaker's tone of voice. In this matter of tone, reticence can be revelation, polished urbanity can, very effectively, suggest a conniving monster, a smooth, measured artistic delicacy may tentatively uncover an unscrupulous, self-interested man. To this person, the idea of stooping to blame anybody is scarcely thinkable. In fact, the act of 'stooping' is quite beyond him.

I choose

Never to stoop.

167

This brief phrase is a key to the speaker's tone thoughout the poem. This is a very "superior" gentleman who gave his young wife 'My gift of a nine-hundred-years-old name'. The problem is, from the speaker's point of view, that the Duchess doesn't really appreciate this:

> she ranked
> My gift of a nine-hundred-years-old name
> With anybody's gift.

The Duchess is 'trifling', indiscriminate, lacking in that capacity to make refined distinctions which might make her worthy of the Duke's company. The Duke, we know, is speaking to an emissary of the Count of Tyrol whose daughter – for her fair 'self', of course – he now pursues, though he deigns to drop the word 'dowry' also. The Duke and the court's emissary are looking at Frà Pandolf's portrait of the dead Duchess, 'Looking as if she were alive'. How did she die? In life, she smiled constantly at people, including her husband. How could he, a sensitive, acute, art-loving soul, tolerate such indiscriminate smiling?

> I gave commands;
> Then all smiles stopped together.

In the painting being considered by the two men, the Duchess 'stands / As if alive'. This *livingness* doesn't bother the Duke; the picture is 'a wonder', and who better to appreciate that wonder than his superbly conscious and sensitive self? Art is a major part of his life. In fact, as he is just about to go downstairs to meet the Count of Tyrol, in order to acquire his next Duchess, his last words have to do with another work of art.

> Notice Neptune, though,
> Taming a sea-horse, thought a rarity,
> Which Claus of Innsbruck cast in bronze for me!

One wonders if Neptune could tame sea-horses as effectively as the Duke of Ferrara can tame spirited women.

Browning's mastery of tone in this poem is subtle and complete. It is an intensely dramatic piece, as polished, in its way, as the man who speaks the lines. In 'My Last Duchess', certain facts of history are transformed into a poem of swirling emotional undercurrents and sinister, continuing resonance.

ELIZABETH BARRETT BROWNING (1806–1861)

'How do I love thee?'

How do I love thee? Let me count the ways.
   I love thee to the depth and breadth and height
   My soul can reach, when feeling out of sight
For the ends of being and ideal grace.
I love thee to the level of every day's
   Most quiet need, by sun and candle-light.
   I love thee freely, as men strive for right;
I love thee purely, as they turn from praise.
I love thee with the passion put to use
   In my old griefs, and with my childhood's faith.
I love thee with a love I seemed to lose
   With my lost saints, – I love thee with the breath,
Smiles, tears, of all my life! and, if God choose,
   I shall but love thee better after death.

1845 [*Sonnets from the Portuguese*, XLIII, 1850]

Elizabeth Barrett Browning became a popular poet in her life-
time, more highly regarded than her husband Robert Browning,
and is best-known now for her *Sonnets for the Portuguese*, and for
her long narrative poem *Aurora Leigh*, once largely forgotten but
later championed by Virginia Woolf before being taken up during
the 1970s and 80s as an early feminist text.

   Born at Coxhoe Hall in Co. Durham, the eldest of twelve chil-
dren, she lived a sheltered life, spending the rest of her childhood
from 1809 at Hope End, a mansion with a large estate outside
Ledbury in Herefordshire. Her family's wealth was largely derived
on both sides from sugar plantations in Jamaica, and their fortunes
collapsed after slavery was abolished, forcing the sale of Hope End.
Her later political writings included poetry and prose campaigning
for female emancipation and against slavery, child labour and
Austria's treatment of Italy.

She suffered from debilitating illnesses for much of her life, with intense headaches, spinal pain (possibly from a mishap while dismounting a horse) and difficulties with mobility, in addition to a probably unrelated lung disease which afflicted her from 1837. Her dependence on opiates for pain relief – laudanum and morphine – would have exacerbated her frail condition. Apart from periods living in Devon, at Sidmouth and Torquay, for her health, she was mostly confined to her bedroom in the new family house in London at 50 Wimpole Street from 1838, fiercely protected by her father.

In 1844 her two-volume *Poems* appeared and was widely acclaimed, not just in Britain but also in America where her admirers included Emily Dickinson. One of the poems included a tribute to Robert Browning, prompting him to write to her in January 1845: 'I love your verses with all my heart, dear Miss Barrett.' This initiated a correspondence and a courtship she reflected upon in a series of highly personal sonnets examining her worries (parental disapproval, her infirmity, him being younger, more gregarious) before accepting the realisation of her hopes in sonnet XLIII, 'How do I love thee'. After they married and eloped to Italy, in 1846, she was disinherited by her father. She didn't show the sonnets to Robert until three years later. Persuaded by him that they should be published, she agreed to their inclusion in a new edition of her *Poems*, in 1850, under title *Sonnets from the Portuguese*, as if they were translations.

After four miscarriages, Elizabeth gave birth to a son in 1849, at the age of 43. Her health deteriorated further during the winter of 1860-61, which they spent in Rome, and she died in her husband's arms on returning to Florence on 29 June 1861.

BK ▪ A question, 'How do I love thee?', is posed in the first line of this candid sonnet; the remaining thirteen lines express eight precise ways in which the question is answered. These involve spiritual depth, breadth and height; everyday steadfastness; freedom, purity, passion, religious intensity; and finally a resolution to love even more resolutely after death. This calm counting of ways of loving gives muscle and sinew to the poem. Seven times she says 'I love thee' and the last line has the phrase 'I shall but love thee'. Yet there is no sense of tedious repetition. There is, though, a sense of conviction, of passionate sincerity which establishes and sustains the speaker's certainty about how she loves. Her own candid counting of 'the ways' wins the reader's heart and mind.

CHARLOTTE BRONTË [?] (1816–1855)
and/or EMILY BRONTË (1818–1848)

Stanzas

Often rebuked, yet always back returning
　　To those first feelings that were born with me,
And leaving busy chase of wealth and learning
　　For idle dreams of things that cannot be:

Today, I will seek not the shadowy region;
　　Its unsustaining vastness waxes drear;
And visions rising, legion after legion,
　　Bring the unreal world too strangely near.

I'll walk, but not in old heroic traces,
　　And not in paths of high morality,
And not among the half-distinguished faces,
　　The clouded forms of long-past history.

I'll walk where my own nature would be leading:
　　It vexes me to choose another guide:
Where the grey flocks in ferny glens are feeding;
　　Where the wild wind blows on the mountain side.

What have those lonely mountains worth revealing?
　　More glory and more grief than I can tell:
The earth that wakes *one* human heart to feeling
　　Can centre both the worlds of Heaven and Hell.

[1850]

Charlotte Brontë gave up writing poetry after the success of her novel *Jane Eyre* (1847). The Brontë sisters' first publication was *Poems by Currer, Ellis, and Acton Bell* (1846), with each adopting the male pseudonyms they were to use for their novels because of prejudice against women writers: Charlotte published as Currer Bell, Emily became Ellis Bell, and Anne was Acton Bell. In the book's second edition (1850) its three separate sections of poems by Currer, Ellis and Acton Bell were followed by 'Selections from the Literary Remains of Ellis and Acton Bell' edited by Currer Bell 'out of the papers left by my sisters' in which this poem was attributed to Ellis Bell, that is Emily Brontë. It authorship has subsequently been questioned by scholars who have argued that Emily couldn't have written some of the lines, and that the poem was actually written – and not just edited – by Charlotte (who added lines and whole stanzas to other poems by Emily). It may be safer to think of it as a collaboration. But regardless of whether it is a work of single or dual authorship, it remains a fine poem, and one which carries a burden.

BK ■ In 'Stanzas', Brontë gives us an exhilarating poem of decision, resolution and belief stemming from her being 'rebuked' because of her tendency to indulge in 'idle dreams of things which cannot be'. Her language is decisive: 'I will seek not the shadowy region'; 'I'll walk, but not in old heroic traces'; 'I'll walk where my own nature would be leading'. And this resolute phrasing, reflecting a strength of will that deepens with each stanza, culminates in an uncompromising act of faith in feeling, a consequence of these 'first feelings' which, as she tells us in the opening stanza, 'were born' with her.

There is a certain loneliness in this poem which leads towards choice, decision and a vigorous individual belief in the value and power of feeling generated by the relationship between the human heart and the earth itself.

How many people actually have such a relationship today? How many contemporary poets observe and celebrate the telling natural beauty of England? And how many dare to assert the revealing *connection* between the earth and the individual heart, resulting in an awakened ability to 'centre' the worlds of good and evil? Brontë's journey from loneliness to choice to decision to connection to belief and understanding is worth close study. The reader my choose to be a fellow traveller, to witness, even share, the joy of her final statement

> The earth that wakes *one* human heart to feeling
> Can centre both the worlds of Heaven and Hell.

EMILY BRONTË (1818–1848)

Remembrance

Cold in the earth, and the deep snow piled above thee!
   Far, far, removed, cold in the dreary grave!
Have I forgot, my only Love, to love thee,
   Severed at last by time's all-wearing wave?

Now, when alone, do my thoughts no longer hover
   Over the mountains, on that northern shore;
Resting their wings where heath and fern-leaves cover
   That noble heart for ever, ever more?

Cold in the earth, and fifteen wild Decembers,
   From those brown hills, have melted into spring –
Faithful, indeed, is the spirit that remembers
   After such years of change and suffering!

Sweet love of youth, forgive, if I forget thee,
   While the world's tide is bearing me along:
Sterner desires and darker hopes beset me,
   Hopes which obscure but cannot do thee wrong.

No other sun has lightened up my heaven;
   No other star has ever shone for me:
All my life's bliss from thy dear life was given –
   All my life's bliss is in the grave with thee.

But, when the days of golden dreams had perished
   And even despair was powerless to destroy,
Then did I learn how existence could be cherished,
   Strengthened, and fed without the aid of joy;

Then did I check the tears of useless passion,
  Weaned my young soul from yearning after thine;
Sternly denied its burning wish to hasten
  Down to that tomb already more than mine!

And, even yet, I dare not let it languish,
  Dare not indulge in memory's rapturous pain;
Once drinking deep of that divinest anguish,
  How could I seek the empty world again?

7 March 1845 [1846]

Emily Brontë invented an imaginary world called Gondal, at the age of 12, with her younger sister Anne. They continued to write poems and stories set in a landscape similar to their Yorkshire moors well into adulthood, with Emily continuing the saga from the age of 12 until her death from consumption at 30 in 1848. The stories have been lost but Emily copied 45 of her Gondal poems written between 1844 and 1848 into a private notebook which has survived. Emily was furious when Charlotte found one of her notebooks in autumn 1845, but following Anne's admission that she also had been writing poems, Charlotte persuaded her sisters that they should publish a selection of their poems. Five of the Gondal poems were among those by Emily included in *Poems by Currer, Ellis, and Acton Bell* (1846), but with all references to Gondal's fictional people and places taken out.

While drawn from her character Augusta's story in her Gondal narrative, the grief evoked in Emily's 'Remembrance' is no less authentic, written by a young woman who had lost her mother and two older sisters by the age of seven. Death and mortality were ever present in the Brontë parsonage at Haworth: the graveyard where Emily herself would be buried is right in front of the house. Her poetry expresses the same world view as her only novel *Wuthering Heights* (1847). She wants to remove herself from what she calls 'the brotherhood of misery' in another poem, 'My Comforter', like her heroine Catherine Earnshaw, while the will to be herself in this life is satisfied only in the moment of death, as when Catherine feels her whole being at one with Heathcliff's. Imagined by a woman

174

not known to have had any romantic associations, the fierce, unconsumated love of Catherine and Heathcliff in *Wuthering Heights* nevertheless convinces totally.

The only poems Emily saw published in her lifetime were the 21 included in the first edition of *Poems*, in 1846, which are among the best of all two hundred eventually published. C. Day Lewis wrote that the effect of the rhythm in 'Remembrance' is 'extremely powerful, extremely appropriate' and that 'it is the slowest rhythm I know in English poetry, and the most sombre'. Only two copies of *Poems* were sold. Emily died from consumption in 1848, the year after *Wuthering Heights* was published to mixed reviews. In 1850 an edition of *Wuthering Heights* appeared under Emily's own name.

BK ■ Emily Brontë's poem, dealing with the complexities of memory, begins with the problem of forgetting. This tension between remembering and forgetting runs through 'Remembrance'. It involves self-accusation, or at least a searing sustained self-scrutiny, remorse, a plea for forgiveness, a sense of emergence from 'memory's rapturous pain' into a state of emotional and mental learning from the entire experience. There's a sense of coming to terms with that world in which the loved one is 'cold in the dreary grave'.

The world and 'the world's tide' insist that the voice of the poem-speaker utter the need to achieve a balance between remembering and forgetting. To drink too deeply of the 'divinest anguish' of remembering 'the days of golden dreams' might mean an inability to face and live in 'the empty world again'; and to forget completely would be to betray a just recognition of love and its meaning.

> No other sun has lightened up my heaven;
>   No other star has ever shone for me:
> All my life's bliss from thy dear life was given –
>   All my life's bliss is in the grave with thee.

The capacity to learn from this recognition shows an admirable, tough ability to balance remembering with forgetting, passion with pragmatism. Yet, even in this hard-won balanced state, memory might prove to be overwhelming if it were allowed to 'languish'. The tough quality of this poem derives from its gritty decision to continue living in a manner unbullied and undrowned by a flood of sad and beautiful memories. 'Remembrance' digs deeply into the complex, sensitive, necessary, cruelty of continuity.

MATTHEW ARNOLD (1822–1888)

Dover Beach

The sea is calm tonight.
The tide is full, the moon lies fair
Upon the straits; on the French coast the light
Gleams and is gone; the cliffs of England stand,
Glimmering and vast, out in the tranquil bay.
Come to the window, sweet is the night-air!
Only, from the long line of spray
Where the sea meets the moon-blanched land,
Listen! you hear the grating roar
Of pebbles which the waves draw back, and fling,
At their return, up the high strand,
Begin, and cease, and then again begin,
With tremulous cadence slow, and bring
The eternal note of sadness in.

Sophocles long ago
Heard it on the Aegean, and it brought
Into his mind the turbid ebb and flow
Of human misery; we
Find also in the sound a thought,
Hearing it by this distant northern sea.

The Sea of Faith
Was once, too, at the full, and round earth's shore
Lay like the folds of a bright girdle furled.
But now I only hear
Its melancholy, long, withdrawing roar,
Retreating, to the breath
Of the night-wind, down the vast edges drear
And naked shingles of the world.

Ah, love, let us be true
To one another! for the world, which seems
To lie before us like a land of dreams,
So various, so beautiful, so new,
Hath really neither joy, nor love, nor light,
Nor certitude, nor peace, nor help for pain;
And we are here as on a darkling plain
Swept with confused alarms of struggle and flight,
Where ignorant armies clash by night.

June 1851 [*New Poems*, 1867]

Matthew Arnold was the eldest son of Thomas Arnold, a much celebrated headmaster of Rugby School. He later taught at Rugby himself before becoming a schools inspector. An urbane, dandyish Victorian, his love of nature connects him with the Romantic tradition, while his deep appreciation of the classics helped to mould a poetic identity which drew on an inner stability and melancholy that set him apart from his contemporaries.

He believed in poetry as a regenerative force in society, as it had been in Sophoclean Greece, but became less convinced of his ability to assert this through poetry than through prose. He published his first collection in 1849, but had written most of his significant poetry by 1853. In his preface to *Poems* (1853) he expressed regret that 'the calm, the cheerfulness, the disinterested objectivity have disappeared: the dialogue of the mind with itself has commenced; the modern problems have presented themselves. [...] We hear already the doubts, we witness the discouragement, of Hamlet and of Faust.'

He was the first Oxford Professor of Poetry to give the lectures in English not Latin. In works such as *Culture and Anarchy* (1869), he extolled the virtues of poetry and the life of the mind while attacking the tastes and manners of the 'Barbarians' (the aristocracy), the 'Philistines' (the mercantile middle class) and the 'Populace'.

In a letter to his mother (5 June 1869), he summarised what he saw as his particular contribution to the English poetic tradition:

> My poems represent, on the whole, the main movement of my
> mind of the last quarter of a century [...] It might be fairly urged

that I have less poetic sentiment than Tennyson, and less intellectual rigour and abundance than Browning; yet, because I have perhaps more of a fusion of the two than either of them, and have more regularly applied that fusion to the main line of modern development, I am likely enough to have my turn, as they have had theirs.

Also in 1869 he published this five-line poem which might serve better as his poetic credo:

Below the surface-stream, shallow and light,
Of what we say we feel – below the stream,
As light, of what we think we feel – there flows
With noiseless current strong, obscure and deep,
The central stream of what we feel indeed.

BK ■ 'Dover Beach' moves from the image of a calm sea to that of a troubled land; from a 'tranquil bay' to a 'darkling plain / Swept with confused alarms of struggle and flight, / Where ignorant armies clash by night'. This movement is in four parts, from the 'sweet' tranquillity of Dover Beach to the confused, violent ignorance of clashing armies. First, the poem's speaker invites his loved one to 'Come to the window' so that they may witness this striking scene, with the gleaming, transient light of the French coast and the glimmering, vast cliffs of England in the 'fair' moonlight, together. Yet it is at this very moment of loving togetherness that the sea, in eight eloquent lines, brings 'The eternal note of sadness in'.

The second part of the poem's movement begins with Sophocles, Arnold's favourite Greek dramatist who heard in the rhythm of the Aegean sea 'the turbid ebb and flow / Of human misery'. This direct linking of the sea's rhythms with the profound rhythms of human feelings is central to 'Dover Beach'. It is a vital part of the poem's resolution to confront the 'eternal'.

The sadness deepens. The ebb and flow of human misery become more insistent. This leads into the third part of the poem's movement. The Sea of Faith, once 'full' like the tide in the poem's second line, and reassuringly wrapped like 'a bright girdle, around the world, is now 'Retreating' from the hearts and minds, the souls of men and women, leaving a scene of epic spiritual desolation, stretching

> down the vast edges drear
> And naked shingles of the world.

The fourth and final part of the poem's logical, passionate movement involves a plea, an act of bleak global analysis and a massive picture of violence, ignorance, darkness (compare Arnold's use of the word 'darkling' with that of Keats and Browning) and a hopelessly rampant confusion which brings to mind aspects of our own torn world. The plea is simple, straight.

> Ah, love, let us be true
> To one another!

The analysis involves the rejection, or the denial, of the tranquil beauty of the poem's opening as a mere 'land of dreams' which doesn't really possess the 'joy', 'love', 'light', 'certitude', 'peace' and 'help for pain' it seems to promise. Instead,

> we are here as on a darkling plain
> Swept with confused alarms of struggle and flight
> Where ignorant armies clash by night.

Arnold is sometimes the victim of critical disparagement. One can only state that he is a comprehensive critic, a superb narrative poet (few narrative poems of either the 19th or the 20th centuries can equal 'Sohrab and Rustum', but, to get the full flavour of its drama, it should be read aloud), and a moving love-poet. 'Dover Beach', for all its bleakness and sense of loss, its vision of spiritual emptiness and blind, dark, universal violence, remains one of the great love-poems in the language. It states, very simply, the one human resource capable of fighting the evil, despair and madness encountered on our 'darkling plain'.

> Ah, love, let us be true
> To one another!

Patrick Kavanagh once said that 'Consciousness is despair'. The quality of Arnold's consciousness in 'Dover Beach' is sensitive and exploratory, intensely aware of present circumstances, past realities, future possibilities. Out of that troubled consciousness he speaks, confronts, connects. His tone is unfailingly straighforward. He copes bravely with his personal heavy bear in a 37-line poem that combines lyric intensity with epic scope.

CHRISTINA ROSSETTI (1830–1894)

Remember

Remember me when I am gone away,
  Gone far away into the silent land;
  When you can no more hold me by the hand,
Nor I half turn to go yet turning stay.
Remember me when no more day by day
  You tell me of our future that you planned:
  Only remember me; you understand
It will be late to counsel then or pray.
Yet if you should forget me for a while
  And afterwards remember, do not grieve:
  For if the darkness and corruption leave
  A vestige of the thoughts that once I had,
Better by far you should forget and smile
  Than that you should remember and be sad.

1849 [1862]

Christina Rossetti was the youngest child of Italian poet and political exile, Gabriele Rossetti, who emigrated to England in 1824 and married the half-English, half-Italian Frances Polidori (sister of Byron's friend and physician John Polidori) in 1826. Her brothers were Dante Gabriel Rossetti, poet and Pre-Raphaelite artist, and art and literary critic, William Rossetti. The children were mostly educated at home in London by their mother, who had trained as a governess. When the Tractarian or Oxford Movement reached London in the 1840s, Christina adopted its Anglo-Catholic practices along with her mother and sister Maria. Her Christian faith was the primary influence on her poetry. Two of her poems became better-known as Christmas carols, 'In the Bleak Midwinter' and 'Love Came Down at Christmas'.

    Her experience as a volunteer helper at St Mary Magdalene Penitentiary in Highgate, a charitable institution for the reclamation of "fallen" women, fed into the writing of her long narrative poem *Goblin Market*, with its theme of salvation through a "sister". Regarded by many as her masterpiece, this became the title-poem of her first commerically published collection, *Goblin Market and Other Poems* (1862), which also included 'Remember' and established her literary reputation. Were it not for its length we would have included *Goblin Market* in this anthology.

The morbidity of much of Christina Rossetti's poetry may be attributable in part to the bouts of serious illness she endured at various times in her life along with the prospect of early death most present in the early 1870s when she was afflicted by Graves' disease, a rare thyroid condition, losing her hair and suffering physical changes to her face and voice. She died from cancer in 1894, two years after undergoing a mastectomy in her own home.

As with Elizabeth Barrett Browning's *Aurora Leigh*, a revaluation of her work by feminist critics, in the 1980s, focussed in particular on *Goblin Market*, brought her work back into prominence, and she is now regarded as one of the major poets of the Victorian period.

BK ■ Three times in the first seven lines of this sonnet, the speaker pleads 'Remember me'. The last six lines bring a change of tone and thinking. If the person to whom the poem is addressed should forget the speaker 'for a while / And afterwards remember', then, the speaker says, 'do not grieve'. The speaker wishes to spare the loved one any further experience of grief, and if this involves forgetting, well,

> Better by far you should forget and smile
> Than that you should remember and be sad.

This concern for the other is born of the possibility that the 'darkness and corruption' may 'leave / A vestige of the thoughts that once' the speaker had. That possible 'vestige' is the source of the generosity and understanding in the final two lines. The poem moves eloquently from an emotional plea, an exhortation, to a stance of magnanimous concern for the other, actually saying that if forgetting brings a smile and remembering brings only sadness, then it is better to forget.

It is revealing, in several aspects, to compare the poem with Emily Brontë's 'Remembrance' [173].

DANTE GABRIEL ROSSETTI (1828–1882)

Sudden Light

I have been here before,
But when or how I cannot tell:
I know the grass beyond the door,
The sweet keen smell,
The sighing sound, the lights around the shore.

You have been mine before, –
How long ago I may not know:
But just when at that swallow's soar
Your neck turned so,
Some veil did fall, – I knew it all of yore.

Has this been thus before?
And shall not thus time's eddying flight
Still with our lives our love restore
In death's despite,
And day and night yield one delight once more?

1853-54 [*Poems: An Offering to Lancashire*, 1863]

Dante Gabriel Rossetti, born Gabriel Charles Dante Rossetti, the elder brother of Christina Rossetti [180], helped to found the Pre-Raphaelite Brotherhood of artists who wanted to achieve the purity of pre-Renaissance art in their work. Through attention to minute detail and from painting outdoors, they sought 'truth to nature'; that in turn led to identification with an idealised, legendary past. Rossetti extended those aspirations by bringing poetry, painting and social idealism together, and then by seeking to reform the applied arts of design, assisted in a new association with two younger artists, Edward Burne-Jones and William Morris. Rossetti's particular contribution to the Brotherhood was through the realisation expressed in his work of the importance of subjective experience, and of perception that is not only visual but psychic.

In 1860 he married their model, Lizzie Siddal, who suffered from constant ill health. When she died two years later from an overdose of laudanum, he buried the only complete manuscript of his poetry with her in Highgate Cemetery. For the next 20 years he shared a house in Chelsea with a menagerie of exotic animals, including two wombats, as well as sharing William Morris's wife Jane at Kelmscott Manor in Oxfordshire when Morris was travelling abroad. In 1869 he had Lizzie Siddal's coffin disinterred to retrieve his poems, which were published with new work in *Poems* (1870).

Unlike his obsessively realistic paintings, his poetry is concerned rather with intensity of emotion, with any detail serving to evoke a mood, as in the timeless moment and sense of *déjà vu* captured in 'Sudden Light'.

BK ■ Many of the poems in this anthology deal with darkness. Rossetti's poem is concerned with light, sudden light, an unexpected bolt of apprehension and insight. The first line is certain and confident ('I have been here before'), the second line uncertain ('But when or how I cannot tell'). This tension between certainty and uncertainty, between knowledge and perplexity, is central to the poem's character and growth. This moment is a repetition of a moment already experienced 'of yore'; the present is the past.

The poem is set in a mind that is both enlightened and perplexed; and the enlightenment is inseparable from the perplexity. This is particularly true of the moment between the lovers in the second stanza. Time is literally unveiled in the present and knowledge of this same moment in the past is confirmed.

> Some veil did fall, – I knew it all of yore.

The final stanza is two questions; the second question, occupying the final four lines, learning from the present and the past, leaps into the future and asks time itself if the future will 'restore' love, in spite of death, and if love's 'delight' will be known 'once more'. 'Sudden Light' handles the mystery of time, its strange relationship with the human heart and mind, with our capacity for recognition, knowledge and ignorance in a way that is itself marked by a beautifully light touch. In his treatment of the mind-time problem, Rossetti anticipates the work of Joyce and Proust. But Rossetti does it with a lighter touch than either of these later, famous giants.

WALT WHITMAN (1819–1892)

Native Moments

Native moments! when you come upon me – Ah you are here now!
Give me now libidinous joys only!
Give me the drench of my passions! Give me life coarse and rank!
Today, I go consort with Nature's darlings – tonight too;
I am for those who believe in loose delights – I share the midnight
  orgies of young men;
I dance with the dancers and drink with the drinkers;
The echoes ring with our indecent calls;
I take for my love some prostitute – I pick out some low person for
  my dearest friend,
He shall be lawless, rude, illiterate – he shall be one condemned by
  others for deeds done;
I will play a part no longer – Why should I exile myself from my
  companions?
O you shunned persons! I at least do not shun you,
I come forthwith in your midst – I will be your poet,
I will be more to you than to any of the rest.

[1860]

Walt Whitman is America's most celebrated public poet, with 'the United States themselves' declared as the subject of his landmark work, *Leaves of Grass* (1855). This had a profound influence on the course of American poetry, celebrating democracy, nature, friendship, love and the body with exuberance in free-ranging, chanting and praising free verse whose cadences echoed the language of the King James Bible. As the book was revised and grew through several subsequent editions from a collection of a dozen poems to a national epic, it divided public and critical opinion, praised by writers such as Emerson and Thoreau but attacked as obscene and profane by those offended by its frank portrayal of sex.

  After leaving school at 11, Whitman found work as an office boy, and then as an apprentice printer, which led to him becoming a journalist for much of his working life. He was sacked from a job as clerk in the Department of the Interior after publishing *Leaves of Grass*, which sold very few copies in the early years. 'Native Moments' was added to the 1860 third edition, and was one of several poems (including 'I Sing the Body Electric') he was asked to remove as obscene by a later publisher in 1882, forcing him to take the book elsewhere. This controversy and the banning of *Leaves of Grass* in Boston turned it into a bestseller.

BK ■ The democracy of poetry lies in its ability, its duty, to present and to represent all facets of life. The outcast and the scapegoat, the shunned and the condemned have as much a right to be voiced in poetry as the lover, the hero, the saint or the 'ordinary' man or woman. In 'Native Moments' Whitman gives us a poem calling for 'libidinous joys', 'life coarse and rank', 'loose delights', 'the midnight orgies of young men', people who are 'lawless, rude, illiterate' and 'condemned', all those 'shunned persons' who are in fact his true 'companions'. Whitman declares himself the voice of these people.

> O you shunned persons! I at least do not shun you,
> I come forthwith in your midst – I will be your poet,
> I will be more to you than to any of the rest.

The old war between poetry and entrenched moralities surfaces here. Good poems can be very insulting to good people. It is within poetry's power to create new moralities: the aboriginal epic innocence of the imagination is not intimidated by established ways of thinking, believing and behaving. This aspect of poetry is often consciously or unconsciously played down. Whitman waves it, the banner of his intention, status, resolution, his calling and function as a poet.

The word 'native' involves what is natural, congenital, innate, home-grown, tribal, deep in the blood as opposed to what is learned or acquired. 'Native Moments' is a map of some of Whitman's most cherished emotional territory. As a poet, he is his own man, embarrassing to some, an inspiration to others, but always an independent, eloquent voice celebrating the value of the exploring mind and the open heart.

EMILY DICKINSON (1830–1886)

'Because I could not stop for Death'

Because I could not stop for Death –
He kindly stopped for me –
The Carriage held but just Ourselves –
And Immortality.

We slowly drove – He knew no haste
And I had put away
My labor and my leisure too,
For His Civility –

We passed the School, where Children strove
At Recess – in the Ring –
We passed the Fields of Gazing Grain –
We passed the Setting Sun –

Or rather – He passed Us –
The Dews drew quivering and Chill –
For only Gossamer, my Gown –
My Tippet – only Tulle –

We paused before a House that seemed
A Swelling of the Ground –
The Roof was scarcely visible –
The Cornice – in the Ground –

Since then – 'tis Centuries – and yet
Feels shorter than the Day
I first surmised the Horses' Heads
Were toward Eternity –

c. 1863 [1890]

■ **Emily Dickinson** was born in Amherst, Massachusetts in 1830. Now considered a lyric genius, she wrote poetry from her teenage years but led an outwardly unexceptional life. Educated at Amherst Academy and South Hadley (Mount Holyoke) Female Seminary, she never married. Her older brother, Austin, married Emily's close friend, Susan Gilbert. Their father was a lawyer and, having no economic need to publish her work, she stayed mostly at home in Amherst throughout her life, living in relative seclusion with her younger sister, Lavinia, after their mother's death in 1882.

She wrote approximately 1,789 extraordinary poems, some of which were sent to family and friends. She also copied them into her own little booklets or 'fascicle bundles'. Some were first written on advertising fliers, wrapping paper, or old letters. Several were sent, from 1862 onwards, to the author Thomas Wentworth Higginson in response to his article in the *Atlantic Monthly* giving practical advice to those seeking publication, but though their correspondence continued, he did not encourage her to publish. However, he and another editor, Mabel Loomis Todd (mistress of Emily's brother Austin) assisted Lavinia when she began the process of publishing Emily's poetry posthumously. Their 1890 selection did not accurately reproduce Emily's poems as Higginson's editing involved substitutions of words and punctuation as well as alterations to line breaks and metre. Even so, her work was well received and further editions followed. Before her death, several poems had been published, anonymously, in newspapers and elsewhere: these were submitted by friends, not Emily herself. Emily wrote her last poems in April 1886. Mabel Loomis Todd published Emily's letters in 1894. The first reliable edition of her *Complete Poems* was edited by Thomas H. Johnson in 1955. The *Complete Letters* appeared in 1958. The text here is from the authoritative edition, *The Poems of Emily Dickinson: reading edition*, ed. R.W. Franklin (The Belknap Press of Harvard University Press, 1999). R.W. Franklin also edited an excellent variorum edition of the complete poems.

[Robyn Bolam, *Eliza's Babes: Four Centuries of Women's Poetry in English*, Bloodaxe Books, 2005]

Brendan especially wanted us to include this Dickinson poem in particular, but hadn't got as far as writing about it when our *Bear* went into hibernation.

ALICE MEYNELL (1847-1922)

Renouncement

I must not think of thee; and, tired yet strong,
    I shun the thought that lurks in all delight –
    The thought of thee – and in the blue Heaven's height,
And in the sweetest passage of a song.

Oh, just beyond the fairest thoughts that throng
    This breast, the thought of thee waits, hidden yet bright;
    Yet it must never, never come in sight;
I must stop short of thee the whole day long.

But when sleep comes to close each difficult day,
    When night gives pause to the long watch I keep,
    And all my bonds I needs must loose apart,

Must doff my will as raiment laid away, –
    With the first dream that comes with the first sleep
    I run, I run, I am gathered to thy heart.

[*Preludes*, 1875]

Alice Meynell was born Alice Thompson in Barnes in 1842. The family led a peripatetic bohemian life around Europe in her early years, mainly in Italy, with Alice and her sister Elizabeth, a painter, being educated by their father Thomas Thompson, son of an unmarried Creole. She began writing poetry in her teens, inspired by the work of Elizabeth Barrett Browning and Christina Rossetti.

    The family settled in London in 1864, where Alice followed her mother Christiana Weller, a concert pianist, in converting to Catholicism, but fell in love with her priest, a young Jesuit, Father Augustus Dignam, who shared her feelings and was sent abroad. Her early poems reflect her sorrow over that relationship, including

'Renouncement', published in her debut collection *Preludes* (1875) under the name of A.C. Thompson. Illustrated by her sister Elizabeth (who later become a celebrated war artist), the book received little public attention but was later praised by Tennyson, Christina Rossetti, George Eliot and Ruskin. Walter de la Mare called her one of the few poets 'who actually think in verse'.

In 1877 she married the journalist Wilfrid Meynell, also a Catholic convert, and they had eight children, one of whom died in infancy. The Meynells edited several literary journals, contributing to a Catholic literary revival, and Alice became a prolific essayist, being made President of the Society of Women Journalists in 1897. As an activist, she embraced many causes, including non-militant suffragism, workers' rights for women and pacifism, working also to improve slum conditions and against cruelty to animals. She was twice considered for the post of Poet Laureate, following the deaths of Tennyson in 1892 and his successor, Alfred Austin, in 1913, the only other woman to have been considered before then being Elizabeth Barrett Browning, a candidate after the death of Wordsworth.

BK ■ [from a letter by BK, 1996] A very moving and beautiful poem. A jewel of I/thee. This is a thrilling poem, perfectly artificed, wholly human. One of the best. It's very dramatic, the drama leading up to the moment of 'doffing the will'; out of which the drama of the last two lines leaps and runs.

GERARD MANLEY HOPKINS (1844–1899)

The Windhover
To Christ our Lord

I caught this morning morning's minion, king-
    dom of daylight's dauphin, dapple-dawn-drawn Falcon, in his riding
    Of the rolling level underneath him steady air, and striding
High there, how he rung upon the rein of a wimpling wing
In his ecstasy! then off, off forth on swing,
    As a skate's heel sweeps smooth on a bow-bend: the hurl and gliding
    Rebuffed the big wind. My heart in hiding
Stirred for a bird, – the achieve of, the mastery of the thing!

Brute beauty and valour and act, oh, air, pride, plume, here
    Buckle! AND the fire that breaks from thee then, a billion
Times told lovelier, more dangerous, O my chevalier!

No wonder of it: shéer plód makes plough down sillion
Shine, and blue-bleak embers, ah my dear,
    Fall, gall themselves, and gash gold-vermilion.

May 1877 [*Poems*, 1918]

Gerard Manley Hopkins was one of the most original English poets of any time, but after the rejection of his major long poem 'The Wreck of the Deutschland' – on the death of five nuns in a shipwreck in 1875 – he made no further attempts to publish his poetry. Victorian readers found it strange, although he did receive some support from friends and fellow poets who read his poems in manuscript, including Robert Bridges and Coventry Patmore. It was Bridges who – as Poet Laureate in 1918 – was to publish the first collected edition of Hopkins' poetry, but a second edition didn't appear until 1930. His work then became highly influential for later poets – from T.S. Eliot and Dylan Thomas to Auden and Ted Hughes – as if Modernism had to have happened for Hopkins' poetry to be accepted and fully appreciated. Hopkins died unread in 1899, the year after Emily Dickinson, his genius and hers unknown to poets and readers of their own time. The poem we agreed upon immediately as our choice for Hopkins was his masterpiece 'The Windhover', but Brendan didn't get as far as writing his commentary. However, he did discuss the poem in a schools television lecture in 1975, 'Gerard Manley Hopkins: The Quest for Essence', which I've transcribed here. This offers such a brilliant and highly original analysis not just of 'The Windhover' but of several other key poems that I wanted to include it in full. This is its first publication in print.[15]

BK ■ Gerard Manley Hopkins was born in Essex, England, in July 1844 into a high church Anglican family which had already achieved a certain cultural distinction. His father had published a book of poems in 1843. Two of his brothers were professional artists, and Gerard himself soon proved his skill at drawing as well as showing his command of language. He won the poetry prize at Highgate School in 1860 and in 1863 he won an exhibition to Balliol College, Oxford, where he read Classics.

In October 1866 Hopkins was received into the Roman Catholic Church by Dr – later Cardinal – Newman. Two years later Hopkins entered the Society of Jesus to begin his training for the priesthood. After his ordination in 1877 he worked in various cities: in London, Liverpool, Glasgow, Chesterfield, Stonyhurst [Stonyhurst College, Clitheroe, Lancashire]. In 1884 he was appointed Professor of Greek at University College, Dublin. He died on the 8th of June 1889. He is buried in Glasnevin.

Many influences contribute to the shaping of Hopkins' genius. Spenser, Milton, Shakespeare and Keats were important formative influences. Important also are the spiritual exercises of St Ignatius, which Hopkins studied, contemplated and practised for over 20 years. Another significant influence on Hopkins was the work of Duns Scotus, a great medieval thinker who had been an Oxford professor. For Hopkins, Duns Scotus was 'of reality the rarest veinèd unraveller'. Scotus was able to isolate and pinpoint the most delicate strands in the most complex intellectual pattern. He believed that each individual has a distinctive form. Each person is unique, inimitable. When we consider that for Hopkins poetry itself is a quest for uniqueness, we see why Scotus with his belief that individuality is the final perfection of any creature appeals so much to Hopkins' imagination.

Scotus's thought helped to confirm the direction of Hopkins' own thinking. If there is one word which gives us the key to that thinking it is the word 'inscape', coined by Hopkins himself. What precisely does 'inscape' mean and how does it affect his poetry? Behind every good poet there lies a certain philosophy. It may not be a totally coherent body of thought, it may not even be logically organised, yet that thought is sufficiently deep and dynamic to inspire some of his best work. I am thinking, for example, of Keats's letters, where in the process of writing to his family and friends he works out his famous doctrine of 'negative capability'. I'm thinking of Eliot's essays on different writers in which often indirectly he gives us the ideas that lie behind the creation of *The Waste Land*.

For Hopkins' philosophy of inscape we have to turn to his letters, notebooks and journals. For example he writes: 'But as air, melody, is what strikes me most of all in music and design in painting, so design, pattern or what I am in the habit of calling "inscape" is what I above all aim at in poetry. Now it is the virtue of design, pattern or inscape to be distinctive, and it is the vice of distinctiveness to become queer.'

It is the virtue of inscape to be distinctive. This is the idea we must grasp if we are to begin to appreciate Hopkins. He wished to define and to communicate his sense of the distinctiveness of his own self, his sense of the distinctiveness of the world in which he lived. It is this sense of distinctiveness which led him to respect the integrity of language, to seek out a personal idiom and to create new, difficult rhythms.

First of all, let's look at his sense of the distinctiveness of his own self. In his comments of the spiritual exercises of St Ignatius Loyola, Hopkins writes:

> I find myself both as man and as myself something most deter-
> mined and distinctive, at pitch, more distinctive and higher
> pitched than anything else I see; I find myself with my pleasures
> and pains, my powers and my experiences, my deserts and guilt,
> my shame and sense of beauty, my dangers, hopes, fears, and all
> my fate, more important to myself than anything else I see. And
> when I ask where does this throng and stack of being, so rich, so
> distinctive, so important, come from/ nothing I see can answer me.
> And this whether I speak of human nature or of my individuality,
> my selfbeing. [...] (as when I was a child I used to ask myself:
> What must it be to be someone else?). Nothing else in nature

comes near this unspeakable stress of pitch, distinctiveness, and selving, this selfbeing of my own.

Now at times that quotation reads like a statement of a man who is almost narcissistically self-absorbed, but if you look closely you will see that Hopkins accepting the distinctiveness of himself is more convinced (a) of the value of other men, and (b) of the existence of God. The inscape of the human individual is a clue to the glory of God. The same is true of objects outside the individual. For example, Hopkins says, looking at a bluebell: 'I do not think I have ever seen anything more beautiful than the bluebell I've been looking at. I know the beauty of Our Lord by it.'

All through Hopkins' letters and journals we find him involved in an act of scrupulous, tireless definition, with the aim of showing the distinctiveness of what he is writing about. His quest is for essence. His manner of doing justice to things is his style of paying absolutely sincere attention, his desire to give full articulate recognition to what confronts his eyes. Further, such recognitions are seen as hints or rumours of the existence of God. God whispers in a poem because a man has paid attention to a bluebell. At his most vigorous Hopkins proclaims this as a universal fact. Even the muck and squalor of 19th-century industrial England could not conceal the divine freshness underlying everything. Now the poem 'God's Grandeur', for example, shows Hopkins at his most buoyant, believing and irrepressible. It is perhaps less subtle as a poem than several of his other poems, but it has a fine, vital enthusiasm, a tone that is infectious and positive.

> The world is charged with the grandeur of God.
>   It will flame out, like shining from shook foil;
>   It gathers to a greatness, like the ooze of oil
> Crushed. Why do men then now not reck his rod?
> Generations have trod, have trod, have trod;
>   And all is seared with trade; bleared, smeared with toil;
>   And wears man's smudge and shares man's smell: the soil
> Is bare now, nor can foot feel, being shod.
>
> And for all this, nature is never spent;
>   There lives the dearest freshness deep down things;
> And though the last lights off the black West went
>   Oh, morning, at the brown brink eastward, springs –
> Because the Holy Ghost over the bent
>   World broods with warm breast and with ah! bright wings.

A striking aspect of Hopkins' genius is his power of concentration. A perfect example of this is 'The Windhover', a poem which Hopkins addresses to 'Christ Our Lord'. The windhover is one of the falcon family, a bird with a hooked, blueish horn bill, distinguished by its rapid, direct flight. It also soars, it frequently and habitually hovers, with tail fanned out, and wings flapping vigorously, followed by a pounce. It is almost a universal bird and can be found from the centre of London to the wildest and remotest mountains and coastal areas. It is a not uncommon suburban bird. Now this is the hovering creature that Hopkins celebrates in his poem. You will be familiar with the noble, chivalric idiom of the opening section of the poem in which Hopkins captures the delicate poise and movements of the bird. The best way to grasp this poem, I think, is to try to see it in your imagination, and then analyse it with your critical intelligence, but if you do not see imaginatively you cannot analyse incisively. You will see that this poem begins in the sky and ends in the earth. What Hopkins establishes is the connection between the two. Just as man in all his limitations may deepen Christ's significance and be in turn deepened by that. Embers in the moment of breaking apart shine in their breaking, they 'gash gold-vermilion'. The windhover, too, will one day break into dust, but that bleak destiny only adds to the fact that the bird's mastery has suggested a mastery that is 'a billion / Times lovelier, more dangerous'.

I'm very much aware that I've simplified this great poem. For example, the word 'buckle' is capable of several interpretations, but I'm trying to stick to the view which I think is most central to Hopkins, and that is that the most beautiful things of this world are poor by comparison with the perfect beauty that is only available in hints and fragments, in brief gleams lighting the individual dark. Creation, beautiful in itself, is still a poor clue left behind by the Holy Ghost, but it is a clue, and that's the important point.

Here is the poem, 'The Windhover'. [BK reads the poem...]

Now in that poem 'God's Grandeur' you remember Hopkins asserted the essential freshness of nature. In 'The Windhover' he celebrated a bird's beauty. In the poem 'Felix Randal' he pays tribute to a man, a blacksmith. When Felix Randal was seriously ill Hopkins had given him holy communion. The poem opens at that point where Hopkins has just heard of Randal's death. Randal was a farrier, one who shoes horses, a shoeing smith, hence one who treats the ailments of horses. During his lifetime Felix Randal had helped horses; now Hopkins remembers how he, as priest, helped Randal. Hearing of Randal's death he thinks of the man. He thinks of his strength, his bony handsomeness; then he thinks of Randal in his sickness, cursing with impatience at the very thought of being sick. Then comes the typical Hopkins meditation, this time a meditation on sickness, its nature, what it does. When Hopkins saw sick people he felt them nearer to him. They became endeared to him and he in turn was himself endeared: 'This seeing the sick endears them to us, us, too, it endears.'

This aspect of Hopkins is not, I think, sufficiently stressed. He was a man of deep and genuine humanity for whom all experience was a sort of spiritual connection with other people. For example, he comforted the sick man Felix Randal, he reached out to Randal, and, in turn, he was reached, touched, deepened by the dying man. His own being is therefore consoled by one whom he consoles. We are witnessing, not a solitary, isolated act of help but a mutual act of assistance. Because it is mutual and not solitary, Hopkins at the end of the poem is free to imagine Felix Randal at his most glorious moment, when he fettled 'for the great grey drayhorse his bright and battering sandal!'

Now this, if you like, is the inscape of Felix Randal, not a dying man at all but a powerful, vibrant living man, a creator of beauty, a glad giver of help. Notice how this poem opens with news of Randal's death, then how it swerves back to his sickness and the spiritual help Hopkins gave him in that sickness. Then there is the brief trenchant meditation on sickness, and finally we get one of the most powerful and exultant images in all of Hopkins' poetry. Felix Randal, 'powerful amidst peers', doing the job that he was very good at. This poem is a beautiful and moving elegy for a working man, yet, though it speaks of sickness and death, the overwhelming impression it leaves is not one of sadness but of joy because its climax is an image of living and masterly creativity.

This is the poem, 'Felix Randal':

Felix Randal the farrier, O is he dead then? my duty all ended,
Who have watched his mould of man, big-boned and hardy-handsome
Pining, pining, till time when reason rambled in it, and some
Fatal four disorders, fleshed there, all contended?

Sickness broke him. Impatient, he cursed at first, but mended
Being anointed and all; though a heavenlier heart began some
Months earlier, since I had our sweet reprieve and ransom
Tendered to him. Ah well, God rest him all road ever he offended!

This seeing the sick endears them to us, us too it endears.
My tongue had taught thee comfort, touch had quenched thy tears,
Thy tears that touched my heart, child, Felix, poor Felix Randal;

How far from then forethought of, all thy more boisterous years,
When thou at the random grim forge, powerful amidst peers,
Didst fettle for the great grey drayhorse his bright and battering sandal!

I think you will agree that a feeling of joyous creation vibrates
through these last lines, yet some of Hopkins's greatest poetry
deals not with joy but with its opposite – or indeed, something at
least very like its opposite – especially during his years in Dublin,
Hopkins suffered the most terrible agonies of spiritual desolation.

I've said from the beginning that Hopkins's primary concern is
with the essence of things. Nothing will do for him but the core,
the heartbeat, the central reality. Whatever Hopkins is writing
about he cuts through to the very centre of it. That's why he's at
once so impassioned and detailed, capable always of what seems
like merciless documentation and chill, clinical precision. This
kind of precision shows the imagination at its most moral and
most courageous. Therefore when Hopkins feels loneliness and
desolation in his heart, when he is severed from all vitality and
energy and happiness, he will write of his loneliness with the same
remorseless power that he once wrote of his joy. Now very few
poets have expressed their sense of desolation as powerfully as
Hopkins. I've spoken of his courage. That, more than anything, is
what it took to write these 'terrible sonnets'. He knew himself. He
had the courage to express himself. Now let me return for a moment
to his comments on the spiritual exercises of St Ignatius Loyola:

> I find myself with my pleasures and pains, my powers and my
> experiences, my deserts and guilt, my shame and sense of beauty,
> my dangers, hopes, fears, and all my fate, more important to
> myself than anything else I see.

The opposite side of that coin of conviction can be seen in the
poem entitled 'I wake and feel the fell of dark'. In that poem
Hopkins says 'I am gall, I am heartburn. God's most deep decree /

Bitter would have me taste: my taste was me'. Here for Hopkins is now the sour taste of mere self, the severed self. This poem explores the hell of the severed self. It seems as if there can be nothing more hideous than this, yet, at the end of the poem, Hopkins suggests an even darker and more terrible world. The poem begins in deep, frightening darkness and ends in a darkness that is even deeper and more frightening. That other, more frightening, world – for Hopkins – is presented in the last words of the poem, the last two words of the poem in fact, almost like a grotesque after-thought:

> I wake and feel the fell of dark, not day.
> What hours, O what black hours we have spent
> This night! what sights you, heart, saw; ways you went!
> And more must, in yet longer light's delay.
>   With witness I speak this. But where I say
> Hours I mean years, mean life. And my lament
> Is cries countless, cries like dead letters sent
> To dearest him that lives alas! away.
>
>   I am gall, I am heartburn. God's most deep decree
> Bitter would have me taste: my taste was me;
> Bones built in me, flesh filled, blood brimmed the curse.
>   Selfyeast of spirit a dull dough sours. I see
> The lost are like this, and their scourge to be
> As I am mine, their sweating selves; but worse.

It is significant that Hopkins characterises the condition of the damned by saying that their damnation consists of the fact that they are 'their sweating selves'. So, the reality of hell resides in the self. In those days, when he felt himself abandoned by God, when he felt lost and sick and severed, Hopkins, in a state of pained bewilderment, wondered why he – who had given what he believed was his entire life to God's work – why he should be so arid, so spiritually barren, while others – who seemed wicked in Hopkins' eyes – prospered easily. It's in this mood of pained perplexity that he wrote the poem entitled 'Thou art indeed just, Lord'. As an epigraph to that poem, Hopkins quotes the following lines from the prophet Jeremiah: 'Righteous art thou, O Lord, when I plead with thee: yet let me talk with thee of thy judgements: Wherefore doth the way of the wicked prosper?' In a series of pained questions Hopkins asks his God why is it that he meets only disappointment while sinners thrive. Looking at nature he witnesses its rich flourishing even as he endures his own inner shrivelling. It seems his creative genius has forsaken him and he has become a famished eunuch. The poem concludes with a prayer for renewal:

> Thou art indeed just, Lord, if I contend
> With thee; but, sir, so what I plead is just.
> Why do sinners' ways prosper? and why must
> Disappointment all I endeavour end?
>   Wert thou my enemy, O thou my friend,
> How wouldst thou worse, I wonder, than thou dost
> Defeat, thwart me? Oh, the sots and thralls of lust
> Do in spare hours more thrive than I that spend,
> Sir, life upon thy cause. See, banks and brakes
> Now, leavèd how thick! lacèd they are again
> With fretty chervil, look, and fresh wind shakes
> Them; birds build – but not I build; no, but strain,
> Time's eunuch, and not breed one work that wakes.
> Mine, O thou lord of life, send my roots rain.

Despite his poems of spiritual desolation, the overwhelming impression one is left with after reading through all of Hopkins's poetry is an impression of tremendous emotional and imaginative energy, and energy, as Blake tells us, is 'eternal delight'.

A poem written in the last year of Hopkins's life entitled 'That Nature is a Heraclitean Fire and of the comfort of the Resurrection' is full of precisely this delightful energy. 'Nature is a Heraclitean Fire': now according to Heraclitus, all things are in a state of flux, of change, being 'differentiations produced by strife of a single mobile principle, the principle of fire'. All creation is part of this Heraclitean flux, all things go from fire to earth, earth to fire, dust to flesh, flesh to dust, and so on. It's as though everything were becoming everything else, as though death were part of life, life part of death. Reality itself is grinding, remorseless, inexhaustible, ever self-transforming. An individual life in the context of history is only the blink of an eye, and all the time Nature goes its own tireless way: 'Million-fuelèd, | nature's bonfire burns on.' Nature's fire is unquenchable, but man's fire soon turns to ashes: 'Manshape, that shone / Sheer off, disseveral, a star, | death blots black out; nor mark / [...] But vastness blurs and time | beats level.'

From the other poems I've read you, you can can appreciate how profound is Hopkins' sense of the littleness and the insignificance of the individual human life. Yet we must also remember that, for Hopkins, because of his belief, man's soul is immortal, he is capable of achieving eternal glory and joy. The end of this poem is an affirmation of that belief. Here, too, Hopkins achieves what I take to be the whole goal of his life. For a moment he sees – he witnesses – the inscape of Christ. Notice again here the mutuality of the situation: nothing is lonely, he is what Christ is, Christ is what he is. Here, in Hopkins's own terms as a poet, the self is redeemed.

In an earlier poem he had said: 'I am gall, I am heartburn.' But now he says 'I am all at once what Christ is.' This achieved identification with the object of all his love is what makes tolerable – even enobling – the thought that Nature is a Heraclitean fire, a cosmic appetite, a vast generating lust, a consuming ravening force. The individual has meaning. For Hopkins, that meaning is in Christ.

> Flesh fade, and mortal trash
> Fall to the residuary worm; | world's wildfire, leave but ash:
> In a flash, at a trumpet crash,
> I am all at once what Christ is, | since he was what I am, and
> This Jack, joke, poor potsherd, | patch, matchwood, immortal diamond,
> Is immortal diamond.

That is a poem of assertion based on belief. One may accept or reject the belief but one must be impressed by the strength and impression of the assertion.

There are many reasons why Hopkins is an important modern poet. He gave the English language an injection of life when it badly needed it and it lay half stupefied in a dull Victorian slumber. He created new beautiful rhythms. He revolutionised metrics. He emphasised the poetic values of concentration and implication. He saw that poetry is a matter of both sound and sense. His poems do enchant the ear as well as stimulate the mind. His meaning is in his music. His music is in his meaning.

If I had to choose one word to describe Hopkins I would choose the word heroic. He was heroic in his life and in his art. His poems show us that he had the courage to venture into the abyss of himself, to confront and to express the full range and depth of his own personality. He knew the meaning of both ecstasy and despair. Between these two emotional poles, his poems move in their brilliance, consoling us, disturbing us, renewing us always.

GEORGE MEREDITH (1828–1909)

Lucifer in Starlight

On a starred night Prince Lucifer uprose.
Tired of his dark dominion swung the fiend
Above the rolling ball in cloud part screened,
Where sinners hugged their spectre of repose.
Poor prey to his hot fit of pride were those.
And now upon his western wing he leaned,
    Now his huge bulk o'er Afric's sands careened,
Now the black planet shadowed Arctic snows.
Soaring through wider zones that pricked his scars
    With memory of the old revolt from awe,
He reached a middle height, and at the stars,
        Which are the brain of heaven, he looked, and sank.
        Around the ancient track marched, rank on rank,
    The army of unalterable law.

[*Poems and Lyrics of the Joy of Earth*, 1883]

George Meredith was a Victorian novelist and poet whose life was as much a tale of mixed fortunes as the stories he told in his fiction and poetry. Born above the family tailoring shop in Portsmouth, he was five when his mother died; and he was eleven when his father went bankrupt after mismanaging the business for many years. Inheritances from his mother and an aunt funded his education at schools where he was able to pass himself off as a gentleman's son.

For some years he tried unsuccessfully to make a living as a journalist. A disastrous marriage to Mary Ellen Nicolls, the widowed daughter of the eccentric writer Thomas Love Peacock, ended when she ran off with the Pre-Raphaelite artist Henry Wallis, inspiring *Modern Love* (1862), his collection of fifty 16-line sonnets about the failure of a marriage. What became known as the Meredithian sonnet cycle provided a formal model for later writers, including Tony Harrison in his *School of Eloquence* sequence (also influenced by Milton's sonnets). With its resounding lines and striking images, 'Lucifer in Starlight' is representative of his later, more prophetic poetry. Meredith developed a philosophy of 'Earth' in which man merges with the life force, discovering love and eternal significance when liberated from egotism. This drove the writing of his fiction, particularly in novels such as *The Ordeal of Richard Feveral* (1859), *The Egoist* (1879) and *Diana of Crossways* (1885), comedies of manners and morals with a social edge. He was more inventive and influential as a novelist than as a poet, especially in his later fiction, experimenting with shifting points of view and unreliable narrators. He has been called one of the earliest English psychological novelists, a precursor of later writers of English modernist novels.

BK ■ In this concentrated, narrative sonnet, evil incarnate seeks the stellar spotlight, finds it, looks at it and sinks back into hell. Satan, 'Tired of his dark dominion', moves his 'huge bulk' over the earth, over 'Afric's sands', 'Arctic snows' and even 'wider zones' which remind him of the 'scars' he picked up during his revolt against God when he and his legions were crushed and condemned to hell. There is a sense here of Satan trying again to glimpse his original state of light. He does, in fact, manage to look briefly at the stars 'which are the brains of heaven'. After one brief glimpse of light, of heaven's intelligence, Satan sinks into that darkness we find so chillingly portrayed by Milton [86] and also, to some extent, by Byron in his poem 'Darkness' [140]. 'Lucifer in Starlight' ends with an image of that 'unalterable law' which Satan unsuccessfully tried to destroy.

> Around the ancient track marched, rank on rank,
> The army of unalterable law.

Like many poets represented here, Meredith deals with the conflict between darkness and light. It is a fundamental and continuing theme for poets; and it involves, despite (or is it because of?) its fundamental nature, the necessity to confront the eternal problem of good and evil in all its complexity. 'Lucifer in Starlight' is a dramatic glimpse into that complexity.

EDWIN ARLINGTON ROBINSON (1869–1935)

Luke Havergal

Go to the western gate, Luke Havergal,
There where the vines cling crimson on the wall,
And in the twilight wait for what will come.
The leaves will whisper there of her, and some,
Like flying words, will strike you as they fall;
But go, and if you listen she will call.
Go to the western gate, Luke Havergal –
Luke Havergal.

No, there is not a dawn in eastern skies
To rift the fiery night that's in your eyes;
But there, where western glooms are gathering,
The dark will end the dark, if anything:
God slays Himself with every leaf that flies,
And hell is more than half of paradise.
No, there is not a dawn in eastern skies –
In eastern skies.

Out of a grave I come to tell you this,
Out of a grave I come to quench the kiss
That flames upon your forehead with a glow
That blinds you to the way that you must go.
Yes, there is yet one way to where she is,
Bitter, but one that faith may never miss.
Out of a grave I come to tell you this –
To tell you this.

There is the western gate, Luke Havergal,
There are the crimson leaves upon the wall.
Go, for the winds are tearing them away, –
Nor think to riddle the dead words they say,

Nor any more to feel them as they fall;
But go, and if you trust her she will call.
There is the western gate, Luke Havergal –
Luke Havergal.

1895 [The Torrent and the Night Before, 1896]

Edwin Arlington Robinson was a prolific American poet best known for his pessimistic poems about the disillusioned folk of Tilbury, a small-town New England community based on Gardiner, Maine, where he spent his 'stark and unhappy' childhood. His Tilbury Town cast of characters includes the eponymous Miniver Cheevy, Reuben Bright, and Richard Cory, the latter thought by Edwin's sister-in-law Emma (whom he had wanted to marry) to be based on his once charismatic brother Herman, whose business ventures failed as he sank into alcholism, dying in poverty. Paul Simon's song 'Richard Cory' is a spin-off from Robinson's poem.

Robinson is one of very few poets whose entire work is almost exclusively concerned with people: their psychology, sensibility and inner life, and what their stories tell us about the human condition. Unable to make a living as a young writer, he worked as a subway inspector in New York before his poetry came to the attention of President Theodore Roosevelt, who secured a post for him at the New York Customs House. His wide popularity came after the publication of his seventh collection, *The Man Against the Sky*, in 1916. He engaged with Arthurian themes in later work, and his book-length poem *Tristram* (1927) was a bestseller. He won the Pulitzer Prize three times. His massive *Collected Poems* runs to over 1500 pages.

'Luke Havergal' is an early poem included in his first collection *The Torrent and the Night Before* (1896), whose publication he paid for himself. Its mysterious protagonist was long assumed by critics – such as Charles Cestre[16] and Ronald Moran[17] – to be a bereaved or lost lover contemplating suicide. He may also be 'a penitent sinner, or a sinner soon to be made penitent', according to Ronald E. McFarland,[18] who suggested a link between the name, Luke Havergal, and the parable of the prodigal son which appears only in Luke's gospel. Robinson wrote to his friend Harry de Forest Smith, in May 1895, that he was 'in the middle of St Luke now and

203

find him magnificent reading';[19] and a letter to Smith from December of that year refers to 'Luke Havergal'.[20] He later wrote another poem on the parable, 'The Prodigal Son' (1932). McFarland goes on to argue for the influence of Dante's *Divine Comedy* – and the *Inferno* in particular – on the writing of 'Luke Havergal', with Robinson known to have been reading the *Divine Comedy* at the time. He expresses his disapproval of Longfellow's 1891 translation in two letters to Smith from autumn 1894.[21] Identifying Robinson's protagonist with Dante's, McFarland views Luke Havergal as 'a sinner who has lost his way in the world without the guidance which had been afforded by his proper object of love. [...] Robinson is stressing the vital point of decision that a man must arrive at and act upon if he is to change his way of living.'[22] This moment of decision is an epiphany in the life of Robinson's protagonist, echoing changes in his own life. Following severe financial losses suffered by the family in the panic of 1893, Robinson had to abandon his studies at Harvard and return to Gardiner.

BK ■ This is a dramatic poem with three characters: the speaker who comes 'out of a grave', Luke Havergal, and 'she'. The speaker exhorts Luke Havergal to 'Go to the western gate' and 'if you listen she will call'. It is a poem of three characters and two worlds. It is consciously repetitive. Much repetition is simply boring but Robinson manages to make repeated phrases such as 'the western gate', 'eastern skies', 'out of a grave', 'to tell you this' and the name 'Luke Havergal' itself contribute to the poem's hypnotic, intimate drama. The mesmeric quality is deepened by the sense of the poem being poised between worlds: natural and supernatural, darkness of the grave and leafy twilight, the western gate and the eastern skies. 'I sing,' Robinson said, 'in my own particular manner, of heaven and hell and now and then of natural things (supposing they exist).' He also said, 'I suppose you will have to put me down as a mystic.'

Hypnotic repetition and the sense of earthly and unearthly drama involving mysterious connections that may or may not happen, emerge strongly when the poem is repeatedly read aloud. It seems easy and overt, yet remains secretive; it is dark yet ultimately hopeful and positive ('if you trust her she will call'). And the name Luke Havergal stays with the reader in an insistent, recurring way. Robinson wished to write a haunted, haunting poem. He succeeded.

OSCAR WILDE (1854-1900)

from The Ballad of Reading Gaol

In Memoriam C.T.W. sometime trooper of the Royal Horse
Guards Obiit H.M. Prison Reading, Berkshire, July 7, 1896

1

He did not wear his scarlet coat,
   For blood and wine are red,
And blood and wine were on his hands
   When they found him with the dead,
The poor dead woman whom he loved,
   And murdered in her bed.

He walked amongst the Trial Men
   In a suit of shabby grey;
A cricket cap was on his head,
   And his step seemed light and gay;
But I never saw a man who looked
   So wistfully at the day.

I never saw a man who looked
   With such a wistful eye
Upon that little tent of blue
   Which prisoners call the sky,
And at every drifting cloud that went
   With sails of silver by.

I walked, with other souls in pain,
   Within another ring,
And was wondering if the man had done
   A great or little thing,
When a voice behind me whispered low,
   'That fellow's got to swing.'

Dear Christ! the very prison walls
  Suddenly seemed to reel,
And the sky above my head became
  Like a casque of scorching steel;
And, though I was a soul in pain,
  My pain I could not feel.

I only knew what hunted thought
  Quickened his step, and why
He looked upon the garish day
  With such a wistful eye;
The man had killed the thing he loved,
  And so he had to die.

                        *

Yet each man kills the thing he loves,
  By each let this be heard,
Some do it with a bitter look,
  Some with a flattering word,
The coward does it with a kiss,
  The brave man with a sword!

Some kill their love when they are young,
  And some when they are old;
Some strangle with the hands of Lust,
  Some with the hands of Gold:
The kindest use a knife, because
  The dead so soon grow cold.

Some love too little, some too long,
  Some sell, and others buy;
Some do the deed with many tears,
  And some without a sigh:
For each man kills the thing he loves,
  Yet each man does not die.

[...]

3

In Debtors' Yard the stones are hard,
    And the dripping wall is high,
So it was there he took the air
    Beneath the leaden sky,
And by each side a Warder walked,
    For fear the man might die.

Or else he sat with those who watched
    His anguish night and day;
Who watched him when he rose to weep,
    And when he crouched to pray;
Who watched him lest himself should rob
    Their scaffold of its prey.

The Governor was strong upon
    The Regulations Act:
The Doctor said that Death was but
    A scientific fact:
And twice a day the Chaplain called,
    And left a little tract.

And twice a day he smoked his pipe,
    And drank his quart of beer:
His soul was resolute, and held
    No hiding-place for fear;
He often said that he was glad
    The hangman's hands were near.

But why he said so strange a thing
    No Warder dared to ask:
For he to whom a watcher's doom
    Is given as his task,
Must set a lock upon his lips,
    And make his face a mask.

[…]

207

That night the empty corridors
    Were full of forms of Fear,
And up and down the iron town
    Stole feet we could not hear,
And through the bars that hide the stars
    White faces seemed to peer.

He lay as one who lies and dreams
    In a pleasant meadow-land,
The watchers watched him as he slept,
    And could not understand
How one could sleep so sweet a sleep
    With a hangman close at hand.

But there is no sleep when men must weep
    Who never yet have wept:
So we – the fool, the fraud, the knave –
    That endless vigil kept,
And through each brain on hands of pain
    Another's terror crept.

Alas! it is a fearful thing
    To feel another's guilt!
For, right within, the sword of Sin
    Pierced to its poisoned hilt,
And as molten lead were the tears we shed
    For the blood we had not spilt.

The Warders with their shoes of felt
    Crept by each padlocked door,
And peeped and saw, with eyes of awe,
    Grey figures on the floor,
And wondered why men knelt to pray
    Who never prayed before.

[…]

4

There is no chapel on the day
    On which they hang a man:
The Chaplain's heart is far too sick,
    Or his face is far too wan,
Or there is that written in his eyes
    Which none should look upon.

So they kept us close till nigh on noon,
    And then they rang the bell,
And the Warders with their jingling keys
    Opened each listening cell,
And down the iron stair we tramped,
    Each from his separate Hell.

Out into God's sweet air we went,
    But not in wonted way,
For this man's face was white with fear,
    And that man's face was grey,
And I never saw sad men who looked
    So wistfully at the day.

I never saw sad men who looked
    With such a wistful eye
Upon that little tent of blue
    We prisoners called the sky,
And at every careless cloud that passed
    In happy freedom by.

[...]

V

I know not whether Laws be right,
 Or whether Laws be wrong;
All that we know who lie in gaol
 Is that the wall is strong;
And that each day is like a year,
 A year whose days are long.

But this I know, that every Law
 That men have made for Man,
Since first Man took his brother's life,
 And the sad world began,
But straws the wheat and saves the chaff
 With a most evil fan.

This too I know – and wise it were
 If each could know the same –
That every prison that men build
 Is built with bricks of shame,
And bound with bars lest Christ should see
 How men their brothers maim.

With bars they blur the gracious moon,
 And blind the goodly sun:
And they do well to hide their Hell,
 For in it things are done
That Son of God nor son of Man
 Ever should look upon!

[...]

VI

In Reading gaol by Reading town
    There is a pit of shame,
And in it lies a wretched man
    Eaten by teeth of flame,
In a burning winding-sheet he lies,
    And his grave has got no name.

And there, till Christ call forth the dead,
    In silence let him lie:
No need to waste the foolish tear,
    Or heave the windy sigh:
The man had killed the thing he loved,
    And so he had to die.

And all men kill the thing they love,
    By all let this be heard,
Some do it with a bitter look,
    Some with a flattering word,
The coward does it with a kiss,
    The brave man with a sword.

1897 [*The Ballad of Reading Gaol*, 1898]

Born in Dublin in 1854, **Oscar Wilde** studied at Trinity College Dublin and Oxford. He married Constance Lloyd in London in 1884 and the couple had two sons. The early 1890s were the period of his greatest artistic fame, when he published *The Portrait of Dorian Gray* and when his most celebrated plays were performed. This was also the time of his homosexual relationship with Lord Alfred Douglas, culminating in his arrest, in 1895, followed by two years' imprisonment with hard labour, which left him physically broken. He began his sentence at Pentonville and Wandsworth jails before being transferred to Reading in November 1895, prior to the arrival of another prisoner, Charles T. Woolridge, a former trooper in the Royal Horse Guards who had murdered his wife.

Woolridge's story and fate were to inspire Wilde to write 'The Ballad of Reading Gaol' after his release.

From December 1896 to March 1897 Wilde worked on his famous letter from prison, *De Profundis*, an attempt to understand the nature of his own life and work, his character and failings, as well as a brilliant meditation on art, love, forgiveness and Christ. Ostracised after his release in 1897, he went into exile in Europe, initially with Douglas, and died in a Paris hotel, in 1900.

Wilde wrote 'The Ballad of Reading Gaol' in Berneval in France in 1897, choosing the ballad form for its spiritual power. In *De Profundis* he'd claimed that Christ was present in other literary ballads, such as Coleridge's 'Rime of the Ancient Mariner', Keats's 'La Belle Dame sans Merci' and Thomas Chatterton's 'Ballad of Charity'; and reading A.E. Housman's *A Shropshire Lad* led to him to publish his ballad as a broadsheet. The key line 'The man had killed the thing he loved' is Wilde's inversion of Bassanio's question to Shylock in Shakespeare's *Merchant of Venice*: 'Do all men kill the things they do not love?'

BK ■ It is possible to doubt, even to reject, a poem's central conviction yet still admire and be moved by the poem as a whole. Not everybody will agree with Wilde's central belief in 'The Ballad of Reading Gaol' that 'each man kills the thing he loves', and yet few will deny the sustained tragic intensity of this poem, or fail to be moved by it. Wilde was a master of paradox and contradiction, a mastery he projected through a brilliant, urbane, anarchic wit. Perhaps there's an ironic paradox in the fact that Wilde, a comic genius, produced this authentically tragic poem; and further that Wilde, a laughing apostle of freedom, conceived this ballad in prison.

The prison-world is evoked with memorable skill. 'The Ballad' is worth comparing with the work of another Dubliner, *The Quare Fellow* by Brendan Behan (1954), a play about prison life and the death penalty. Behan's play made a strong impact on the world of drama in the middle of the 20th century. Wilde's depiction of prison life is really an evocation of namelessness, of outcast anonymity (the only human name to appear in the poem is that of Christ). The man to be hanged is 'He'; the man watching him is 'I'; the prison warders are 'watchers'; the Chaplain is simply 'the Chaplain'. The words most frequently chosen to describe the prisoners are 'wistful' and 'wistfully'. 'Wistful' means 'affected with or betraying vague yearnings or mournfulness or unsatisfied desire to understand' (*The Concise Oxford Dictionary*, 1982). This 'unsatisfied desire to understand' is a crucial part of the 'pain' suffered by the prisoners, and by the man who has 'got to swing'.

> I only knew what hunted thought
>   Quickened his step, and why
> He looked upon the garish day
>   With such a wistful eye;
> The man had killed the thing he loved,
>   And so he had to die.

In this world of 'watchers', that man about to be hanged

>   sat with those who watched
>   His anguish night and day;
> Who watched him when he rose to weep
>   And when he knelt to pray;
> Who watched him lest himself should rob
>   Their scaffold of its prey.

And yet, despite all the vigilant 'watchers', 'The Ballad of Reading Gaol' has an atmosphere of haunting, desolate emptiness, a populated void. This terrible emptiness on the faces and in the souls of all the 'watchers' is what strikes Wilde on the day of the hanging.

> I never saw sad men who looked
>   With such a wistful eye
> Upon that little tent of blue
>   We prisoners called the sky,
> And at every happy cloud that passed
>   In such strange freedom by.

The four stanzas dealing with 'Law' and 'Laws' and their insistence on prisons 'built with bricks of shame' are as challenging today as when Wilde wrote them. These stanzas, written from the prisoners' perspectives, concisely convey the horrors of prison life. It is not just a man's body that is sentenced to prison; it is his consciousness, his identity, his very being. Wilde gives the phrase 'behind bars' a shocking new meaning: prisons are Colleges of crime.

> With bars they blur the gracious moon,
>   And blind the goodly sun:
> And they do well to hide their Hell,
>   For in it things are done
> That Son of God nor son of Man
>   Ever should look upon!

The poem ends emphatically as it began. A nameless, hanged man is buried in a nameless grave.

> In Reading gaol by Reading town
>   There is a pit of shame,
> And in it lies a wretched man
>   Eaten by teeth of flame,
> In a burning winding-sheet he lies,
>   And his grave has got no name.

'The Ballad of Reading Gaol' is not given here in its entirety, yet this extract is sufficient to convey the loneliness, fear, violence, desolation and education in crime that constitute prison life. Wilde's own life ended in cold, pained loneliness. His articulate understanding of that condition helped him to write a poem that even today challenges the whole concept of imprisonment and punishment with penetrating, eloquent power.

A.E. HOUSMAN (1859-1936)

'Good creatures, do you love your lives'

Good creatures, do you love your lives
   And have you ears for sense?
Here is a knife like other knives,
   That cost me eighteen pence.

I need but stick it in my heart
   And down will come the sky,
And earth's foundations will depart
   And all you folk will die.

Date of writing unknown [*More Poems*, XXVI, published 1936]

Alfred Edward Housman was a brilliant classical scholar, born in Worcestershire, who became a highly popular poet some years after the publication of his collection, *A Shropshire Lad,* in 1896. George Orwell attributed the book's popularity with Edwardian youth and with young soldiers in particular to its nostalgia for the countryside; its pessimistic 'adolescent' themes of murder, suicide, unhappy love and doomed or early death; and its 'bitter, defiant paganism, a conviction that life is short and the gods are against you, which exactly fitted the prevailing mood of the young'. Death is part of nature in a hostile universe abandoned by God, while youthful beauty is cherished for only as long as it lasts. Its author's unrequited homosexual leanings are barely disguised but were largely responsible for his later collection, *More Poems* – from which this poem is taken – not being published until after his death, in 1936. Most of the poems are untitled and none is dated. They are likely to have been written over five decades.

    Another poem, 'Oh who is that young sinner with the handcuffs on his wrists?' was written after the trial of Oscar Wilde but not known until his brother Laurence included it in Housman's posthumous *Collected Poems* in 1939.

When I questioned Brendan's choice of 'Good creatures, do you love your lives' as our Housman poem – and not a lyric from *A Shropshire Lad* – suggesting he might be reading himself into what could almost have been one of his own poems, he responded by letter with an impassioned defence, included here in lieu of his unwritten commentary.

BK ■ I chose Housman's 'Good creatures' because it is a poem where Housman steps outside the borders of his customary heroic nostalgia into that emotion for which his beautifully shaped and often moving nostalgia is a mask – a sort of bitter, slightly mocking moment of emotional precision with a twisted, obverse character. I believe that poets can spend a lifetime writing of feelings that are not *ultimately* precise because the poets do not permit themselves to go their full emotional journey; they rather settle on *aspects* of that ultimate precision, becoming preoccupied, even obsessed with those aspects which *do* have their own truths, but truths by the way, on the journey (I tend to do this myself, slipping down laneways, byways in myself), so that they do not allow themselves to discover the full, terrifying fluency of the discovery of that *truest* obsession, in the sense that Keats discovered uncertainty, the authority of uncertainty; Yeats, mastery/measurement/masks; Kavanagh, honesty/passivity; Baudelaire, a spiritual but humourless preoccupation with the sordid.

In 'Good creatures, do you love your lives', Housman was asking of others the question he may have asked himself in darkness or nightmare but not in nostalgia-hungry daylight. Remember – I do love some of his poems, but when I found this one, I believe I found Housman. I do *not* think I'm reading myself into the verses – if I tried to, they would bang the door in my face.

THOMAS HARDY   (1840–1928)

The Voice

Woman much missed, how you call to me, call to me,
Saying that now you are not as you were
When you had changed from the one who was all to me,
But as at first, when our day was fair.

Can it be you that I hear? Let me view you, then,
Standing as when I drew near to the town
Where you would wait for me: yes, as I knew you then,
Even to the original air-blue gown!

Or is it only the breeze, in its listlessness
Travelling across the wet mead to me here,
You being ever dissolved to wan wistlessness,
Heard no more again far or near?

    Thus I; faltering forward,
    Leaves around me falling,
Wind oozing thin through the thorn from norward,
    And the woman calling.

December 1912 [1914]

Thomas Hardy was born in Dorset, the son of a stonemason, leaving school at 16 to train as an architect. He worked in London from 1862 for five years before returning to Dorset, meeting his first wife, Emma Gifford, while working on the restoration of a church in Cornwall. His early romance novel, *A Pair of Blue Eyes* (1873), was inspired by their passionate courtship. They married in 1874, moving in 1885 to Max Gate in Dorchester, the house he designed, where he lived for the rest of his life. His novels were all published between 1871 and 1897, most notably *Far from the Madding Crowd* (1874), *The Mayor of Casterbridge* (1886), *Tess of* *the d'Urbervilles* (1891) and *Jude the Obscure* (1895), mostly set in the fictionalised region of Wessex (most of south-west England). He had always written poetry and regarded himself as primarily a poet, but didn't publish his first collection until 1898, devoting himself to poetry after the attacks on the 'obscenity' of *Jude the Obscure*.

When Emma died suddenly on the morning of 27 November 1912, the couple had been estranged for 20 years. She had become increasingly religious and found her husband's late novels deeply upsetting. Written in the month after her death, 'The Voice' is one of a sequence of 21 elegies he published as *Poems 1912-13* in his 1914 collection *Satires of Circumstance* in which he struggled with his grief, and with regret and remorse at his neglect of her in the later years of their marriage. The following March he travelled to Cornwall, revisiting the places where they had fallen in love. Other poems in the series describe his feelings of being haunted by her there. He was also wrestling with guilt over his feelings for his young secretary, Florence Dugdale, who moved into Max Gate in 1913. They married in early 1914.

BK ■ Thomas Hardy's narrative and dramatic genius, his dark, musical honesty, his technical skill, his resolute scrutiny of feelings, his awareness of the past's influence on the present, and his ability to listen to various kinds of voices – all these are present in 'The Voice', making it a forceful, haunting poem. The voice of the 'Woman much missed' tells him that she is not the woman who had changed 'from the one who was all' to him, but the woman he knew 'at first, when our day was fair'. He wishes to see her as he knew her then, dressed in her 'original air-blue gown!'.

Doubt enters, and he wonders if it is she at all, or 'only the breeze, in its listlessness'. What is this voice? What is its source? The last stanza, formally different from the others, its architecture less solid, presents the speaker 'faltering forward', leaves falling about him in the wind, 'And the woman calling'.

This final image of the man, at once fascinated and faltering, captures the mesmeric quality of the voice of 'the woman calling'. The reader will still ask, 'Or is it only the breeze?'. This sense of a driven, lonely man, compelled by, yet unsure of that hypnotic voice from a past at once vivid and 'dissolved', drives the poem 'forward', not falteringly but with well-stitched verbal precision and concentrated dramatic power.

CHARLOTTE MEW (1869-1928)

Madeleine in Church

Here, in the darkness, where this plaster saint
    Stands nearer than God stands to our distress,
And one small candle shines, but not so faint
    As the far lights of everlastingness
I'd rather kneel than over there, in open day
    Where Christ is hanging, rather pray
      To something more like my own clay,
        Not too divine;
    For, once, perhaps my little saint
    Before he got his niche and crown,
Had one short stroll about the town;
It brings him closer, just that taint
      And anyone can wash the paint
Off our poor faces, his and mine!

Is that why I see Monty now? equal to any saint, poor boy, as good
                                  as gold,
But still, with just the proper trace
Of earthliness on his shining wedding face;
And then gone suddenly blank and old
The hateful day of the divorce:
Stuart got his, hands down, of course
Crowing like twenty cocks and grinning like a horse:
But Monty took it hard. All said and done I liked him best, –
He was the first, he stands out clearer than the rest.
      It seems too funny all we other rips
    Should have immortal souls; Monty and Redge quite damnably
    Keep theirs afloat while we go down like scuttled ships. –
      It's funny too, how easily we sink,
      One might put up a monument, I think
    To half the world and cut across it 'Lost at Sea!'
I should drown Jim, poor little sparrow, if I netted him tonight –

No, it's no use this penny light-
Or my poor saint with his tin-pot crown –
The trees of Calvary are where they were,
When we are sure that we can spare
The tallest, let us go and strike it down
And leave the other two still standing there.
I, too, would ask Him to remember me
If there were any Paradise beyond this earth that I could see.

Oh! quiet Christ who never knew
The poisonous fangs that bite us through
And make us do the things we do,
See how we suffer and fight and die,
How helpless and how low we lie,
God holds You, and You hang so high,
Though no one looking long at You,
Can think You do not suffer too,
But, up there, from your still, star-lighted tree
What can You know, what can You really see
Of this dark ditch, the soul of me!

We are what we are: when I was half a child I could not sit
Watching black shadows on green lawns and red carnations burning in the sun
Without paying so heavily for it
That joy and pain, like any mother and her unborn child were almost one.
I could hardly bear
The dreams upon the eyes of white geraniums in the dusk,
The thick, close voice of musk,
The jessamine music on the thin night air,
Or, sometimes, my own hands about me anywhere –
The sight of my own face (for it was lovely then) even the scent of my own hair,
Oh! there was nothing, nothing that did not sweep to the high seat
Of laughing gods, and then blow down and beat
My soul into the highway dust, as hoofs do the dropped roses of the street.
I think my body was my soul,
And when we are made thus
Who shall control

Our hands, our eyes, the wandering passion of our feet,
Who shall teach us
To thrust the world out of our heart; to say, till perhaps in death,
When the race is run,
And it is forced from us with our last breath
'Thy will be done'?
If it is Your will that we should be content with the tame, bloodless things.
As pale as angels smirking by, with folded wings.
Oh! I know Virtue, and the peace it brings!
The temperate, well-worn smile
The one man gives you, when you are evermore his own:
And afterwards the child's, for a little while,
With its unknowing and all-seeing eyes
So soon to change, and make you feel how quick
The clock goes round. If one had learned the trick –
(How does one though?) quite early on,
Of long green pastures under placid skies,
One might be walking now with patient truth.
What did we ever care for it, who have asked for youth,
When, oh! my God! this is going or has gone?

There is a portrait of my mother, at nineteen,
With the black spaniel, standing by the garden seat,
The dainty head held high against the painted green
And throwing out the youngest smile, shy, but half haughty and half sweet.
Her picture then: but simply Youth, or simply Spring
To me today: a radiance on the wall,
So exquisite, so heart-breaking a thing
Beside the mask that I remember, shrunk and small,
Sapless and lined like a dead leaf,
All that was left of oh! the loveliest face, by time and grief!

And in the glass, last night, I saw a ghost behind my chair –
Yet why remember it, when one can still go moderately gay – ?
Or could – with any one of the old crew,
But oh! these boys! the solemn way
They take you and the things they say –

This 'I have only as long as you'
When you remind them you are not precisely twenty-two –
Although at heart perhaps – God! if it were
Only the face, only the hair!
If Jim had written to me as he did today
A year ago – and now it leaves me cold –
I know what this means, old, old, *old!*
Et avec ça – mais on a vécu, tout se paie.

That is not always true: there was my Mother – (well at least the dead are free!
Yoked to the man that Father was; yoked to the woman I am, Monty too;
The little portress at the Convent School, stewing in hell so patiently;
The poor, fair boy who shot himself at Aix. And what of me – and what of me
But I, I paid for what I had, and they for nothing. No, one cannot see
How it shall be made up to them in some serene eternity.
If there were fifty heavens God could not give us back the child who went or
never came
Here, on our little patch of this great earth, the sun of any darkened day,
Not one of all the starry buds hung on the hawthorn trees of last year's May,
No shadow from the sloping fields of yesterday;
For every hour they slant across the hedge a different way,
The shadows are never the same.

'Find rest in Him!' One knows the parsons' tags –
Back to the fold, across the evening fields, like any flock of baa-ing sheep
Yes, it may be, when He has shorn, led us to slaughter, torn the bleating soul
in us to rag
For so He giveth His belovèd sleep.
Oh! He will take us stripped and done,
Driven into His heart. So we are won:
Then safe, safe are we? in the shelter of His everlasting wings –
I do not envy Him his victories, His arms are full of broken things.

But I shall not be in them. Let Him take
The finer ones, the easier to break.
And they are not gone, yet, for me, the lights, the colours, the perfumes,
Though now they speak rather in sumptuous rooms,
In silks and in gem-like wines;

Here, even, in this corner where my little candle shines
And overhead the lancet-window glows
With golds and crimsons you could almost drink
To know how jewels taste, just as I used to think
There was the scent in every red and yellow rose
Of all the sunsets. But this place is grey,
And much too quiet. No one here,
Why, this is awful, this is fear!
Nothing to see, no face,
Nothing to hear except your heart beating in space
As if the world was ended. Dead at last!
Dead soul, dead body, tied together fast.
These to go on with and alone, to the slow end:
No one to sit with, really, or to speak to, friend to friend:
Out of the long procession, black or white or red
Not one left now to say 'Still I am here, then see you, dear, lay here your head.'
Only the doll's house looking on the Park
Tonight, all nights, I know, when the man puts the lights out, very dark.
With, upstairs, in the blue and gold box of a room, just the maids' footsteps
                                                                    overhead,
Then utter silence and the empty world – the room – the bed –
The corpse! No, not quite dead, while this cries out in me,
But nearly: very soon to be
A handful of forgotten dust –
There must be someone. Christ! there must,
Tell me there *will* be someone. Who?
If there were no one else, could it be You?

How old was Mary out of whom you cast
So many devils? Was she young or perhaps for years
She had sat staring, with dry eyes, at this and that man going past
Till suddenly she saw You on the steps of Simeon's house
And stood and looked at You through tears.
I think she must have known by those
The thing, for what it was that had come to her.
For some of us there is a passion, I suppose
So far from earthly cares and earthly fears

That in its stillness you can hardly stir
            Or in its nearness, lift your hand,
So great that you have simply got to stand
Looking at it through tears, through tears.
Then straight from these there broke the kiss,
            I think You must have known by this
The thing, for what it was, that had come to You:
            She did not love You like the rest,
It was in her own way, but at the worst, the best,
            She gave you something altogether new.
And through it all, from her, no word,
            She scarcely saw You, scarcely heard:
Surely You knew when she so touched You with her hair,
            Or by the wet cheek lying there,
And while her perfume clung to You from head to feet all through the day
            That You can change the things for which we care,
But even You, unless You kill us, not the way.

This, then was peace for her, but passion too.
I wonder was it like a kiss that once I knew,
            The only one that I would care to take
Into the grave with me, to which if there were afterwards, to wake.
            Almost as happy as the carven dead
            In some dim chancel lying head by head
We slept with it, but face to face, the whole night through –
One breath, one throbbing quietness, as if the thing behind our lips was
                                                    endless life,
    Lost, as I woke, to hear in the strange earthly dawn, his 'Are you there?'
            And lie still, listening to the wind outside, among the firs.

So Mary chose the dream of Him for what was left to her of night and day,
It is the only truth: it is the dream in us that neither life nor death nor
                                    any other thing can take away:
    But if she had not touched Him in the doorway of the dream could she
                                            have cared so much?
    She was a sinner, we are what we are: the spirit afterwards, but
                                                    first, the touch.

224

And He has never shared with me my haunted house beneath the
                                                                    trees
Of Eden and Calvary, with its ghosts that have not any eyes for tears,
And the happier guests who would not see, or if they did, remember
                                                                   these,
               Though they lived there a thousand years.
                 Outside, too gravely looking at me, He seems to stand,
                  And looking at Him, if my forgotten spirit came
                           Unwillingly back, what could it claim
                           Of those calm eyes, that quiet speech,
                 Breaking like a slow tide upon the beach,
                       The scarred, not quite human hand? –
         Unwillingly back to the burden of old imaginings
         When it has learned so long not to think, not to be,
Again, again it would speak as it has spoken to me of things
               That I shall not see!

I cannot bear to look at this divinely bent and gracious head:
          When I was small I never quite believed that He was dead:
          And at the Convent school I used to lie awake in bed
Thinking about His hands. It did not matter what they said,
He was alive to me, so hurt, so hurt! And most of all in Holy Week
               When there was no one else to see
          I used to think it would not hurt me too, so terribly,
                    If He had ever seemed to notice me
                    Or, if, for once, He would only speak.

1914-15 [*The Farmer's Bride*, 1916]

Born in London, **Charlotte Mew** lived for most of her life with
her family in Bloomsbury. Three of her brothers died in childhood,
another was committed to an asylum, while her youngest sister
Freda spent her later years as a patient in a mental hospital on the
Isle of Wight where she died in 1958. After her father's death in
1898, she lived in reduced financial circumstances, mostly with her
mother and younger sister Anne, a painter, and was said to have
renounced marriage because of hereditary insanity in the family,

but this may well have been cover for her being a lesbian. Her first short story was published in *The Yellow Book* in 1894, and her first collection *The Farmer's Bride* by Harold Monro's Poetry Bookshop in 1916. Following the deaths of her mother in 1923 and sister Anne in 1927, Charlotte committed suicide by drinking disinfectant in 1928. A posthumously published collection, *The Rambling Sailor*, appeared in 1929.

'Madeleine in Church' is one of a number of her dramatic monologues written in the voice of a female or male persona, often exploring the passion of women, and is certainly the most ambitious and innovative of these. Charlotte Mew's concerns link her with 19th-century women poets who wrote in more traditional styles but her poetic technique has much more in common with 20th-century modernist poets.

Charlotte Mew was one of the poets Brendan especially wanted in the anthology but hadn't covered in his commentaries when *The Heavy Bear* went into hibernation. He did, however, present this case for her inclusion in one of the letters we exchanged while drawing up our selection:

BK ■ Charlotte Mew simply has to be brought to people's attention again. There is something at once heroic and strangulated in the woman, something as fluent as the Shannon in spate and as tight as a mackerel's arse that makes for a poetry in which these polar feelings find expression in lines striding like Olympic runners and also lines like clenched fists. There's no doubt that 'Madeleine in Church' is a major poem, a major *bridgepoem* between Victorianism and modernism, and I think we should simply go for it. The poem *deserves* to be read and studied by a new generation (and also by an old one). I'd plead with you about this one – the ould bear last night in sleep asked me to ask you to print this one for the benefit of especially young beasts in the making. The music of her expression is more soaring than Eliot's, of whom she reminds me at times. But she is more candid about her lack of candour; and she is genuinely *passionate* – a passionate poet in all her senses, before the armies of irony marched into the house of poetry and took it over. Some of 'Madeleine in Church' I don't understand, but I hope to go into it, and through it, again and again. So whatcha think, Neil Óg?

WALTER DE LA MARE (1873–1956)

The Listeners

'Is there anybody there?' said the Traveller,
    Knocking on the moonlit door;
And his horse in the silence champed the grasses
    Of the forest's ferny floor:
And a bird flew up out of the turret,
    Above the Traveller's head:
And he smote upon the door again a second time;
    'Is there anybody there?' he said.
But no one descended to the Traveller;
    No head from the leaf-fringed sill
Leaned over and looked into his grey eyes,
    Where he stood perplexed and still.
But only a host of phantom listeners
    That dwelt in the lone house then
Stood listening in the quiet of the moonlight
    To that voice from the world of men:
Stood thronging the faint moonbeams on the dark stair,
    That goes down to the empty hall,
Hearkening in an air stirred and shaken
    By the lonely Traveller's call.
And he felt in his heart their strangeness,
    Their stillness answering his cry,
While his horse moved, cropping the dark turf,
    'Neath the starred and leafy sky;
For he suddenly smote on the door, even
    Louder, and lifted his head: –
'Tell them I came, and no one answered,
    That I kept my word,' he said.
Never the least stir made the listeners,
    Though every word he spake
Fell echoing through the shadowiness of the still house
    From the one man left awake:

227

Ay, they heard his foot upon the stirrup,
  And the sound of iron on stone,
And how the silence surged softly backward,
  When the plunging hoofs were gone.

[1912]

Walter de la Mare was an English poet and short story writer
known especially for this poem. Many of his poems and stories have
a similar childlike or dreamlike vision and a supernatural dimension,
often with an air of mystery and an undercurrent of melancholy. He
left school at 16 and for the next 18 years worked in the statistics
department of Anglo-American Oil in London. A Civil List pension
awarded in 1908 enabled him to become a full-time writer. 'The
Listeners' appeared in his second collection, *The Listeners* (1912).
His classic children's collection, *Peacock Pie*, followed in 1913.

BK ■ The reader of this poem is somewhat like the Traveller in it:
he is fascinated by what he cannot really reach, compelled by an
energy he cannot define or communicate with. Yet the energy is
there, present and listening, but not responding. The Traveller's
passionate eagerness to communicate meets only the silent, patient,
unassailable power of the listeners. It feels like a contest in which
silence easily overcomes language. Three times the Traveller knocks
but gets no reply, not even when he says, 'Tell them I came, and
no one answered,/ That I kept my word.' The Traveller has lived
up to some duty, fulfilled some promise, and wants to let 'them'
know this. But the listeners don't make even 'the least stir' although
'they heard his foot upon the stirrup' as he rides away.

  There are two worlds in this poem but they do not touch each
other. The Traveller's vulnerable need to speak his heart and mind
is no match for the listeners' unbreakable silence. He is severed,
disconnected, driven by a desire, to connect. In a poem called
'The Traveller', de la Mare speaks of 'the all-but-uttered, and yet
out of reach'. 'The Listeners' is pitched on the threshold of a
door that will not open, sheltering beings 'out of reach'. Perhaps
these two worlds are within us. Perhaps we are all travellers and
listeners. Does a listening heart answer a speaking poem? Does a
listening poem respond to a pleading heart?

ROBERT FROST (1874–1967)

The Road Not Taken

Two roads diverged in a yellow wood,
And sorry I could not travel both
And be one traveler, long I stood
And looked down one as far as I could
To where it bent in the undergrowth;

Then took the other, as just as fair,
And having perhaps the better claim,
Because it was grassy and wanted wear;
Though as for that, the passing there
Had worn them really about the same,

And both that morning equally lay
In leaves no step had trodden black.
Oh, I kept the first for another day!
Yet knowing how way leads on to way,
I doubted if I should ever come back.

I shall be telling this with a sigh
Somewhere ages and ages hence:
Two roads diverged in a wood, and I –
I took the one less traveled by,
And that has made all the difference.

October 1914 [First published in *The Atlantic Monthly*, 1915]

Robert Frost was the most popular American poet of the 20th century. Joseph Brodsky wrote of Frost: 'He is generally regarded as the poet of the countryside, of rural settings – as a folksy, crusty, wisecracking old gentleman farmer, generally of positive disposition. In short, as American as apple pie. […] Now, this is obviously a romantic caricature. […] Nature, for this poet, is neither friend nor foe, nor is it the backdrop for human drama; it is this poet's terrifying self-portrait.' [23]

Born in San Francisco, Frost moved with his family to New England at the age of 11. Most of his best-known poems are set in the New Hampshire farmland where he raised chickens, but his first two collections, *A Boy's Will* (1913) and *North of Boston* (1914), were written when he lived in England, from 1912 to 1915, where he also met Ezra Pound and Edward Thomas. Much of that time was spent in Gloucestershire where his friendship with Thomas became highly influential in the development of the work of both poets. His third collection, *Mountain Interval* (1916), assembled while still in England, brought his work to wider public attention in the US, including poems such as 'The Road Not Taken' and 'Birches', both first published in *The Atlantic Monthly*, in August 1915. It was Thomas's poem, 'The Signpost' ('I read the sign. Which was shall I go?'), written and sent to Frost in December 1914, which encouraged Frost in a line of thinking about his friend which led to the writing the following autumn of 'The Road Not Taken', which was to become America's most popular modern poem.

In his Edward Thomas biography, *Now All Roads Lead to France* (2011), Matthew Hollis tells how the poem was instrumental in Thomas's fateful decision to enlist, after many months of wavering, reading it as a spur to action, contrary to how Frost saw the poem:

> Noble, characteristic, wise: in the years since its composition, 'The Road Not Taken' has been understood by some as an emblem of individual choice and self-reliance, a moral tale in which the traveller takes responsibility for their own destiny. But it was never intended to be read as such by Frost, who was well aware of the playful ironies contained within it, and would go on to warn audiences, 'You have to be careful of that one; it's a tricky poem – very tricky.' Frost knew that reading the poem as straight morality tale would pose a number of difficulties. [...]
>
> 'The Road Not Taken' is typical of Frost's skill with perspective and with mirrors: behind the neat, unfussy frontage is an experience of great depth and subtlety, and no small amount of wit. For the poem to appear wise to some and ironic to others is a credit to the sophisticated way in which Frost had become the poet 'for all sorts and kinds': no wonder it stands as such a beguiling poem in the minds of readers; no wonder it has been taken so much to heart.[24]

The poem also carried that more personal, misconstrued message, Frost said later, for 'a friend who had gone off to war, a person who, whichever road he went, would be sorry he didn't go the other'.[25]

BK ■ Robert Frost wrote that 'Poetry provides the one permissible way of saying one thing and meaning another. People say, "Why don't you say what you mean?" We never do that, do we, being all of us too much poets. We like to talk in parables and in hints and in indirections.' Frost's faith in indirectness recalls Yeats's statement that 'The poet never speaks directly as to someone at a breakfast table; there is always a phantasmagoria.' There are many differences between these two poets but they share this belief in the power of the indirect statement, although Yeats can be, in fact, very direct at times.

Frost cultivates indirectness of tone, theme and language, like a cute countryman who never wants to tell you the full story in case you might get to know too much about him. This foxy shrewdness, this air of reserved and masterly cunning, combined with a capacity for almost proverbial wisdom, gives many of Frost's poems a paradoxical air of showy caution, exhibitionistic reserve. This is a crucial part of their attraction: they are at once chatty and formal, confidentially revealing and consciously protected, even hidden. At times Frost seems to be playing a game in which he won't let his spondee know what his trochee is doing.

'The Road Not Taken' is a delightful poem about choice and its consequences. Two roads go in different directions from a certain point; the traveller must choose; he does, opting for the one 'less traveled by', and that choice 'has made all the difference'.

This poem will mean something deeply personal to practically everyone. Nearly everybody has had to make such choices in life; for most of us, there is some road 'not taken'. Frost's poem is an echoing metaphor for states of mind marked by wondering what might have been if one had taken such and such a course of action. To take the one 'less traveled by' as Frost does is to look back after 'ages and ages' and recognise 'the difference' made to his life. But what is that difference? 'We like to talk in parables and in hints and indirections.' Frost leaves it up to the reader to ponder, to wonder, to discover whatever 'difference' he or she can. The choice is made, the road taken, the old fox has been and gone. The world is different. How different?

EDWARD THOMAS (1878–1918)

Adlestrop

Yes. I remember Adlestrop –
The name, because one afternoon
Of heat the express-train drew up there
Unwontedly. It was late June.

The steam hissed. Someone cleared his throat.
No one left and no one came
On the bare platform. What I saw
Was Adlestrop – only the name

And willows, willow-herb, and grass,
And meadowsweet, and haycocks dry,
No whit less still and lonely fair
Than the high cloudlets in the sky.

And for that minute a blackbird sang
Close by, and round him, mistier,
Farther and farther, all the birds
Of Oxfordshire and Gloucestershire.

8 January 1915 [First published in *Poems*, 1917]

Edward Thomas wrote a lifetime's poetry in two years. Already a dedicated prose writer and influential critic, he became a poet only in December 1914, at the age of 36, kick-started into poetry by his conversations with Robert Frost. Often viewed as a "war poet", he wrote nothing directly about the trenches, finishing his last poem in January 1917 before embarking for France. And yet all his poetry was written during the war and is shadowed by its presence.

Thomas was plagued by self-recrimination over whether or not he should follow friends and fellow writers who had enlisted, these doubts surfacing in a number of poems reflecting on the state of

England during the war. Over-age, he was under no obligation to do so, but in July 1915 he finally volunteered, joining the Artists' Rifles as a private. In November 1916 he was commissioned as a 2nd Lieutenant with Artillery, arriving at Arras on the front line in February 1917, where he was killed on 9 April. While on leave he had arranged for the publication of his first poetry collection, *Poems*, using the pseudonym Edward Eastaway with a dedication to Robert Frost. That collection appeared after his death in 1917.

'Adlestrop' translates memories from the golden summer of 1914 – before the outbreak of war in August – into a poetic epiphany. Edward and Helen Thomas were travelling from London to visit the Frosts in Ledbury on 24 June 1914 when their express train made an unscheduled stop at the country station of Adlestrop in Gloucestershire. His field notebook records how 'through the willows could be heard a chain of blackbirds song at 12.45 and one thrush and no man seen, only a hiss of engine letting off steam'. They stopped at another signal outside Campden 'by banks of long grass willowherb and meadowsweet', with 'another stop like this outside Colwell on 27th with thrush singing on hillside above'. The poem conflates details from these three stops on two journeys.

BK ■ Some of the best lyric poems deal with moments that are personal, vivid, calm and memorable. A train stops 'unwontedly' at a station named Adlestrop. It is late June, hot, there is a sound of hissing steam and someone clearing his throat, the platform is bare, the scene of trees, grass, flowers and haycocks is peaceful and still as the June sky itself. A blackbird sings, and suddenly the world becomes pure birdsong in which 'all the birds / Of Oxfordshire and Gloucestershire' play their part. All this lasts a moment, or as Edward Thomas puts it, 'for that minute'.

'Adlestrop' celebrates the name of that quiet station; it is this name, rhythmically local and homely when one says it over and over to oneself, that Thomas remembers and which leads him on to other striking names: Oxfordshire, Gloucestershire. 'Naming these things is the love-act and its pledge' wrote Patrick Kavanagh in his poem 'Hospital'. Twice, Edward Thomas says he remembers 'the name'. And for a brief 'minute' of peace, wonder and birdsong, that name, Adlestrop, becomes the source and scene of an articulate act of rapt personal attention to nature's music.

ISAAC ROSENBERG (1890–1918)

Break of Day in the Trenches

The darkness crumbles away.
It is the same old druid Time as ever,
Only a live thing leaps my hand,
A queer sardonic rat,
As I pull the parapet's poppy
To stick behind my ear.
Droll rat, they would shoot you if they knew
Your cosmopolitan sympathies.
Now you have touched this English hand
You will do the same to a German
Soon, no doubt, if it be your pleasure
To cross the sleeping green between.
It seems you inwardly grin as you pass
Strong eyes, fine limbs, haughty athletes,
Less chanced than you for life,
Bonds to the whims of murder,
Sprawled in the bowels of the earth,
The torn fields of France.
What do you see in our eyes
At the shrieking iron and flame
Hurled through still heavens?
What quaver – what heart aghast?
Poppies whose roots are in man's veins
Drop, and are ever dropping;
But mine in my ear is safe –
Just a little white with the dust.

June 1916 [First published in *Poetry* (Chicago), December 1916; *Poems*, 1922]

■ **Isaac Rosenberg** was the son of Jewish immigrants from Eastern Europe, and grew up in the East End of London. He left school at 14 to become an apprentice engraver. Later, he received financial help to study art at the Slade School but remained undecided between poetry and art. Edward Marsh, editor of the 'Georgian' anthologies, noticed his poetry. Rosenberg wrote to Marsh in 1916: 'The Homer for this war has yet to be found.' He told another friend that he disliked Rupert Brooke's 'begloried sonnets' because war 'should be approached in a colder way, more abstract, with less of the million feelings everybody feels; or all these should be concentrated in one distinguished emotion'. Rosenberg hated war ("Now is the time to go on an exploring expedition to the North Pole") but in 1915 he enlisted in the Suffolk Regiment to help his family out financially.

[Edna Longley, *The Bloodaxe Book of 20th Century Poetry*, 2000]

Rosenberg joined a 'bantam battalion' for undersized recruits, and was sent to France with the King's Own Royal Lancaster Regiment in June 1916. He was killed returning from a night patrol at dawn on 1 April 1918 at Fampoux near Arras. Growing up in a poor household, his artistic gifts were nevertheless encouraged at home and school, and he began writing poetry very early, in 1905 at the age of 15. Only ten per cent of his poems actually relate to the war. He published two collections, *Night and Day* (1912) and *Youth* (1915), and a verse play, *Moses*, during his pre-embarkation leave in May 1916, but his great war poems of 1916-17 weren't published in a single volume until after the war, in 1922. These included 'Dead Man's Dump' and 'Returning, we hear the Larks', also candidates for this anthology, but after much discussion we decided in favour of 'Break of Day in the Trenches', with Brendan planning to link it in his commentary with Owen's 'Strange Meeting'. In his preface to Rosenberg's *Collected Works* (1937), Siegfried Sassoon wrote:

> Rosenberg was not consciously a 'war poet'. But the war destroyed him, and his few but impressive 'Trench Poems' are a central point in this book. They have the controlled directness of a man finding his voice and achieving mastery of his material [...] They are all of them fine poems, but 'Break of Day in the Trenches' has for me a poignant and nostalgic quality which eliminates critical analysis. Sensuous front-line existence is there, hateful and repellent, unforgettable and inescapable.

SIEGFRIED SASSOON (1886–1967)

Base Details

If I were fierce, and bald, and short of breath,
  I'd live with scarlet Majors at the Base,
And speed glum heroes up the line to death.
  You'd see me with my puffy petulant face,
Guzzling and gulping in the best hotel,
  Reading the Roll of Honour. 'Poor young chap,'
I'd say – 'I used to know his father well;
  Yes, we've lost heavily in this last scrap.'
And when the war is done and youth stone dead,
I'd toddle safely home and die – in bed.

Rouen, 4 March 1917 [*Counter-Attack and Other Poems*, 1918]

■ **Siegfried Sassoon** was the son of wealthy Anglo-Jewish parents. Before 1914 he lived a leisured life, golfing, hunting, writing derivative poetry. He joined up on the first day of the Great War, and won a Military Cross which he later renounced. Sassoon had become radicalised by the losses at the Battle of the Somme and by meeting leftwing pacifist intellectuals. His famous protest against the politics of the war – 'A Soldier's Declaration' – was printed in the *Times* and quoted in parliament. To prevent Sassoon from being court-martialled, Robert Graves, a fellow-officer in the Royal Welch Fusiliers, got him admitted to Craiglockhart War Hospital near Edinburgh where the psychological effects of war were treated. There he wrote the poems in *Counter-Attack* (1918), and met and influenced Wilfred Owen. Sassoon returned to action: another expression of solidarity with ordinary soldiers. His most significant postwar writings are memoirs that obsessively revisit his lost generation, partly in an effort to exorcise survivor-guilt. [...] His verse-satires attack the ignorance or indifference that sustains both the war and war-rhetoric.

[Edna Longley, *The Bloodaxe Book of 20th Century Poetry*, 2000]

BK ■ Like Wilfred Owen, Siegfried Sassoon fought in the First World War. Unlike Owen, he survived it and went on to have a long, productive life as a writer.

Sassoon believed that a poem should have a 'full and living voice' and possess 'the true vocal cadence of something urgently communicated'. The voice in 'Base Details' is certainly 'full and living' and it embodies 'the true vocal cadence' of what Sassoon wishes to say vigorously and clearly, something that is indeed 'urgently communicated'. With unconcealed satirical anger, Sassoon paints a contrast between the 'scarlet Majors at the Base', who are 'bald, and short of breath', with 'puffy petulant' faces and the young 'glum heroes' whom they, the Majors, 'speed [...] up the line to death', even as they themselves are 'Guzzling and gulping in the best hotel', drivelling clichés.

Much of the power of 'Base Details' stems from the way Sassoon slips easily and lethally into the identity of one of these scarlet Majors. As the writer of this poem, therefore, he enjoys the perspective afforded by his occupying a double identity, just as the title 'Base Details' covers both important military matters and lowly, ignoble ways of thinking and acting. In the end, with the war over 'and youth stone dead', the scarlet Major imagined by Sassoon is content to 'toddle safely home and die – in bed'. The pompous, puffy, petulant, guzzling, gulping scarlet Major has become a safe toddler far removed from young soldiers 'in foul dug-outs, gnawed by rats'.

Sassoon threw his Military Cross into the sea and became a devoted pacifist. 'Base Details' dramatises one source, at least, of his lifelong hatred and denunciation of war. It is a strong, controlled, enraged poem.

WILFRED OWEN   (1893–1918)

Strange Meeting

It seemed that out of battle I escaped
Down some profound dull tunnel, long since scooped
Through granites which titanic wars had groined.

Yet also there encumbered sleepers groaned,
Too fast in thought or death to be bestirred.
Then, as I probed them, one sprang up, and stared
With piteous recognition in fixed eyes,
Lifting distressful hands, as if to bless.
And by his smile, I knew that sullen hall, –
By his dead smile I knew we stood in Hell.

With a thousand pains that vision's face was grained;
Yet no blood reached there from the upper ground,
And no guns thumped, or down the flues made moan.
'Strange friend,' I said, 'here is no cause to mourn.'
'None,' said that other, 'save the undone years,
The hopelessness. Whatever hope is yours,
Was my life also; I went hunting wild
After the wildest beauty in the world,
Which lies not calm in eyes, or braided hair,
But mocks the steady running of the hour,
And if it grieves, grieves richlier than here.
For by my glee might many men have laughed,
And of my weeping something had been left,
Which must die now. I mean the truth untold,
The pity of war, the pity war distilled.
Now men will go content with what we spoiled,
Or, discontent, boil bloody, and be spilled.
They will be swift with swiftness of the tigress.
None will break ranks, though nations trek from progress.

Courage was mine, and I had mystery,
Wisdom was mine, and I had mastery:
To miss the march of this retreating world
Into vain citadels that are not walled.
Then, when much blood had clogged their chariot-wheels,
I would go up and wash them from sweet wells,
Even with truths that lie too deep for taint.
I would have poured my spirit without stint
But not through wounds; not on the cess of war.
Foreheads of men have bled where no wounds were.

'I am the enemy you killed, my friend.
I knew you in this dark: for so you frowned
Yesterday through me as you jabbed and killed.
I parried; but my hands were loath and cold.
Let us sleep now....'

January–March 1918 [First published in *Wheels: an anthology of verse*, 1919;
first collected in *Poems*, ed. Siegfried Sasson, 1920]

Wilfred Owen was the foremost British poet of the First World
War, but only five of his poems were published in his lifetime.
Working as a tutor in France when war was declared, he returned
home during the summer of 1915, enlisted with the Artists' Rifles
in October, and was later commissioned as a 2nd Lieutenant. Arriv-
ing in France on 1 January 1917, he joined the 2nd Manchester
Regiment on the front line at Serre.

His trench poems draw on his experiences of four months in
France, from January 1917. That June he was sent to Craiglockhart
War Hospital near Edinburgh, suffering from shellshock, where he
met Siegfried Sassoon in August. Their discussions prompted his
best work. 'Strange Meeting' was written some months later,
probably in Scarborough. He returned to France and was shot
while helping his men to cross the Sambre-Oise Canal on 4
November 1918, aged 25, a week before the Armistice was signed.

BK ■ There are two voices in 'Strange Meeting': that of the speaker/
narrator, and that of the man he killed only 'yesterday'. The dialogue
is visionary and humane and amounts to one of the most eloquent

revelations and denunciations of the horrors and waste of war in English poetry. Probably the most eloquent.

'Strange' is a strange word. It captures what is perhaps the most fascinating aspect of poetry itself, but also of so much 'ordinary' experience, if we stood back and looked at it. Strange. If familiarity breeds contempt, the sense of strangeness can breed wonder, tolerance and respect. It can lead us to appreciate what we might otherwise ignore. In 'Strange Meeting' the voice of the soldier who is addressed as 'Strange friend', killed by the speaker/narrator, occupies 30 of the poem's 44 lines. The poem allows him space to speak of past, present and future, of 'the undone years, / The hopelessness', 'the wildest beauty in the world', the laughter and legacy of his 'glee' and 'weeping' that 'must die now', of 'the truth untold', 'The pity of war', and 'the cess of war'. The poem's ending reconciles the reality of killing with an invitation to sleep and peace.

> 'I am the enemy you killed, my friend.
> I knew you in this dark: for so you frowned
> Yesterday through me as you jabbed and killed.
> I parried; but my hands were loath and cold.
> Let us sleep now....'

'Strange Meeting' is like a compressed Dantean vision of Hell, but a Hell in which the killed soldier, the 'Strange friend', lifts his 'distressful hands as if to bless' and offers a 'smile' to his killer.

Owen has written lines that feel like a love-poem set in Hell. In a preface to the book of poems he never saw published, he wrote:

> This book is not about heroes. English poetry is not yet fit to speak of them. Nor is it about deeds, or lands, nor anything about glory, honour, might, majesty, dominion, or power, except War. Above all I am not concerned with Poetry. My subject is War, and the pity of War. The Poetry is in the pity. Yet these elegies are to this generation in no sense consolatory. They may be to the next. All a poet can do today is warn. That is why the true Poets must be truthful.

The world, it would appear, has not really heeded Owen's desire to 'warn'. But 'Strange Meeting' survives as a great, enlightening, challenging war-poem/love-poem that could have emanated only from a brilliant mind and a noble heart. Its immense, calm, technical skill serves to underline its humane, responsible spirit of visionary revelation.

W.B. YEATS (1865–1939)

The Second Coming

Turning and turning in the widening gyre
The falcon cannot hear the falconer;
Things fall apart; the centre cannot hold;
Mere anarchy is loosed upon the world,
The blood-dimmed tide is loosed, and everywhere
The ceremony of innocence is drowned;
The best lack all conviction, while the worst
Are full of passionate intensity.

Surely some revelation is at hand;
Surely the Second Coming is at hand.
The Second Coming! Hardly are those words out
When a vast image out of *Spiritus Mundi*
Troubles my sight: somewhere in sands of the desert
A shape with lion body and the head of a man,
A gaze blank and pitiless as the sun,
Is moving its slow thighs, while all about it
Reel shadows of the indignant desert birds.
The darkness drops again; but now I know
That twenty centuries of stony sleep
Were vexed to nightmare by a rocking cradle,
And what rough beast, its hour come round at last,
Slouches towards Bethlehem to be born?

1919 [First published in *The Dial*, November 1920]

Leda and the Swan

A sudden blow: the great wings beating still
Above the staggering girl, her thighs caressed
By the dark webs, her nape caught in his bill,
He holds her helpless breast upon his breast.

How can those terrified vague fingers push
The feathered glory from her loosening thighs?
And how can body, laid in that white rush,
But feel the strange heart beating where it lies?

A shudder in the loins engenders there
The broken wall, the burning roof and tower
And Agamemnon dead.
                                          Being so caught up,
So mastered by the brute blood of the air,
Did she put on his knowledge with his power
Before the indifferent beak could let her drop?

1923 [First published in *The Dial*, June 1924]

William Butler Yeats was born in Sandymount, of southern Irish Protestant gentry parentage, and grew up in Dublin, London and his mother's home county of Sligo (where he is buried at Drumcliff under Ben Bulben). Influenced at first by his reading of Shelley, Spenser and Pre-Raphaelite verse, he drew on Irish mythology, William Blake and mystical writings of various kinds in his early poetry. He became a central figure in the Irish literary revival as a poet, playwright and author of *The Celtic Twilight* (1893), and was involved in the management and staging of plays at the Abbey Theatre from 1904. He later become a senator of the Irish Free State (1922-28) and was awarded the Nobel Prize in 1923.

The biographical complications of Yeats's life and the complexities and contradictions of his work are such as to make to any summary such as this largely futile. With Yeats being Brendan Kennelly's primary influence (signalled in 1959 by the title he chose for his debut collection, *Cast a Cold Eye*), he should have written on Yeats here, but as with Kavanagh, this was a case of leaving till last some of the poets he felt closest to, only for the project to stall. We veered between choosing 'The Second Coming' and 'Leda and the Swan' as our Yeats poem for this anthology. As with Kavanagh, I've had to extract a poem commentary by him from another essay ('Poetry and Violence')[26] so that 'Leda and the Swan' could be included. But since 'The Second Coming' was the poem he'd wanted to write about in the end, I've included both poems. To provide a more apposite introduction offering the reader more context, this is preceded here by an excerpt from another of his essays ('Irish Poetry to Yeats').[27] I was tempted to include Brendan's poem 'Late Yeats'[28] – about Yeats's sexual problems – as an endpiece to his consideration of Yeats, having added his poem on Kavanagh elsewhere, but decided that its flippancy would be undermining.

BK ■ There was tremendous poetic energy in 19th-century Ireland. Yet there was something lacking: a centralising force, a unifying spirit. W.B. Yeats, himself an important part of 19th-century poetry, was such a spirit, with a vision for Ireland unequalled in her tradition, as well as the intelligence and energy to turn that vision into reality. Carrying his experience of the 19th century and its mythology in his heart and head, he stepped into 20th-century Ireland, a great poet with a great poet's ideals. Never did a country so badly need a poet. Never did a poet work so tirelessly for his country.

The Irish literary revival was largely the work of W.B. Yeats. It is not simply that Yeats went from the tinsel brilliance of conventional Pre-Raphaelite verse to a bare, sensual, symbolic poetry; but his development is parallel, almost identical with, his changing views of a changing Ireland. Three poems illustrate this. 'To Ireland in the Coming Times' is youthful and idealistic, and shows the young poet consciously trying to identify himself with the unsung makers of the Irish tradition. 'September 1913' is bitter and disillusioned: Yeats here is middle-aged and openly disgusted by the self-righteous materialism of Irish society. The Easter Rebellion and the Civil War followed; a new Ireland stumbled into existence and Yeats played his part in the uncertain, exciting creation of the young state. In 'The Statues' he applauds the heroism that made this birth possible and asserts Ireland's dignity in the face of the overwhelming 'filthy modern tide'. Yeats is Ireland's greatest poet, not least because he learned to confront the challenging complexities of Irish life. He recognised that Ireland is always capable of treachery and squalor, but he was also aware of its capacity for heroism and nobility. He witnessed and experienced 'the weasel's twist, the weasel's tooth'. Yet he exhorted later generations to be, and to continue to be, the 'indomitable Irishry'.[29]

BK ■ At the back of most of the poems I've discussed is some kind of response to the violence inherent in sexuality. The Church uses this violence to keep women down; one man uses it to establish his own mastery, another to renew both himself and his mate while his mate does the same. It would appear that poetry tells us that violence is inevitable and universal, that it has to do with vital and consequential change, that it appeals to the imagination of a person even as it threatens or even appalls that same person's daily life. Or to put it another way: there are certain forces which, simultaneously, attract the imagination and repel the reason. Yeats's last poem 'Under Ben Bulben' is a celebration of what violence can lead to.

> You that Mitchel's prayer have heard,
> 'Send war in our time, O Lord!'
> Know that when all words are said
> And a man is fighting mad,
> Something drops from eyes long blind,
> He completes his partial mind,
> For an instant stands at ease,
> Laughs aloud, his heart at peace.
> Even the wisest man grows tense
> With some sort of violence
> Before he can accomplish fate,
> Know his work or choose his mate...

The imagination instinctively realises that violence exists everywhere, and has its own purpose. It goes further: violence is a kind of motive-power, a sort of emotional fuel, a key to developed action, a source of creative thinking, a restless, stirring, challenging origin of art and civilisation.

Poetry, like the moth to the flame, is drawn towards violence. But poetry does not perish because of this attraction. In fact, poetry is animated, vitalised, refreshed by the contact. This is so, I think, because poetry is neither moral nor immoral. It is amoral, it exists beyond conventional morality. If poetry merely reflected conventional morality, it would exist only in Christmas bards and after-dinner speeches. But poetry creates its own new fierce, vigorous code of morality. It was Synge who said that 'before verse can be human again it must learn to be brutal'.[30] This is the real crux. If poetry is to be real, challenging, primitive and sophisticated at once, then it must observe and imitate that fundamental principle of life: in a million different ways, under the guise of politeness, concern, do-gooding, converting, enlightening, educating, loving – people do violence to each other. *Not* to perceive and explore this in poetry is to open the floodgates of sentimentality and sententious moralising. That is why I personally believe that poetry, far from being consolatory and uplifting like some Victorian pill to send you asleep, radiant with beautiful thoughts, poetry is dangerous, particularly if it is constantly and attentively read. Not all of it is like this; but a surprising amount of it is.

Let us look, for example, at Yeats's 'Leda and the Swan'. It is a poem about rape. The poem does not condemn rape; neither does it condone it; it *presents* it. And yet, if the poem could be said to teeter between condemning and condoning, I think that, after many readings, it could be argued that phrases such as 'feathered glory', 'loosening thighs', 'strange heart', 'white rush', and the sheer power of 'engenders there' – all these veer towards a dramatisation of the *energy* of the rapist, and not the plight of the victim. In the *present* act of violence, the future is born. Violence begets violence. Agamemnon is dead at the moment of the rape of Leda. Time and its fierce dramas are concentrated, focussed in that violent sexual act. We are appalled at the barbarism of the truth. The god, in the shape of a swan, rapes the girl. The poem, beautifully made, contains this violence within its elegant framework. The formal elegance makes the violence more savagely real, and forces the intellect to accommodate, in one mental feat, the coincidence of act and consequence. Morality, as we tend to understand it, has no place here. The present is furiously incensed, that the future may be unleashed.

Poetry tends to recognise and demonstrate what a conventional morality will tend to outlaw and condemn. The imagination when

245

it is probing, serves no system, obeys no law but its own longing for exciting truth. What we call 'violence' is only a part of that excitement; gentleness, love, pity and mercy also come under its defining and dramatising scrutiny. [...]

Poetry, by definition, is always breaking through boundaries and categories. To try to inhibit or limit that function is to do violence to the very nature of poetry, to make it the sweet, biddable, musical slave of our expectations. The poetry that deals with violence is more concerned with its *own* compulsions than with the expectations of others. It will not flatter or comfort or console; it will disturb, challenge, even threaten. Above all, it threatens our complacency. And, in a world that seems hell-bent on its own destruction, that threat to complacent unawareness is a valuable service.[31]

HART CRANE (1899–1932)

My Grandmother's Love Letters

There are no stars tonight
But those of memory.
Yet how much room for memory there is
In the loose girdle of soft rain.

There is even room enough
For the letters of my mother's mother,
Elizabeth,
That have been pressed so long
Into a corner of the roof
That they are brown and soft,
And liable to melt as snow.

Over the greatness of such space
Steps must be gentle.
It is all hung by an invisible white hair.
It trembles as birch limbs webbing the air.

And I ask myself:

'Are your fingers long enough to play
Old keys that are but echoes:
Is the silence strong enough
To carry back the music to its source
And back to you again
As though to her?'

Yet I would lead my grandmother by the hand
Through much of what she would not understand;
And so I stumble. And the rain continues on the roof
With such a sound of gently pitying laughter.

[1920]

Hart Crane was one of the most significant modernist poets of the 20th century. Robert Lowell called him 'the Shelley of my age' and 'the great poet of that generation'. The sensational aspects of his life have tended to obscure the greatness of his poetry. Born in 1899 in Garrettsville, Ohio, the son of a confectionery manufacturer, he survived an unhappy childhood in Cleveland presided over by warring parents who divorced when he was 17. For the next seven years he moved between Cleveland and New York, taking jobs as a labourer in a shipyard and in his father's factory, and as an advertising copywriter. He led a wild, precarious life during the 1920s in Brooklyn, Europe and the Caribbean: asserting his homosexuality, tormented by his fickle genius, depressed, sick, poor and usually drunk. In 1929 he spent several months in France, trying to finish his American epic, *The Bridge*, but his time there was beset with trouble: heavy drinking, escapades with sailors in Marseille, and a fight with police in Paris which earned him six days in prison.

Hart Crane's major work included *White Buildings* (1926) and *The Bridge* (1930), two landmarks in American literature, but neither book was well received at the time, which added to his depression and self-doubt. Inspired by Whitman and Melville, *The Bridge* is a metaphorical fusion of personal feeling with the myths and history of America, and an optimistic reply from the New World to Eliot's *Waste Land*: 'I take Eliot as a point of departure toward an almost complete reverse of direction,' he wrote. 'His pessimism is amply justified, in his case. But I would apply as much of his erudition and technique as I can absorb and assemble towards a more positive, or (if I must put it so in a skeptical age) ecstatic goal.' When Crane created his new visionary poetry, he found his own American symbols, man-made or untamed, in modern cities of concrete and steel, and in the luxuriant Florida Keys and Caribbean islands. We didn't think it would work to present an excerpt from *The Bridge*, choosing instead one of our favourite poems from *White Buildings*.

While in Mexico on a Guggenheim Fellowship in 1931-32, Crane fell in love with his friend Malcolm Cowley's wife Peggy, apparently trying to change his nature, but returning to New York on the SS *Orizaba* he was beaten up for making sexual advances towards a crew member. Just before noon on 27 April 1932, he walked the length of the ship to the stern, jumped overboard and was drowned. Apparently, his last words were 'Goodbye, everybody!'

D.H. LAWRENCE (1885–1930)

Snake

A snake came to my water-trough
On a hot, hot day, and I in pyjamas for the heat,
To drink there.

In the deep, strange-scented shade of the great dark carob tree
I came down the steps with my pitcher
And must wait, must stand and wait, for there he was at the trough
            before me.

He reached down from a fissure in the earth-wall in the gloom
And trailed his yellow-brown slackness soft-bellied down, over
                the edge of the stone trough
And rested his throat upon the stone bottom,
And where the water had dripped from the tap, in a small clearness,
He sipped with his straight mouth,
Softly drank through his straight gums, into his slack long body,
Silently.

Someone was before me at my water-trough,
And I, like a second-comer, waiting.

He lifted his head from his drinking, as cattle do,
And looked at me vaguely, as drinking cattle do,
And flickered his two-forked tongue from his lips, and mused
            a moment,
And stooped and drank a little more,
Being earth-brown, earth-golden from the burning bowels
            of the earth
On the day of Sicilian July, with Etna smoking.

The voice of my education said to me
He must be killed,

For in Sicily the black, black snakes are innocent, the gold
        are venomous.

And voices in me said, If you were a man
You would take a stick and break him now, and finish him off.

But must I confess how I liked him,
How glad I was he had come like a guest in quiet, to drink
        at my water-trough
And depart peaceful, pacified, and thankless,
Into the burning bowels of this earth?

Was it cowardice, that I dared not kill him?
Was it perversity, that I longed to talk to him?
Was it humility, to feel so honoured?
I felt so honoured.

And yet those voices:
If you were not afraid, you would kill him!

And truly I was afraid, I was most afraid,
But even so, honoured still more
That he should seek my hospitality
From out the dark door of the secret earth.

He drank enough
And lifted his head, dreamily, as one who has drunken,
And flickered his tongue like a forked night on the air, so black,
Seeming to lick his lips,
And looked around like a god, unseeing, into the air,
And slowly turned his head,
And slowly, very slowly, as if thrice adream,
Proceeded to draw his slow length curving round
And climb again the broken bank of my wall-face.

And as he put his head into that dreadful hole,
And as he slowly drew up, snake-easing his shoulders,
        and entered farther,
A sort of horror, a sort of protest against his withdrawing into

that horrid black hole,
Deliberately going into the blackness, and slowly drawing
      himself after,
Overcame me now his back was turned.

I looked round, I put down my pitcher,
I picked up a clumsy log
And threw it at the water-trough with a clatter.

I think it did not hit him,
But suddenly that part of him that was left behind convulsed
      in an undignified haste,
Writhed like lightning, and was gone
Into the black hole, the earth-lipped fissure in the wall-front,
At which, in the intense still noon, I stared with fascination.

And immediately I regretted it.
I thought how paltry, how vulgar, what a mean act!
I despised myself and the voices of my accursed human education.

And I thought of the albatross,
And I wished he would come back, my snake.

For he seemed to me again like a king,
Like a king in exile, uncrowned in the underworld,
Now due to be crowned again.

And so, I missed my chance with one of the lords
Of life.
And I have something to expiate:
A pettiness.

Taormina, Sicily, July 1920 (?) [Published in *Birds, Beasts and Flowers*, 1923]

■ Like Hardy, whose work he studied closely, **David Herbert Lawrence** is a novelist-poet whose poetry may be his finest achievement. Lawrence was born in Eastwood, Nottinghamshire, the fourth son of a coalminer and a former teacher. His parents' conflicting class-values shaped his literary personality. Lawrence's most celebrated novel, *Sons and Lovers*, and his first book of poems, *Love Poems and Others*, were both published in 1913. In 1911, partly owing to the threat of TB (from which he was to die), Lawrence ceased to be a teacher. With his wife Frieda, he began to lead a nomadic life: always seeking (in Australia, New Mexico and elsewhere) a utopian alternative to the restrictions and repressions of England.

Lawrence wrote many kinds of poem, including poems (sometimes in dialect) that recreate the Nottinghamshire of his childhood. [...] *Birds, Beasts and Flowers* (1923) is usually considered his best book. The natural world purges the didacticism and sexual theorising that can unbalance Lawrence's writings. There is, indeed, an anthropomorphic element in his animal poems. Yet each poem's rhythm persuasively mimics a creature's unique qualities, its otherness and place in the cosmos, while the tone of human address also seems fitted to the occasion. Lawrence's way of building a poem on subtly paced repetitions was influenced by the Bible and by Walt Whitman. He criticised both the 'static perfection' of traditional stanzas, and 'free-versifiers' (like Eliot) who merely 'break the lovely form of material verse'. He saw his own verse as 'direct utterance from the instant, whole man'. The living movement of Lawrence's poetry best conveys his gospel of sensory 'life': a gospel that has both rejected and absorbed the nonconformist religion in which he was reared. W.H. Auden, for whom Lawrence was a 'pilgrim' rather than a 'citizen', calls his messianic approach to verse and life 'very protestant indeed'. 'Bavarian Gentians' and 'The Ship of Death' (inspired by Etruscan culture and tombs) are great visionary poems. [...]

[Edna Longley, *The Bloodaxe Book of 20th Century Poetry*, 2000]

D.H. Lawrence was always a seminal poet and novelist for Brendan, which makes the lack of a commentary by him on Lawrence's poem especially regrettable. This poem, 'Snake' – which he called 'a beautiful harrowing drama' – was his immediate first choice in our deliberations over which Lawrence poem to pick.

EDNA ST VINCENT MILLAY (1892–1950)

'What lips my lips have kissed…'

What lips my lips have kissed, and where, and why,
I have forgotten, and what arms have lain
Under my head till morning; but the rain
Is full of ghosts tonight, that tap and sigh
Upon the glass and listen for reply,
And in my heart there stirs a quiet pain
For unremembered lads that not again
Will turn to me at midnight with a cry.

Thus in the winter stands the lonely tree,
Nor knows what birds have vanished one by one,
Yet knows its boughs more silent than before:
I cannot say what loves have come and gone,
I only know that summer sang in me
A little while, that in me sings no more.

[First published in *Vanity Fair*, November 1920]

Edna St Vincent Millay was born in Rockland, Maine, and grew up in Camden, Maine, with her divorced mother. Her middle name came from St Vincent's Hospital in New York which had saved her uncle's life, and she insisted on being called Vincent during her school years. She wrote poems from an early age, gaining immediate renown when her poem 'Renascence' appeared in *The Lyric Year* in 1912. She published her first collection, *Renascence and Other Poems*, after graduating from Vassar College, in 1917, and was soon part of the bohemian community of Greenwich Village, where she became involved as a social, political and anti-war activist known for her unconventional life style including relationships with men and women, writing popular fiction under the pseudonym Nancy Boyd to support herself. In 1920 she published *A Few Figs from Thistles* including 'The First Fig', a generation-defining poem she later came to hate for its lines: 'My candle burns at both ends; / It will not last the night; / But ah, my foes and oh my friends—/ It gives a lovely light!'

In 1923 she became only the third woman to win a Pulitzer Prize for Poetry, for her fourth collection, *The Ballad of the Harp-Weaver* (1922), which included 'What lips my lips have kissed'. That year she married Eugen Jan Boissevain, a Dutch businessman, and in 1925 they moved into Steepletop, the farmhouse in the Berkshire foot-hills near Austerlitz in New York State, where they lived for the rest of their lives. Now called the Edna St Vincent Millay House, the Millay Colony was founded next door, after her death, by her sister Norma. Her later collections include *Fatal Interview* (1931), a sequence of 52 sonnets recounting her affair with a much younger man, George Dillon, with whom she translated Baudelaire's *Les Fleurs du Mal* (1936). She suffered from ill health in her later years after a car accident in 1936 left her with a severely damaged spine, requiring many operations and daily morphine injections to ease the constant pain. She died at home, aged 58, the year after Eugen, from a heart attack and a fall downstairs.

BK ■ Remembering and forgetting figure in many poems in this book. Edna St Vincent Millay has forgotten nights of love, 'but the rain / Is full of ghosts tonight' and the 'quiet pain' in her heart is for 'unremembered lads' she will not love again. These lads are ghosts tapping at her mind for attention. Remembering what and who have been forgotten brings a moment of knowledge, of definitive insight into lost loves. She speaks of 'the lonely tree' that doesn't 'know' what birds have vanished, yet 'knows' that 'its boughs are more silent than before'. Her moment of knowledge springs from this.

> I only know that summer sang in me
> A little while, that in me sings no more.

Many poems deal with this moment of truth achieved through the exercise of memory and the realisation of what it means to forget. The fluent, gentle nostalgia of 'What lips my lips have kissed' serves to underline the reality of that achieved moment of truth. Memory can be soft and self-forgiving, a warm deceiver. It can also be severe and self-accusing, a pitiless revealer. There is more of the latter than the former in this poem, which is vulnerable and courageous.

LANGSTON HUGHES (1902–1967)

The Negro Speaks of Rivers

I've known rivers:
I've known rivers ancient as the world and older than the flow of
  human blood in human veins.

My soul has grown deep like the rivers.

I bathed in the Euphrates when dawns were young.
I built my hut near the Congo and it lulled me to sleep.
I looked upon the Nile and raised the pyramids above it.
I heard the singing of the Mississippi when Abe Lincoln went
  down to New Orleans, and I've seen its muddy bosom turn all
  golden in the sunset.

I've known rivers:
Ancient, dusky rivers.

My soul has grown deep like the rivers.

[First published in *The Crisis*, June 1921]

■ **Langston Hughes** was born in 1902 in Joplin, Missouri, and
was a central figure in the Harlem Renaissance of the 20s. In 1921,
'The Negro Speaks of Rivers' became his first poem to be published
nationwide, and his debut collection, *The Weary Blues* followed in
1926. He was the first African-American to make a living from
writing, and his pioneering efforts brought black literature and
music to national attention, undoubtedly opening the way for a
subsequent generation of black writers. The syncopated rhythms
of his 'jazz poetry' were absorbed even further afield: not only by
the Beats and the East and West Coast scenes of the 50s, but in
Britain, in the work of Christopher Logue, Michael Horovitz, and

the 'Underground' poets Trocchi, Mitchell and others. For some, Hughes's writing was not militant enough (he sought 'change through the force of his art'), but his hymns to civil rights remain some of the most moving and memorable ever written, including his Whitmanesque 'I, too, sing America'. He founded black theatre groups in Harlem, Chicago and Los Angeles, and prolifically published poetry, short stories and cultural history, as well as two autobiographies and a *Selected Poems* (1959).

[W.N. Herbert & Matthew Hollis, *Strong Words: modern poets on modern poetry*, 2000]

Langston Hughes described how he came to write 'The Negro Speaks of Rivers' in *The Big Sea* (1940), the first volume of his autobiography:

> Now it was just sunset, and we crossed the Mississippi, slowly, over a long bridge. I looked out the window of the Pullman at the great muddy river flowing down toward the heart of the South, and I began to think what that river, the old Mississippi, had meant to Negroes in the past – how to be sold down the river was the worst fate that could overtake a slave in times of bondage.... Then I began to think about other rivers in our past – the Congo, and the Niger, and the Nile in Africa – and the thought came to me: 'I've known rivers,' and I put it down on the back of an envelope I had in my pocket, and within the space of ten or fifteen minutes, as the train gathered speed in the dusk, I had written this poem, which I called 'The Negro Speaks of Rivers'. (p.55)

BK ■ Langston Hughes, an African American poet, captures the turbulent flow of his people's history as he meditates on 'ancient' rivers such as the Euphrates, the Congo, the Nile and Mississippi. This charged, rivery poem injects into the poet's being the depth and energy of the rivers themselves. That repeated line, 'My soul has grown deep like the rivers', suggests the atrocities and heroisms, despairs and hopes of history that pour into, appal and educate the individual soul. Langston Hughes's rivers, like William Blake's chartered Thames and James Joyce's singing Liffey, help to deepen and strengthen him as a human being.

MARIANNE MOORE (1887–1972)

A Grave

Man looking into the sea,
taking the view from those who have as much right to it as you have to it
                                                              yourself,
it is human nature to stand in the middle of a thing,
but you cannot stand in the middle of this;
the sea has nothing to give but a well excavated grave.
The firs stand in a procession, each with an emerald turkey-foot at the top,
reserved in their contours, saying nothing;
repression, however, is not the most obvious characteristic of the sea;
the sea is a collector, quick to return a rapacious look.
There are others besides you who have worn that look—
whose expression is no longer a protest; the fish no longer investigate them
for their bones have not lasted:
men lower nets, unconscious of the fact that they are desecrating a grave,
and row quickly away—the blades of the oars
moving together like the feet of water-spiders as if there were no such
                                                              thing as death.
The wrinkles progress among themselves in a phalanx—beautiful under
                                                              networks of foam,
and fade breathlessly while the sea rustles in and out of the seaweed;
the birds swim through the air at top speed, emitting cat-calls as
                                                              heretofore—
the tortoise-shell scourges about the feet of the cliffs, in motion beneath
                                                              them;
and the ocean, under the pulsation of lighthouses and noise of bellbuoys,
advances as usual, looking as if it were not that ocean in which dropped
                                                              things are bound to sink—
in which if they turn and twist, it is neither with volition nor consciousness.

[First published in *The Dial*, July 1921]

■ **Marianne Moore** was born near St Louis, Missouri, and in 1896 moved to Pennsylvania, where her mother was a teacher. Her father, whom she never met, spent his life after her birth in psychiatric care. Moore studied Biology and Histology at Bryn Mawr College, graduating in 1909, and after a brief spell in New Jersey moved to New York City with her mother in 1918, where she worked as a librarian. Her first collection, *Poems*, published in 1921, was followed by *Observations* (1924). She joined *The Dial* in 1925, and was its final editor, from 1926 to 1929, publishing Eliot, Pound, Hart Crane and Valéry. [...]

Moore is a key figure within Modernism and of particular importance to the women who write after her. Sylvia Plath, for example, when trying to place herself within a female poetic lineage in her journals, refers to Moore, along with Edith Sitwell, as a 'poetic fairy godmother'. Moore had a long friendship with Elizabeth Bishop, whom she met in 1934. In her memoir of Moore, 'Efforts of Affection', Bishop wonders whether 'the feminist critics' knew that Moore had 'paraded with the suffragettes, led by Inez Milholland on her white horse, down Fifth Avenue? Once, Marianne told me, she "climbed a lamppost" in a demonstration for votes for women... in long skirt and petticoats and a large hat.'[32]

[Deryn Rees-Jones, *Modern Women Poets*, Bloodaxe Books, 2005]

Marianne Moore's poem 'A Grave' has also been published with the title 'A Graveyard'. It is one of several early poems to draw on sea imagery to express her sense of the relation between the real and the imagined. The sea and sea life are seen as ungraspable, ever changing, as in 'A Jelly-Fish' (1909) in which she describes the creature as 'Visible, invisible,/ A fluctuating charm.[...] It floats away/ From you.' Our first list included other Moore poems we both loved ('The Pangolin', 'New York', 'England', 'The Mind Is an Enchanting Thing' and 'What Are Years'), but then I suggested 'A Grave', which I remembered copying into a notebook I carried with me in my 20s, telling Brendan how I used to think about this poem on visits to the Northumberland coast while staring at the sea. Brendan was looking out the window at the sea as we were talking on the phone and immediately started picking up echoes between lines in the poem and what he was seeing.

WALLACE STEVENS   (1879–1955)

The Snow Man

One must have a mind of winter
To regard the frost and the boughs
Of the pine-trees crusted with snow;

And have been cold a long time
To behold the junipers shagged with ice,
The spruces rough in the distant glitter

Of the January sun; and not to think
Of any misery in the sound of the wind,
In the sound of a few leaves,

Which is the sound of the land
Full of the same wind
That is blowing in the same bare place

For the listener, who listens in the snow,
And, nothing himself, beholds
Nothing that is not there and the nothing that is.

[First published in *Poetry*, October 1921]

Wallace Stevens was born in Reading, Pennsylvania, and educated at Harvard and New York Law School, working for most of his life as an executive for an insurance company in Hartford, Connecticut. 'The Snow Man' appeared in his 1923 collection *Harmonium*. Influenced by his reading of – and discussions with – his friend the philosopher, George Santayana, the poem embodies Stevens's 'perspectivism': the principle that perception and knowledge of anything depend on the interpretive perspectives of those observing it. Writing of this poem, Robert Pack (1958) observes that 'Stevens dramatises the action of a mind as it becomes one with the scene it perceives, and at that instant, the mind having ceased to bring something of itself to the scene, the scene then ceases to exist fully.'[33] In what could almost be a gloss on 'The Snow Man', Stevens considers the significance of art in *The Necessary Angel* (1951): 'The world about us would be desolate except for the world within us.'[34]

■ Wallace Stevens exploited a dichotomy between his exterior life (comfortably middle-class American) and the interior world of the poet (richly symbolic and metaphysical) to produce a body of work that is almost a subversion of his environment. His daily routines as vice-president of an insurance company in Connecticut appeared to involve a self-abnegation to bourgeois values. But in the astonishing baroque vocabulary of *Harmonium* (1923) and the more symbolically-charged work of his middle period, *The Man with the Blue Guitar* (1937), and above all in the late poems of *Transport to Summer* (1947), in particular, 'Notes Toward a Supreme Fiction', he reveals himself as a self-appointed priest of his own cult of the imagination. Capable of an extraordinarily sensual response to his transcendental subject-matter, his mastery of tone has proven significant to another conflater of the mundane with the transformative powers of language, John Ashbery.

The Necessary Angel (1951), his collection of essays, is in many ways as striking as his poetry. Stevens aligns himself with a Shelleyan vision of the poet as the creator of the imaginative models by which we, knowingly or not, live our lives. In a sense, he posits poetry as the supreme ideology.

[W.N. Herbert & Matthew Hollis, *Strong Words: modern poets on modern poetry*, 2000]

ELINOR WYLIE (1885–1928)

Full Moon

My bands of silk and miniver
Momently grew heavier;
The black gauze was beggarly thin;
The ermine muffled mouth and chin;
I could not suck the moonlight in.

Harlequin in lozenges
Of love and hate, I walked in these
Striped and ragged rigmaroles;
Along the pavement my footsoles
Trod warily on living coals.

Shouldering the thoughts I loathed,
In their corrupt disguises clothed,
Mortality I could not tear
From my ribs, to leave them bare
Ivory in silver air.

There I walked, and there I raged;
The spiritual savage caged
Within my skeleton, raged afresh
To feel, behind a carnal mesh,
The clean bones crying in the flesh.

[*Black Armour*, 1923]

Elinor Wylie was an American poet and novelist whose sensuous, formally traditional poetry, lyrically close to English metaphysical poets, had a similar appeal to the work of Edna St Vincent Millay, but whose readership was fed by her notoriety as a society figure known for many affairs and marriages in 1920s New York. She died from a stroke at 43. Brendan called this 'A burning poem, the last verse all fiery rage […] a beautiful, explosive, barbaric poem.'

E.E. CUMMINGS (1894–1962)

'next to of course god america i'

'next to of course god america i
love you land of the pilgrims' and so forth oh
say can you see by the dawn's early my
country 'tis of centuries come and go
and are no more what of it we should worry
in every language even deafanddumb
thy sons acclaim your glorious name by gorry
by jingo by gee by gosh by gum
why talk of beauty what could be more beaut-
iful than these heroic happy dead
who rushed like lions to the roaring slaughter
they did not stop to think they died instead
then shall the voice of liberty be mute?'

He spoke. And drank rapidly a glass of water

1926 [1926]

Edward Estlin Cummings was born in Cambridge, Massachusetts, the son of a Unitarian minister. Like his parents, his religious beliefs were influenced by the New England Transcendentalists. He grew up knowing many family friends from that cultural and intellectual milieu, including the philosopher William James. After graduating from Harvard, he spent several months in the US Army's ambulance corps in France, much of that time detained in a French military internment camp under suspicion of espionage. His experimental memoir-novel, *The Enormous Room* (1922), draws on that experience, showing his distrust of both officialdom and convention. This sonnet 'next to of course god america i' was published in his fourth collection, *is 5* (1926), with other unpatriotic anti-war poems, with an introduction in which he argued that poetry should be viewed not as a 'product' but a 'process'.

It was his publishers, not Cummings himself, who began printing his name all in lower case, playing upon the subversion of typographical convention in his poetry, and this came to be how his name was printed in anthologies, but in recent years his estate has insisted that publishers print his name with capital letters, as we have done here.

Cummings was a prolific as well as a popular poet, the author of 12 volumes of highly distinctive, often eccentric poetry. According to Randall Jarrell, 'No one else has ever made avant-garde, experimental poems so attractive to the general and the special reader.' Readers familiar with Brendan Kennelly's satirical epics, *The Book of Judas* and *Poetry My Arse,* are unlikely to be surprised by the inclusion of a Cummings poem in this anthology.

BK ■ E.E. Cummings is a daring experimenter in poetry and much of his appeal comes from his sophisticated audacity in playing with language and form. Introducing his *Collected Poems* (1938) he wrote: 'The poems to come are for you and me and are not for mostpeople.' He is convinced that 'Life, for mostpeople, simply isn't.' One senses in these words the spirit of the ludic satirist at work (or at play) in 'next to of course god america i'. The voice in the poem seems like that of a politician making a speech; and Cummings's definition of a politician is well known: 'an arse upon / which everything has sat except a man'.

Like much good satire, this poem is both funny and acerbic, the almost breathless rhetoric of insincerity making the poor man gulp a glass of water to clear his throat and even, one suspects, his conscience.

It is sometimes said that Cummings is not a 'profound' poet. Maybe not. But he is spirited, lively, fresh, experimental. He returns time and again, chuckling, into one's head. He might even draw a smile from the heavy bear himself.

ARCHIBALD MacLEISH (1892–1982)

Ars Poetica

A poem should be palpable and mute
As a globed fruit,

Dumb
As old medallions to the thumb,

Silent as the sleeve-worn stone
Of casement ledges where the moss has grown –

A poem should be wordless
As the flight of birds.

*

A poem should be motionless in time
As the moon climbs,

Leaving, as the moon releases
Twig by twig the night-entangled trees,

Leaving, as the moon behind the winter leaves,
Memory by memory the mind –

A poem should be motionless in time
As the moon climbs.

*

A poem should be equal to:
Not true.

For all the history of grief
An empty doorway and a maple leaf.

For love
The leaning grasses and two lights above the sea –

A poem should not mean
But be.

[1926]

Archibald MacLeish was born in Glencoe, Illinois. His father
was Scottish, the son of a poor shopkeeper, who'd fled Glasgow
for London before heading for Chicago at the age of 18, while his
mother was a Hillard, a descendant of Mayflower pilgrims.

MacLeish studied at Yale from 1911 to 1915, served in France,
and completed his education after the war at Harvard Law School,
intending to become a lawyer. His most significant poetry was
written after he gave up the law for the muse, moving with his
wife and two children in 1923 to a flat on the Boulevard St Michel
in Paris. His collection *Streets of the Moon* (1926) includes the
poems he wrote there. His less effective, more public writing –
including long poems, plays, essays and speeches – followed his
return from France, in 1928, much of it addressed to the concerns
of his time. Writing in *Poetry* in 1931, Harriet Monroe praised
'the ability of this poet to interpret his age: he has the thinking
mind, the creative imagination, the artistic equipment of beautiful
words and rhythms'.

He held various public offices, including Librarian of Congress,
from 1939 to 1944, and was Boylston Professorship of Rhetoric and
Oratory at Harvard from 1949 to 1962, an endowed chair later
held by Seamus Heaney. A highly respected man of letters and
thinker in the post-war years, MacLeish never gained much of a
readership for his poetry outside the US, apart from for anthology
perennials such as 'You, Andrew Marvell' from his 1930 collection,
New Found Land, and 'Ars Poetica' from *Streets of the Moon*.

BK ■ There are almost as many definitions of poetry as there are
poets. Because poets constantly explore language, rhythm, images,
ways of writing, they tend at times to be somewhat authoritarian
in their descriptions or definitions of what poetry is or should be.

265

Indeed, that phrase 'should be' occurs five times in 'Ars Poetica'; it is, in fact, the actual conclusion of the poem.

> A poem should not mean
> But be.

could be abbreviated to, simply,

> A poem should be.

That is what MacLeish means. But then we read his conclusion again; it says 'A poem should not mean'. Meaning is out. But can there be a poem without 'meaning'? And what is 'meaning'? What is the meaning of 'meaning'? Poetry leads into philosophy. It leads into a lot of physical and metaphysical areas.

For MacLeish, a poem should be 'palpable', 'mute', 'Dumb', 'Silent', 'wordless', 'motionless in time'; it should be 'equal to: not true'.

MacLeish uses words to tell us a poem should be 'wordless'; and it is arguable that, in spelling out his own honest concept of what a poem 'should be', he is conveying his own concept of meaning. He is aggressively didactic. And yet that authoritarian stance is made gentle and acceptable by his precise, vivid, sensuous images. Phrases such as 'globed fruit', 'old medallions', 'the sleeve-worn stone / Of casement ledges where the moss has grown', 'flight of birds', 'the night-entangled trees', 'An empty doorway and a maple leaf', 'The leaning grasses and two lights above the sea' – such phrases offset the forceful didacticism of his tone.

They even seem to collaborate with it, to drive home his beliefs about the very nature of a poem's being, its own life, its life in the reader's mind. 'Ars Poetica' is complex, contradictory and challenging, a densely layered poem to explore for hours on end, either by oneself or with interested friends. Its lyrical didacticism tends to open up lively discussion about the nature of poetry.

T.S. ELIOT (1888–1965)

Journey of the Magi

'A cold coming we had of it,
just the worst time of the year
For a journey, and such a long journey:
The ways deep and the weather sharp,
The very dead of winter.'
And the camels galled, sore-footed, refractory,
Lying down in the melting snow.
There were times we regretted
The summer palaces on slopes, the terraces,
And the silken girls bringing sherbet.
Then the camel men cursing and grumbling
And running away, and wanting their liquor and women,
And the night-fires going out, and the lack of shelters,
And the cities hostile and the towns unfriendly
And the villages dirty and charging high prices:
A hard time we had of it.
At the end we preferred to travel all night,
Sleeping in snatches,
With the voices singing in our ears, saying
That this was all folly.

Then at dawn we came down to a temperate valley,
Wet, below the snow line, smelling of vegetation,
With a running stream and a water-mill beating the darkness,
And three trees on the low sky.
And an old white horse galloped away in the meadow.
Then we came to a tavern with vine-leaves over the lintel,
Six hands at an open door dicing for pieces of silver,
And feet kicking the empty wine-skins.
But there was no information, and so we continued
And arrived at evening, not a moment too soon
Finding the place; it was (you may say) satisfactory.

All this was a long time ago, I remember,
And I would do it again, but set down
This set down
This: were we led all that way for
Birth or Death? There was a Birth, certainly,
We had evidence and no doubt. I had seen birth and death,
But had thought they were different; this Birth was
Hard and bitter agony for us, like Death, our death.
We returned to our places, these Kingdoms,
But no longer at ease here, in the old dispensation,
With an alien people clutching their gods.
I should be glad of another death.

1927 [1927]

■ **Thomas Stearns Eliot** wrote the most famous poem of the
20th century, *The Waste Land* (1922). The poem has contexts in his
American background as well as its London foreground. Eliot grew
up in St Louis, Missouri, but spent long holidays on the east coast.
His grandfather, a zealous Unitarian minister from Boston, was a
founder of Washington University, St Louis. Religion and education
became motifs in Eliot's criticism, as did an ideal of unified trad-
ition. He measured this ideal, at once literary and cultural, against
the difficulty of attaining it under modern conditions. Disliking
the heterogeneity of American culture, he mythologised what he
called 'the mind of Europe'. In 1906 Eliot went to Harvard, and
trained as an academic philosopher. But he was converted to poetry
by Arthur Symons's *The Symbolist Movement in Literature* (1899),
earlier an influence on Yeats. Eliot's moody urban impressions are
indebted to Symons's poetry, as well as more directly to French
symbolists such as Jules Laforgue. From 1914, Eliot lived in Eng-
land. He tried, but failed, to join the US Navy after America
entered the war. Rescued from a job in Lloyds Bank, Eliot founded
and edited *The Criterion* (1922-39), and from 1925 had a powerful
role with the publishers Faber and Faber. He was awarded the
Nobel Prize in 1948. [...]
   The Waste Land has been called a 'pre-conversion' poem. Its

underlying quest for spiritual meaning can be detected in the 'inexplicable' symbol of 'Magnus Martyr'. In 1928 Eliot termed himself 'classical in literature, royalist in politics, and Anglo-Catholic in religion'. His sequence *Four Quartets* (1943) mystically blends an Anglican version of Englishness with the 'way' to God. Some readers follow George Orwell in preferring Eliot's earlier poetry of 'glowing despair' to his later poetry of 'melancholy faith'.

[Edna Longley, *The Bloodaxe Book of 20th Century Poetry*, 2000]

'The Journey of the Magi' is a dramatic monologue – influenced by Eliot's reading of Robert Browning – and was one of the first poems he wrote following his conversion to Anglo-Catholicism, in 1926. Published in August 1927 by Faber & Gwyer (later Faber & Faber) in a pamphlet illustrated by E. McKnight Kauffer, it was one of five poems he contributed to Faber's *Ariel* series. These were later included in his collected editions as the *Ariel poems* (1927-1931). It was followed in 1930 by his 'conversion poem', *Ash Wednesday*, a long poem about his struggle to find faith in the form of a religious meditation unlike any of his earlier work.

The speaker in 'The Journey of the Magi' is one of the three Magi or wise men who followed the Star of Bethlehem on a long journey in search of a revelation which turned out to be the infant Christ born in a stable according to the biblical accounts. He gives voice to Eliot's feelings of alienation and disillusionment at a changed world in which he no longer feels he belongs, echoing Matthew Arnold's sentiments in 'Dover Beach' [176]. The famous first five lines are in quotes because they are adapted from a passage in the 'Nativity Sermon' of Lancelot Andrewes preached before James I on Christmas Day in 1622: 'A cold coming they had of it at this time of the year, just the worst time of the year to take a journey, and specially a long journey. The ways deep, the weather sharp, the days short, the sun farthest off, *in solsitio brumali*, the very dead of winter.' In later years the Magus sees Christ's birth as bringing about the death of the old order. Eliot uses symbols to suggest and compress, such as 'three trees against a low sky', an image projecting time forward to the crucifixion.

PATRICK KAVANAGH (1905–1967)

Shancoduff

My black hills have never seen the sun rising,
Eternally they look north towards Armagh.
Lot's wife would not be salt if she had been
Incurious as my black hills that are happy
When dawn whitens Glassdrummond chapel.

My hills hoard the bright shillings of March
While the sun searches in every pocket.
They are my Alps and I have climbed the Matterhorn
With a sheaf of hay for three perishing calves
In the field under the Big Forth of Rocksavage.

The sleety winds fondle the rushy beards of Shancoduff
While the cattle-drovers sheltering in the Featherna Bush
Look up and say: 'Who owns them hungry hills
That the water-hen and snipe must have forsaken?
A poet? Then by heavens he must be poor.'
I hear and is my heart not badly shaken?

1934 [1938]

Epic

I have lived in important places, times
When great events were decided: who owned
That half a rood of rock, a no-man's land
Surrounded by our pitchfork-armed claims.
I heard the Duffys shouting 'Damn your soul'
And old McCabe stripped to the waist, seen

270

Step the plot defying blue cast-steel –
'Here is the march along these iron stones'.
That was the year of the Munich bother. Which
Was most important? I inclined
To lose my faith in Ballyrush and Gortin
Till Homer's ghost came whispering to my mind
He said: I made the *Iliad* from such
A local row. Gods make their own importance.

[1951]

Born in 1904 at Inniskeen, in Co. Monaghan, **Patrick Kavanagh**
left school at 13 to work on the family farm. The relentless toil of
scraping a living in rural Ireland which he railed against in his long
poem *The Great Hunger* (1942) was one he knew in his bones:

> Clay is the word and clay is the flesh
> Where the potato-gatherers like mechanised scarecrows move
> Along the side-fall of the hill – Maguire and his men.
> If we watch them for an hour is there anything we can prove
> Of life as it is broken-backed over the Book
> Of Death? [...]
>
> Poor Paddy Maguire, a fourteen-hour day
> He worked for years. It was he that lit the fire
> And boiled the kettle and gave the cows their hay.

Kavanagh wasn't going to be Paddy Maguire. He wanted to be a
poet. In 1939, after 20 years on the farm, he left for Dublin to try
to make his way as a poet on the strength of his first collection,
Ploughman and Other Poems (1936). But that book and his auto-
biographical novel, *The Green Fool* (1938), saw him labelled as a
peasant poet, just as John Clare had been in England. Like Clare,
he was soon disillusioned by the literary world, meeting Dublin
writers who romanticised rural Ireland ('the dregs of the old Literary
Revival'), and earning a pittance as a hack reviewer and journalist.
The Monaghan of memory and imagination became his inner refuge;
he was 'never in any doubt about the social and artistic validity of
his parish' ('The Parish and the Universe'). He mellowed with his
work in later decades, publishing his *Collected Poems* in 1964, three
years before his death from a heart attack.

271

Kavanagh's genius was mostly unrecognised in his lifetime, but he is now regarded as one of Ireland's greatest poets, popular as well as critically acclaimed. His work and example have influenced many later poets, including Brendan Kennelly, Seamus Heaney and Paul Muldoon, all of whom have shared his belief in the capacity of the local, or parochial, to reveal the universal, while Paul Durcan has been inspired by his social anger and 'spiritual courage'.

His gruff abrasive manner and alcoholism can't have helped, as Brendan recalled in an interview with Theo Dorgan on RTÉ's *Imprint Later,* in 1999: 'I loved him. I loved his poetry. I met him a few times, and he was very disgruntled, hard to talk to, and yet totally genuine. I'm very attracted by the kind of person who can write so beautifully and yet be inarticulate and dismissive. He'd throw you away from him if you were trying to talk to him. I tried to talk to him a few times in pubs and then finally one day he did turn to me, and he talked about football.'

In his anthology, *Between Innocence and Peace* (1993), Brendan wrote of Kavanagh's work: 'It's as fresh today as when I stumbled across it 40 or more years ago. Time and again Kavanagh wrote out of humility and achieved sublimity.' In our discussions about which poem to include in *The Heavy Bear*, he began by advocating 'Spring Day' as a necessary 'direct address to poets', but we ended up agreeing on 'Epic'. Brendan especially wanted to write on Kavanagh for this anthology, but hadn't produced his piece when our project stalled. To honour our choice and to offer more of his insights into a single Kavanagh poem, I've included two poems here, 'Epic' and another of our candidates, the earlier 'Shancoduff', paired with slightly edited extracts from two of Brendan's essays from *Journey into Joy: Selected Prose* (1994), which include some discussion of 'Shancoduff' as well as being relevant to 'Epic'. I've also added Brendan's poem about Kavanagh, 'A Man I Knew',[35] which he loved to recite when asked about him.

BK ■ Yeats's Cuala Press published Patrick Kavanagh's long poem, *The Great Hunger*, in 1942. Kavanagh went on to denounce Yeats as being 'protected by ritual' in his poem, 'An Insult'; he also criticised him severely in several essays. This was Kavanagh's way of distancing himself from Yeats. He went on to explain and express his own vision, a vision which in the end has, ironically, some remarkable similarities to Yeats's. Kavanagh called it 'comedy' in his essay 'Signposts'; Yeats called it 'tragic joy' in 'The Gyres'. Kavanagh's castigating references to Yeats and others helped him to create for himself that space, that freedom from other poets' work (even as they are deeply aware of it) that most poets need. Poets' vicious denunciations of the work of others can be forms of self-liberation.

Yeats's tendency towards rhetorical pomposity may be due to his compulsion to mythologise and dramatise everyone, including himself. His aesthetic compels him to be always at the centre of the poem's action, determined not to fall apart. Beckett and Kavanagh, in their different ways, reject the inflated feelings consequent on dramatic mythologising, Kavanagh especially denouncing Yeats's 'myth of Ireland as a spiritual entity' (in 'From Monaghan to Grand Canal') and proceeding in a defiant and convincing manner to write about the most ordinary situations, events, people: the life of a street, the 'undying difference in the corner of a field' ('Why Sorrow'), cubicles and wash-basins in a chest hospital, the canal in Dublin, bogs and small 'incurious' hills in Monaghan ('Shancoduff'), pubs, coffee-shops, mundane aspects of life as he saw it about him. All this, however, was coloured by an intense inner life, a religious conviction that 'God is in the bits and pieces of Everyday', as he wrote in *The Great Hunger*. The result is a delightful body of poetry in which the mundane is transfigured by the mystical, and the mystical is earthed in the mundane. [...] [36]

The poems in Kavanagh's early work, *Ploughman and Other Poems*, are beautifully simple. Yet they contain certain elements which endure into his later work, though in a transfigured way. In the note to his *Collected Poems*, Kavanagh tells us that, for him, poetry is 'a mystical thing, and a dangerous thing'. It is mystical because it is concerned with man's dialogue with God, the foundation-stone of all Kavanagh's work, the source of his humour and sanity.

In the best of his early poems Kavanagh looks into himself, desiring this detachment, the key to not-caring about the 'important'. He is trying, in the poetic sense, to keep his soul pure. He looks out from himself at the natural beauty of Monaghan and sees the black hills that do not care, that are 'incurious'. A certain kind of curiosity not only killed the cat and turned Lot's wife into salt – it could also mar the detachment of the poet, and meddle with the happiness that comes from observation and expression:

My black hills have never seen the sun rising,
Eternally they look north towards Armagh
Lot's wife would not be salt if she had been
Incurious as my black hills that are happy
When dawn whitens Glassdrummond chapel.

Kavanagh said once that a poet's journey is the way 'from simplicity
back to simplicity'. The simplicity of Kavanagh's 'Shancoduff' is
the simplicity of Blake's 'London', the simplicity that stems from
a totally coherent and lucid vision. In an essay called 'Pietism and
Poetry', Kavanagh says that 'The odd thing about the best modern
poets is their utter simplicity'. I would further add that only the
man who sees completely can be completely simple. Kavanagh
knew this in his heart, and it can be said of him that he is the
only great modern poet who never wrote an obscure poem. He
recognised that, in most cases, obscurity is simply a failure of the
poet's imagination, the sanctuary of the inadequate. (In a couple
of cases, such as Wallace Stevens and some of Yeats, it is a measure
of the depth of their enquiry.)

This simplicity, present from the beginning in Kavanagh's
work, is characteristic of his achieved comic vision. He saw that
his simplicity was a gift from the gay, imaginative God; that it
was the most difficult thing in the world to achieve; and that if
sophistication has any meaning at all (and no word in the English
language is more abused or misunderstood) it means that the poet
has the courage to be utterly himself, his *best* self, and that nothing
else will do. In 'Shancoduff', Kavanagh is simple in this sense.
He obviously thought a great deal about the nature of simplicity
and came up with a few sentences that should be stamped on the
brow of every modern poet and critic:

> There are two kinds of simplicity, the simplicity of going away
> and the simplicity of return. The last is the ultimate in sophis-
> tication. In the final simplicity we don't care whether we appear
> foolish or not. We talk of things that earlier would embarrass. We
> are satisfied with being ourselves, however small.[37]

Because Kavanagh passionately believed in his own conception
of simplicity, he was impatient, both in his own work and in the
work of others, with whatever violated that conception. A poet's
critical judgements are always, at bottom, necessary justifications
of his own most dearly held aesthetic.[38]

A Man I Knew

(i.m. Patrick Kavanagh)

1

'I want no easy grave,' he said to me,
'where those who hated me can come and stare,
slip down upon a servile knee,
muttering their phoney public prayer.
In the wilds of Norfolk I'd like to lie,
no commemorative stone, no sheltering trees,
far from the hypocrite's tongue and eye,
safe from the praise of my enemies.'

2

A man I knew who seemed to me
the epitome of chivalry
was constantly misunderstood.
The heart's dialogue with God
was his life's theme and he
explored its depths assiduously
and without rest. Therefore he spat
on every shoddy value that
blinded men to their true destiny –
the evil power of mediocrity,
the safety of the barren pose,
all that distorted natural grace.
Which is to say, almost everything.
Once he asked a girl to sing
a medieval ballad. As her voice rang out,
she was affronted by some interfering lout.

This man I knew spat in his face
and wished him to the floor of hell.
I thought then, and still think it well
that man should wear the spittle of disgrace
for violating certain laws.

Now I recall my friend because
he lived according to his code
and in his way was true to God.
Courage he had and was content to be
himself, whatever came his way.
There is no other chivalry.

[1968]

BRENDAN KENNELLY

RUTH PITTER (1897–1992)

The Coffin Worm

which consider

The Worm unto his love: lo, here's fresh store;
Want irks us less as men are pinched the more.
Why dost thou lag? thou pitiest the man?
Fall to, the while I teach thee what I can.
Men in their lives full solitary be:
We are their last and kindest company.
Lo, where care's claws have been! those marks are grim;
Go, gentle Love, erase the scar from him.

Hapless perchance in love (most men are so),
Our quaint felicity he could not know:
We and our generation shall sow love
Throughout that frame he was not master of;
Flatter his wishful beauties; in his ear
Whisper he is at last beloved here;
Sing him (and in no false and siren strain)
We will not leave him while a shred remain
On his sweet bones: then shall our labour cease,
And the imperishable part find peace
Even from love; meanwhile how blest he lies,
Love in his heart, his empty hands, his eyes.

[*A Mad Lady's Garland*, 1934]

Ruth Pitter was born in Ilford, Essex, the daughter of two school-teachers. Hilaire Belloc helped to publish her *First Poems* in 1920, and her work was later championed by writers including Yeats, Larkin and Kathleen Raine. Influenced by C.S. Lewis, her faith became central to her poetry, as she recalled: 'For much of my life I lived more or less as a Bohemian, but when the second war broke out, Lewis broadcast several times, and also published some little books (notably *The Screwtape Letters*), and I was fairly hooked. I came to know him personally, and he came here several times. Lewis's stories, so very entertaining but always about the war between good and evil, became a permanent part of my mental and spiritual equipment.'[39]

In her own introduction to her *Poems 1922-66*, Ruth Pitter wrote that she was brought up to love art and poetry, and started writing herself when she was 'about five'. Poetry, for her, was a lifelong passion. She would sacrifice 'all consolations' to attain 'the ineffable communion with the earth itself'. Since childhood, writing poetry was an attempt to 'express something of the secret meanings which haunt life and language'.

In her introduction to Ruth Pitter's *Collected Poems*, Elizabeth Jennings quotes extensively from that earlier autobiographical preface, clearly seeing parallels with her own work, noting how Ruth Pitter writes of 'the silent music, the dance in stillness' present in all things. The poet's task is to capture it and hold it down, to find words for what seems inexpressible, to pack imagery with nuance to suggest order in the many contradictions of creation:

> Making a poem is a mysterious act; poets and critics have always tried to define it but no one has ever been able to catch it in one simple phrase. Ruth Pitter says that 'It begins in that secret movement of the poet's being in response to the secret dynamism of life'. [...] As she becomes more adept at making her subjects and themes inseparable from form and music, so her observations of Nature appear more exact and simple [...] the closer she keeps to the life of natural creatures, the more frequent does the visionary element in her work appear. [...] Ruth Pitter's style may often appear simple but this is a hard-won simplicity of tone, of form, a simplicity which leads to the profound. [...] She is aware of many great truths. Her mind works on the contradictions in Christianity and the forces of Nature.[40]

For many years Ruth Pitter earned her living as a decorative furniture and ornamental tray painter in Suffolk, opening her own business after the war with her lifelong friend, Kathleen O'Hara. She became a frequent guest on many radio programmes and appeared regularly on BBC Television's *The Brains Trust* during the 1940s and 50s. In 1955 she became the first woman to receive the Queen's Gold Medal for Poetry, and was appointed CBE in 1979. Her *Collected Poems* was published in her 93rd year, in 1990.

ELIZABETH DARYUSH   (1887–1977)

'Anger lay by me all night long'

Anger lay by me all night long,
　His breath was hot upon my brow,
He told me of my burning wrong,
　All night he talked and would not go.

He stood by me all through the day,
　Struck from my hand the book, the pen;
He said: 'Hear first what *I've* to say,
　And sing, if you've the heart to, then.'

And can I cast him from my couch?
　And can I lock him from my room?
Ah no, his honest words are such
　That he's my true-lord, and my doom.

[*The Last Man & Other Verses*, 1936]

■ The daughter of the poet, Robert Bridges, **Elizabeth Daryush** published her first collection of poems, *Charitessi 1911*, anonymously in 1912, the year before her father became the Poet Laureate. *Verses* was published in 1916, and *Sonnets from Hafez and Other Verses* in 1921, under the name Elizabeth Bridges. She married Ali Akbar Daryush in 1926 and they moved to Persia before returning to Britain in 1929. Disowning her first three collections of poems, she wrote prolifically after the death of her father during the 1930s [...] Daryush described her use of syllabics in 1934: 'The poems without line-capitals are written in syllabic metres (by which I mean metres governed only by the number of syllables to the line, and in which the number and position of the stresses may be varied at will) and are so printed as a reminder to the reader to follow strictly the natural speech-rhythm and not to look for stresses where there are none intended.'

　　Donald Davie, in an article in *Poetry Nation*, in 1975,[41] praises Daryush, demanding a reevaluation of her work, comparing her at times with Thomas Hardy. Roy Fuller has connected her work with that of her exact contemporary, Marianne Moore, while Jane Dowson has suggested that her work 'paved the way for the metrical ranges of Auden and other poets who popularised syllabic metre after 1939' (*Women Poets of the 1930s*, p.57). Her *Collected Poems*, with an introduction by Davie, was published in 1976.

[Deryn Rees-Jones, *Modern Women Poets*, Bloodaxe Books, 2005]

Despite the strong advocacy of Elizabeth Daryush's work over many years by Yvor Winters – taken up belatedly by Donald Davie – few readers are familiar with her work now. Brendan also hadn't read her until I posted him a copy of her out-of-print *Collected Poems* for him to read through in Ballybunion, together with a photocopy of Davie's essay on her work, prompting him to annotate our list with the comments copied below.

'Anger lay by me all night long' is from her 1936 collection, *The Last Man & Other Verses*, which Winters believed marked a shift in her work as she became 'increasingly conscious...of social injustice, of the mass of human suffering',[42] prompting this from Davie:

> Elizabeth Daryush, unlike her father Robert Bridges and unlike a greater poet of whom she sometimes reminds us, Thomas Hardy, is a poet in whom we can discern a development, not merely technical but thematic also, a deepening and changing attitude to the world she lives in. Quite simply, she has not lived through the first three quarters of the twentieth century in England without registering and responding to the profound changes that have transformed the world of the English gentry which, as the daughter of Robert Bridges, she was born to.[43]

BK ■ Her note on syllabic metres, while essentially aimed at herself, is a coherent and sharp concern with the mathematics of the music of poetry. [...] Further, she's at her best, not when her consciousness is dominated by syllabics, but when she goes instinctively for pictures, for scenes with memorable dramatic reverberations. So I would suggest (a) 'I saw the daughter of the sun: she stood'. (b) 'The Warden's daughter'. (c) 'Anger lay by me all night long'. [...] She was in a tough position as a poet, the father a Big Man, and she ached to be filled by a rage to knock a Big House. She has written some excellent poems. 'He said: "The city is a forest"' is an interesting candidate too, on page 154 of *Collected Poems*.'

SHEILA WINGFIELD (1906–1992)

from Beat Drum, Beat Heart

Where is the lumber-room of what was important?
The bric-à-brac of old feelings? Finished, put away.
And where the motes of ideas we breathed for our *now*?
Lost corridors, stray paths in the woods to our *here*?
Forgotten, of no account. In me, I feel
New space, new time, strangely askew and on whose
Axes spin my world, as you and I –
The man, the woman – tremble face-to-face.
The air is filled with power, hesitancy,
And awareness sharp as a blade's edge:
The lightest gesture, the least sign, can alter
Our whole fate. Opposed like this, we know,
We two, the other's soul is the most threatening
And immediate fact there's ever been –
You are so whole and real, he says, and keeps
Back tears; she, Nothing can stop the force
Of this great hour: I, as a woman, know
That from this confrontation a momentous
Grace or plight will come. It is the reason
I was born a peasant in the rain
Or one who trails her mantle through the hall;
Centuries have waited and prepared
For, with mimed passion and mock battles –
Yes, for this one and overpowering cause:
A cause whose glare lights up the skies and roofs,
Streets, spires and alleys of the mind
With an intensity so sacrificial
That its blazing flash and burning shadow
Fill with unseen, heroic acts. What
Can profane, he thinks, such faith as this? And she:
In finding you, I find myself, will cry.

For now I understand all twofold things;
How dark and light, matter and spirit, gut
And brain can be acquainted, how they accord:
Angel and beast in me are one because
The midway heart is held between
What's private, base, and what's diffused and rare,
Binding the two as the sun's power can weld
The soil, where his foot rests, into quick life
With upper levels of the air. Through me
All contraries of grief and joy are strung:
I am rage and mercy, impulse and slow patience,
Folly and wisdom; I am the rain-filled wind,
The blade that suffers drought. I've tolled
A bell of duty harshly; groaned and wept
For mercy like a saint on a stone floor.
Some fear me, and of one I go in terror;
I am those Fates with scant hair and red eyes
And brittle bones, who so disdain the young;
I am the thread that stretches to be nicked.
I am a parody and extreme, but round me
Natural things are stupid, without substance:
People with idiot faces, in nameless houses,
Going on errands that can have no meaning.
Aloof from others, I still speak for them
And must fulfil them. Bending my ear to catch
The oracle, at the same time it's I,
Fume-crazy croaking sibyl, who predict it.
[...]

Should anyone ask, Where are these battlefields?
Perhaps in the country house
Where a clammy mist falls over the garden,
Fills muddied lanes
And surges into an empty room.

Perhaps in some Park.
Municipal ducks, freezing lake,

Reeds like straw,
And an old bottle caught in the ice.

Perhaps by sand near prickled,
Sea-pitted coral rocks,
Where fond hope and insufficiency
Are the same as anywhere else;
While in the heat
Roads blind you with whiteness.

These are my Flanders, Valley Forge, Carthage.

Late 1930s [1946]

■ Born in Hampshire to an English father and an Irish mother,
Sheila Wingfield (*née* Beddington) spent much of her married
life in Ireland. She attended Roedean School and a finishing
school in Paris before marrying Viscount Powerscourt, who lived
at Powerscourt House, near Enniskerry, Co. Wicklow, Ireland. She
wrote secretly at first and her poems were initially published in
the *Dublin Magazine*, in the 1930s. Her first 'imagistic' collection
(though she claimed never to have heard the term), *Poems*, appeared
in 1938. Her most ambitious and successful work, *Beat Drum, Beat
Heart*, was published in 1946, though it had been written prior to
the war. *Beat Drum, Beat Heart* draws on the writing of Whitman
and D.H. Lawrence to examine the gender divide in wartime. [...]
Her work was widely praised, notably by Yeats, who admired it
for its 'style distinction...precise and subtle vocabulary', as well as
by Elizabeth Bowen. Her *Collected Poems 1938-1983* was published
by Enitharmon, in 1983.

[Deryn Rees-Jones, *Modern Women Poets*, Bloodaxe Books, 2005]

Brendan selected this extract from Sheila Wingfield's *Beat Drum,
Beat Heart*, which is from part three, 'Women in Love'.

W.H. AUDEN (1907–1973)

In Memory of W.B. Yeats

(d. Jan. 1939)

I

He disappeared in the dead of winter:
The brooks were frozen, the airports almost deserted,
And snow disfigured the public statues;
The mercury sank in the mouth of the dying day.
What instruments we have agree
The day of his death was a dark cold day.

Far from his illness
The wolves ran on through the evergreen forests,
The peasant river was untempted by the fashionable quays;
By mourning tongues
The death of the poet was kept from his poems.

But for him it was his last afternoon as himself,
An afternoon of nurses and rumours;
The provinces of his body revolted,
The squares of his mind were empty,
Silence invaded the suburbs,
The current of his feeling failed: he became his admirers.

Now he is scattered among a hundred cities
And wholly given over to unfamiliar affections;
To find his happiness in another kind of wood
And be punished under a foreign code of conscience.
The words of a dead man
Are modified in the guts of the living.

But in the importance and noise of tomorrow
When the brokers are roaring like beasts on the floor of the Bourse,

And the poor have the sufferings to which they are fairly accustomed,
And each in the cell of himself is almost convinced of his freedom;
A few thousand will think of this day
As one thinks of a day when one did something slightly unusual.

What instruments we have agree
The day of his death was a dark cold day.

II

You were silly like us: your gift survived it all;
The parish of rich women, physical decay,
Yourself. Mad Ireland hurt you into poetry.
Now Ireland has her madness and her weather still,
For poetry makes nothing happen: it survives
In the valley of its saying where executives
Would never want to tamper; it flows south
From ranches of isolation and the busy griefs,
Raw towns that we believe and die in; it survives,
A way of happening, a mouth.

III

Earth, receive an honoured guest;
William Yeats is laid to rest:
Let the Irish vessel lie
Emptied of its poetry.

In the nightmare of the dark
All the dogs of Europe bark,
And the living nations wait,
Each sequestered in its hate;

Intellectual disgrace
Stares from every human face,
And the seas of pity lie
Locked and frozen in each eye.

Follow, poet, follow right
To the bottom of the night,
With your unconstraining voice
Still persuade us to rejoice;

With the farming of a verse
Make a vineyard of the curse,
Sing of human unsuccess
In a rapture of distress;

In the deserts of the heart
Let the healing fountain start,
In the prison of his days
Teach the free man how to praise.

February 1939 [First published in *The New Republic*, 8 March 1939. Auden cut three stanzas from part III, and made other amendments for the later revised text used here. The four lines quoted by Brendan in his recollection of meeting Auden below were among the cuts.]

■ **Wystan Hugh Auden** was so influential in the 1930s that some critics name a whole poetic generation after him. Auden grew up near Birmingham, and studied English at Oxford. His *Poems* (1930) and Michael Roberts's anthology, *New Signatures* (1932), seemed to announce a new poetic movement with a leader who was taking poetry in a left-wing direction. Auden's chief disciples, Stephen Spender and Cecil Day Lewis, misread his early poetry as a call for revolution. In fact, it was conditioned by a complex of factors: rebellion against his middle-class public school background, homosexual alienation, nine months in Berlin, anxiety about England ('this island now'), psychoanalysis, Marxism, youthful anarchism. Perhaps Auden's greatest appeal was the panache with which his poetry of highly concentrated statement grabbed words and images from the full range of modern living: politics, science, technology, popular culture, the city. [...] He left behind his false position as leader of the literary Left when he and Christopher Isherwood sailed for America in January 1939. In 1946, Auden became a US citizen. [...]

Auden's end-of-the-30s poems are powerful because they dramatise his conflicts about art and politics [...] His elegy for Yeats and 'September 1, 1939' (the date when Hitler invaded Poland) combine intensified images of historical 'offence' with moral language that heralds his commitment to Anglicanism. Auden went on arguing with himself about poetry even after he ceased to believe in its directly political effect.

[Edna Longley, *The Bloodaxe Book of 20th Century Poetry*, 2000]

Auden was awarded an honorary degree in 1964 by Swarthmore College, near Philadelphia, where Brendan was visiting professor in November 1971 when Auden returned to give a lecture and poetry reading as well as joining Brendan's class for an informal discussion. The Quaker college's guest of honour was less than pleased to discover there was no wine or liquor at the reception held for him, but Brendan came to the rescue by leaving his whiskey flask in the toilet for him to find. Brendan talked about meeting Auden in an interview with Aengus Fanning published in the *Sunday Independent* (15 April 2001) to mark the publication of his collection *Glimpses*. His poem, 'Making nothing happen', is from that collection and these comments are from that interview:

BK ■ Auden was the writer in residence at Swarthmore College, and he came back the year I was visiting professor there to give seminars and tutorials. He was a receptive teacher, a good listener, and a good encourager.

Making nothing happen

Auden smiled and slyly said
'Yeats had a cold heart
and a warm head.'

Auden said this to me about Yeats in Swarthmore. I thought it was a very astute thing to say. He had written the beautiful and famous eulogy to Yeats, which is full of praise, but there are moments in it where he obviously has something on his mind:

Time that with this strange excuse
Pardoned Kipling and his views,
And will pardon Paul Claudel,
Pardons him for writing well.

Auden thought Yeats was a bit pompous, that his ideas were muddled, that he had a coldness about him that he didn't like. I disagree with that, and I believe Yeats was a great poet, but I thought the line was epigrammatic enough to record.

I had memorised the opening of Auden's essay on the poetry of Robert Frost, because I thought it was incredibly beautiful. It was about beauty and ugliness. Auden was suggesting that in poetry you can have beauty and vileness in the same poet, and that they can work together to make a poem. Auden came over to me he said: 'It is true about the Irish; they do remember things.' He was delighted that had I remembered the lines. He was stuck for a drop of whiskey and I gave him some; I was drinking at the time. He sent three bottles the next morning around to where I was staying.

I thought he had a wonderful face, the greatest face I had ever seen. I remember writing a poem for an old Dublin magazine in the 1950s about his face, based on a mountain actually Ben Bulben because I was reared up there for a while. I used to go back to see the rivulets and the little streams pouring down the side of the mountain. His face was like that; it was full of suffering and thought and determination. That was the kind of person he was. He kept writing until the end. He lived in New York at one time and he used to make enough money in two or three months touring universities doing readings in America and then he'd have nine months free to write.

He was very interesting when he spoke about his typical day. He drank a lot, and ate, and wrote. He had a dinner each evening, beginning at six o'clock, and whether the dinner was finished or not, he got up and left at 10 o'clock. The people could continue with the dinner, but he'd go to bed, and he was up every morning at five. I thought that was strange discipline. A mixture of discipline and a kind of wildness bordering on excess. He was a great drinker, a great eater, and a great thinker.

I've been reading Auden's lectures on Shakespeare recently, he's very original. Kavanagh greatly admired him and he admired Kavanagh. His lectures on Shakespeare actually use, here and there, old Irish poetry. He was a great reader and he had a great feeling for the old poetries of the world, mythologies and the beautiful early unashamed lyricism that perhaps we have lost or have compromised. Kavanagh didn't lose that lyricism either.

KEITH DOUGLAS   (1920–1944)

How to Kill

Under the parabola of a ball,
a child turning into a man,
I looked into the air too long.
The ball fell in my hand, it sang
in the closed fist: *Open Open*
Behold a gift designed to kill.

Now in my dial of glass appears
the soldier who is going to die.
He smiles, and moves about in ways
his mother knows, habits of his.
The wires touch his face: I cry
NOW. Death, like a familiar, hears

and look, has made a man of dust
of a man of flesh. This sorcery
I do. Being damned, I am amused
to see the centre of love diffused
and the waves of love travel into vacancy.
How easy it is to make a ghost.

The weightless mosquito touches
her tiny shadow on the stone,
and with how like, how infinite
a lightness, man and shadow meet.
They fuse. A shadow is a man
when the mosquito death approaches.

c. August 1943 [1946]

■ When **Keith Douglas** was killed during the Allied invasion of Normandy, he left behind poetry whose major importance is still being realised. Douglas calls his ancestry 'Scottish and pre-Revolution French'. As a schoolboy at Christ's Hospital, London, he already published poems. At Merton College, Oxford, he was encouraged by Edmund Blunden, a soldier-poet of the Great War. Partly owing to a broken love affair, partly owing to a constant desire to be where the action was, Douglas joined up when war was declared. In 1941 he went to Palestine as an officer in the Nottinghamshire Sherwood Rangers. His vivid prose account of the North African Campaign, *Alamein to Zem Zem* (1946), updates the 1930s theme of 'journey to a war'. Douglas's poetry, too, moved on. In a different way from Dylan Thomas, he reasserted poetry's cosmic scope. [...] Yet – as 'Cairo Jag' underlines – history is part of that larger, richer picture, and war has changed the meaning of political poetry. In 'Poets in This War' (1943) Douglas criticises supposedly political poets for being 'curiously unable to react', and 'the nation's public character' for remaining 'as absurdly ignorant and reactionary as ever'. A year later he wrote: 'For me, it is simply a case of fighting *against* the Nazi regime.'

Douglas was as wary of repeating the trench poets ('hell cannot be let loose twice') as of repeating the 1930s. He could move on because he adjusted his language and imagery to the historical moment, to the poetic moment. Douglas's belief that 'every word must work for its keep' became a means of critique: 'my object... is to write true things, significant things in words each of which works for its place in a line. My rhythms...are carefully chosen to enable the poems to be *read* as significant speech'. [...] Douglas's talent as a visual artist shapes his poetry's self-image as a lens or spectacle. His desert arena, although less hellish than the trench landscape, is an equally macabre cosmic theatre. 'How to Kill' re-writes Owen's 'Strange Meeting' for that theatre. Douglas returns to the action of killing the enemy and identifies it with his poem's procedure. For Ted Hughes, a great admirer, all his work is a 'balancing act in words, which draws the reader into the same imperilled concentration as Douglas's own'.

[Edna Longley, *The Bloodaxe Book of 20th Century Poetry*, 2000]

LOUIS MacNEICE   (1907–1963)

Prayer before Birth

I am not yet born; O hear me.
Let not the bloodsucking bat or the rat or the stoat or the
    club-footed ghoul come near me.

I am not yet born, console me.
I fear that the human race may with tall walls wall me,
    with strong drugs dope me, with wise lies lure me,
        on black racks rack me, in blood-baths roll me.

I am not yet born; provide me
With water to dandle me, grass to grow for me, trees to talk
    to me, sky to sing to me, birds and a white light
        in the back of my mind to guide me.

I am not yet born; forgive me
For the sins that in me the world shall commit, my words
    when they speak to me, my thoughts when they think me,
        my treason engendered by traitors beyond me,
            my life when they murder by means of my
                hands, my death when they live me.

I am not yet born; rehearse me
In the parts I must play and the cues I must take when
    old men lecture me, bureaucrats hector me, mountains
        frown at me, lovers laugh at me, the white
            waves call me to folly and the desert calls
                me to doom and the beggar refuses
                    my gift and my children curse me.

I am not yet born; O hear me,
Let not the man who is beast or who thinks he is God
    come near me.

I am not yet born; O fill me
With strength against those who would freeze my
  humanity, would dragoon me into a lethal automaton,
    would make me a cog in a machine, a thing with
      one face, a thing, and against all those
        who would dissipate my entirety, would
          blow me like thistledown hither and
            thither or hither and thither
              like water held in the
                hands would spill me.

Let them not make me a stone and let them not spill me.
Otherwise kill me.

London, 1944 [First published in *Springboard: poems 1941-1944* (1944)]

Louis MacNeice (1907-63) was born in Belfast, the son of a
rector (later a bishop), and educated in England. When his close
friends W.H. Auden and Christopher Isherwood left for America
at the start of the Second World War, MacNeice stayed behind,
working for the BBC for the next 20 years. He later died from
pneumonia after going down pot-holes to record sound effects for
a radio play. Somewhat overshadowed by Auden during the 1930s,
MacNeice is the quintessential poet of flux, openness and possibil-
ities. Many of his poems defend individual freedom and tolerance,
and kick against conformism and restrictive ideologies. In 'Snow',
he writes that: 'World is crazier and more of it than we think, /
Incorrigibly plural. I peel and portion / A tangerine and spit the pips
and feel / The drunkenness of things being various.' In 'Entirely',
written over half a century ago when the threat was from fascism
or communism, MacNeice opposes the fundamentalist view of the
world as 'black or white entirely', seeing life as 'a mad weir of
tigerish waters / A prism of delight and pain'. His 'Prayer before
Birth', written towards the end of the war, is a plea to God or
humanity to enter the world as a free person, as a being not to be
destroyed or used against others.
  My preferred choices of MacNeice poems for this anthology

were 'Entirely', 'Snow', or an extract from *Autumn Journal*, but Brendan prevailed with 'Prayer before Birth', which fortunately he had previously written about in his essay, 'Derek Mahon's Humane Perspective' (1989), published in *Journey into Joy*. An extract from that essay appears here in lieu of a new commentary, preceded by some more general remarks from another essay, 'Louis MacNeice: An Irish Outsider' (1985), also included in *Journey into Joy*.

BK ■ Louis MacNeice felt that in Ireland he was an outsider from birth. [...] And this sense of being an outsider in Ireland is, in a deeper sense, characteristic of what we may call MacNeice's spiritual life, his developed stance as a poet. All through his poetry we encounter a man who doesn't really seem to belong anywhere, except perhaps in the fertile, mysterious, consoling and challenging land of language itself, where every fresh discovery is inextricably bound up with a new mystery. Yet even there, where a poet might reasonably be expected to feel unreasonably at home, the recurring doubts and uncertainties gnaw away at his mind and imagination. MacNeice is one of the most intelligent of all Irish poets; he is also, in his work, one of the loneliest. [...]

MacNeice is an excellent poet, a skilful craftsman, a shrewd critic of both literature and society, a thinker who makes complex thoughts lucid and shapely, a considerable dramatist, a disciplined classicist, an assured translator and an attractive personality. He achieved all this while remaining a loner. [...]

He clings to his individual moral honesty with an unrelenting grip even as he is deeply aware of its artistic limitations and defects. [...] MacNeice's stubborn honesty helps to account for his strengths and weaknesses as a poet. He is a celebrant and critic of urban life; he has, therefore, a keen eye for the characters that abound in cities [...] he has a profound respect for the integrity of the individual and a vehement hatred for the forces which violate that respect (as in 'Prayer before Birth'); his exploration of time concentrates, for the most part, on the present so that even his most personal poetry, his love poetry, for example, deals with the present fleetingness, or the fleeting presence of love.[44]

BK ■ MacNeice's 'Prayer before Birth' is the prayer of the ironic romantic outsider who is not subject to the delusion of self pity, but who because of his detachment understands and states a valid sense of pity for all that the unborn self must endure. This poem depends very much on its rhythm, the rhythm of prayer, the prayer of the unborn, written by a man who knows something of the killing ways of the world. It is essentially a prayer to be human, to become human in the sense that it is aware of all those forces that are waiting like so many mechanical assassins to diminish one's humanity and to shrivel the potential of one's nature. This may be an appropriate moment to pay tribute to MacNeice, the humanistic source of much Ulster poetry.

I call MacNeice a source because his poetry points to the one thing that is absent from most Irish life and literature. *He is a source of alternatives*, another way of seeing, another way of experiencing. MacNeice perceives, tolerates, cherishes and celebrates *difference*. He proposes an alternative to prejudice in the North, an alternative to lethargy in the South. A humanistic alternative to piosity. This poem is a true prayer. It has the rhythm of the prayer that is said in private but has public reverberations.

In his 'Prayer before Birth' MacNeice is praying for the unborn, which means most of us who flatter ourselves that we are alive.[45]

DYLAN THOMAS (1914–1953)

Do Not Go Gentle into That Good Night

Do not go gentle into that good night,
Old age should burn and rave at close of day;
Rage, rage against the dying of the light.

Though wise men at their end know dark is right,
Because their words had forked no lightning they
Do not go gentle into that good night.

Good men, the last wave by, crying how bright
Their frail deeds might have danced in a green bay,
Rage, rage against the dying of the light.

Wild men who caught and sang the sun in flight,
And learn, too late, they grieved it on its way,
Do not go gentle into that good night.

Grave men, near death, who see with blinding sight
Blind eyes could blaze like meteors and be gay,
Rage, rage against the dying of the light.

And you, my father, there on the sad height,
Curse, bless, me now with your fierce tears, I pray.
Do not go gentle into that good night.
Rage, rage against the dying of the light.

1947 [First published in *Botteghe Oscure*, 1951]

■ **Dylan Thomas** called himself 'unnational', 'a border case':
'Regarded in England as a Welshman (and a waterer of England's
milk), and in Wales as an Englishman… I should be living in a
small private leper-house in Hereford or Shropshire, one foot in

Wales and my vowels in England.' Thomas grew up in Swansea, where his father was Senior English Master at the Grammar School. Elocution lessons explain the English 'vowels' of the resonant voice in which he later gave readings of poetry. A talented broadcaster, Thomas wrote the famous radio-play *Under Milk Wood*. His Welsh base became Laugharne, Carmarthenshire, where 'Over Sir John's hill' is set. Thomas died during an American reading tour. Alcohol may not have been wholly to blame.

The "Welshness" of Thomas's poetry consists, first, in its religious intensity. He creates a life-affirming version of Welsh nonconformism (Chapel) with its tradition of eloquent preaching and passionate hymn-singing. Secondly, he has absorbed two contrasting landscapes: Swansea, his 'ugly lovely' 'sea town', and the 'Welsh Wales' of his childhood holidays in Carmarthenshire. 'Fern Hill' reconstructs that Eden as a poetic source which identifies the physical world with the music of language. Thomas's earlier poetry is less relaxed and 'tuneful'. Criticised for letting his unconscious 'flow', he replied that his poems were, rather, 'hewn'. [...] He tries to say everything at once about life and death, womb and world, spirit and flesh, eternity and time. His poetry is also 'driven' by his effort to exorcise a sense of the body's sinfulness. He said: 'I hold a beast, an angel, and a madman in me.' At times, Thomas's cadences float free of a content whose obscurities resist analysis. Yet the 'force' and ambition of his work had an incalculable effect on later poetry. His readings, as well as poems, re-emphasised poetry's primary appeal to the ear. Louis MacNeice says: 'When his first work appeared it was astonishingly new, and yet went back to the oldest of our roots.'

[Edna Longley, *The Bloodaxe Book of 20th Century Poetry*, 2000]

Brendan grew up knowing Dylan Thomas's poetry from *Under Milk Wood* and Thomas's thunderous readings on the radio. The villanelle 'Do Not Go Gentle into That Good Night' was the Thomas poem he most wanted us to include.

First published in a journal in 1951 and then in his 1952 collection, *In Country Sleep, And Other Poems*, it was thought to have been addressed to Thomas's dying father, who died in December 1952, but was actually written five years earlier during a family visit to Florence, in 1947.

STEVIE SMITH (1902–1971)

The River God

I may be smelly and I may be old,
Rough in my pebbles, reedy in my pools,
But where my fish float by I bless their swimming
And I like the people to bathe in me, especially women.
But I can drown the fools
Who bathe too close to the weir, contrary to rules.
And they take a long time drowning
As I throw them up now and then in a spirit of clowning.
Hi yih, yippity-yap, merrily I flow,
O I may be an old foul river but I have plenty of go.
Once there was a lady who was too bold
She bathed in me by the tall black cliff where the water runs cold,
So I brought her down here
To be my beautiful dear.
Oh will she stay with me will she stay
This beautiful lady, or will she go away?
She lies in my beautiful deep river bed with many a weed
To hold her, and many a waving reed.
Oh who would guess what a beautiful white face lies there
Waiting for me to smooth and wash away the fear
She looks at me with. Hi yih, do not let her
Go. There is no one on earth who does not forget her
Now. They say I am a foolish old smelly river
But they do not know of my wide original bed
Where the lady waits, with her golden sleepy head.
If she wishes to go I will not forgive her.

[1950]

■ Florence Margaret Smith was nicknamed 'Stevie' because her fringe resembled that of the jockey Steve Donaghue. Aged three, she moved with her mother and sister [from Hull] to her aunt's home in Palmers Green, a North London outer suburb. She lived in this 'house of female habitation' for the rest of her life. She also stayed in the same job: spending 30 years as private secretary to the magazine publishers Sir George Newnes and Sir Neville Pearson. During the 1930s Smith published two novels, including *Novel on Yellow Paper* (1936), and two books of poems: *A Good Time Was Had By All* (1937) and *Tender Only to One* (1938). Yet her reputation grew unevenly, although her distinctively voiced readings later became famous. Critics were puzzled by Smith's false-naive style; her strange cast of characters; the childlike drawings that accompanied certain poems; her indifference to literary hierarchy or fashion; the sudden switches from comedy to theology, from doggerel to dirge, from waving to drowning.

[Edna Longley, *The Bloodaxe Book of 20th Century Poetry*, 2000]

■ Many of her poems are accompanied by what she calls her 'doodling', and it could be argued that these oblique 'supplements' to the poems are as essential to interpretation as the illustrations of Blake, whom she greatly admired. Smith has been championed by writers as different as Larkin and Heaney. Her quirky "dialogic" poems which so often revise the work of male writers to her own ends, and her interest and transformation of fairytale and myth, make her an essential, if inimitable, figure in the development of women's poetry. Smith herself did not consider gender an important factor in poetry: 'Differences between men and women poets are best seen when the poets are bad...But neither odd lives nor sex really signify, it is a person's poems that stand to be judged.' (*Me Again*, p.181).

[Deryn Rees-Jones, *Modern Women Poets*, Bloodaxe Books, 2005]

The subject and speaker of Stevie Smith's poem 'The River God' was said by her to be the River Mimram in Hertfordshire, whose name was said – possibly erroneously – to have been derived from a Celtic river god. It was first collected in her 1950 collection, *Harold's Leap*.

TED HUGHES (1930–1998)

The Thought-Fox

I imagine this midnight moment's forest:
Something else is alive
Beside the clock's loneliness
And this blank page where my fingers move.

Through the window I see no star:
Something more near
Though deeper within darkness
Is entering the loneliness:

Cold, delicately as the dark snow
A fox's nose touches twig, leaf;
Two eyes serve a movement, that now
And again now, and now, and now

Sets neat prints into the snow
Between trees, and warily a lame
Shadow lags by stump and in hollow
Of a body that is bold to come

Across clearings, an eye,
A widening deepening greenness,
Brilliantly, concentratedly,
Coming about its own business

Till, with a sudden sharp hot stink of fox
It enters the dark hole of the head.
The window is starless still; the clock ticks,
The page is printed.

[1957]

from The Burnt Fox

At Cambridge University in my third and final year I read *Archae-ology and Anthropology*. But for my first two years, from 1951 to 1953, I read *English*. Like plenty of others, I had assumed that the course in English would help my own writing. Students of English were expected to produce a weekly essay. Though I felt a strong liking for my supervisor, and could not have been more interested in the subject, I soon became aware of an inexplicable resistance in myself, against writing these essays. [...]

Once again I had finished up at two a.m., exhausted, sitting in my college room at my table, bent over a page of foolscap that had about four lines written across the top of it – my opening sentence in its latest state. My desk lamp light fell on the paper. Close to my left was my high curtained window. In front of me, beyond my table, was my bed, the head at the far end. To my right, across the room, were the wooden steps that climbed to my door, on which hung my gown. At last I had to give up and go to bed.

I began to dream. I dreamed I had never left my table and was still sitting there, bent over the lamplit piece of foolscap, staring at the same few lines across the top. Suddenly my attention was drawn to the door. I thought I had heard something there. As I waited, listening, I saw the door was opening slowly. Then a head came round the edge of the door. It was about the height of a man's head but clearly the head of a fox – though the light over there was dim. The door opened wide and down the short stair and across the room towards me came a figure that was at the same time a skinny man and a fox walking erect on its hind legs. It was a fox, but the size of a wolf. As it approached and came into the light I saw that its body and limbs had just now stepped out of a furnace. Every inch was roasted, smouldering, black-charred, split and bleeding. Its eyes, which were level with mine where I sat, dazzled with the intensity of the pain. It came up until it stood beside me. Then it spread its hand – a human hand as I now saw, but burned and bleeding like the rest of him – flat palm down on the blank space of my page. At the same time it said: 'Stop this – you are destroying us.' Then as it lifted its hand away I saw the blood-print, like a palmist's specimen, with all the lines and creases, in wet, glistening blood on the page.

I immediately woke up. The impression of reality was so total, I got out of bed to look at the papers on my table, quite certain that I would see the blood-print there on the page.

1993 [1994]

Ted Hughes was one of the dominant figures in post-war British poetry, serving as Poet Laureate from 1984. Born in Mytholmroyd, Yorkshire, in 1930, he grew up around the farms and moors of the Calder valley, closely connected with its wildlife and landscape. 'The Thought-Fox' was included in his first collection, *The Hawk in the Rain* (1957). In 1956 he met and married the poet Sylvia Plath, who was to take her own life in 1963. In his final collection, *Birthday Letters* (1998), written over many years and published just months before his death, he gives his own account of their relationship.

Interviewed on Thames Television in 1988, Ted Hughes described how 'The Thought-Fox' was prompted by a strange dream he had while studying English literature at Cambridge in the early 1950s, which was the catalyst for requesting a transfer to Anthropology. He expanded that account in a short prose piece in *Winter Pollen: Occasional Prose* (1994) quoted from above.

He also discussed the writing of 'The Thought-Fox' in *Poetry in the Making: A Handbook for Writing and Teaching* (1967). The poem clearly exemplifies his belief that poetry is the unmediated expression of the poet's hidden, inner self which is 'the voice of what is neglected or forbidden' and that 'to live removed from this inner universe of experience is also to live removed from ourself, banished from ourself and our real life'.

The fox becomes an image for poetry itself, for the poetry he wanted to write but felt was being suffocated by academic study. One of his earliest published poems, 'The Thought-Fox' also summons echoes with two poets who had become among the most important and influential in his reading at that time. The first line, 'I imagine this midnight moment's forest' echoes the 'forest of the night' burning bright in William Blake's 'The Tyger' [131], while Hughes's alliteration echoes the opening of Gerard Manley Hopkins's 'The Windhover' [190] ('I caught this morning morning's minion') about another creature, the kestrel, which – like Hughes's fox – symbolises the poetic imagination, but also Christ.

SYLVIA PLATH   (1932–1963)

Morning Song

Love set you going like a fat gold watch.
The midwife slapped your footsoles, and your bald cry
Took its place among the elements.

Our voices echo, magnifying your arrival. New statue.
In a drafty museum, your nakedness
Shadows our safety. We stand round blankly as walls.

I'm no more your mother
Than the cloud that distils a mirror to reflect its own slow
Effacement at the wind's hand.

All night your moth-breath
Flickers among the flat pink roses. I wake to listen:
A far sea moves in my ear.

One cry, and I stumble from bed, cow-heavy and floral
In my Victorian nightgown.
Your mouth opens clean as a cat's. The window square

Whitens and swallows its dull stars. And now you try
Your handful of notes;
The clear vowels rise like balloons.

19 February 1961 [First published in *The Observer*, May 1961; *Ariel*, 1965]

Sylvia Plath was born in Boston, Massachusetts. Her father, Otto
Plath, was a Prussian immigrant entomologist who taught both
German and biology at Boston University, and was an expert on bees;
her mother, Aurelia, was an American of Austrian descent. Otto's
death when Plath was eight gave her a psychic shock which reverb-
erates through her poetry, most searingly in her poem 'Daddy'.

She attended Smith College from 1950, taking up a guest editor-ship on *Mademoiselle* magazine during the summer of 1953. On returning home she suffered a breakdown, underwent electro-convulsive therapy, and attempted suicide, experiences she late drew upon for her novel *The Bell Jar*, published under the pseudonym of Victoria Lucas in January 1963, a month before her death.

After graduating from Smith in 1955, she took up a two-year Fulbright scholarship at Cambridge, where she met Ted Hughes – already a lauded poet – at a party. They married within months after a rapid courtship. She returned with Hughes to the US in 1957 to take up a teaching post at Smith College. In Boston, along with Anne Sexton, she attended Robert Lowell's poetry workshops. Her first collection, *The Colossus*, was published in 1960.

In September 1962 she and Hughes separated after he began an affair with Assia Wevill. She left their Devon home, taking their two children, Frieda and Nicholas, to London, renting a flat where Yeats had once lived. That autumn, depressed, hurt and extremely agitated, she went through a period of fevered creativity, writing most of her greatest poems in the course of a few months. In February 1963, in the middle of the most severe winter for decades, she gassed herself, having sealed the doors between her and the children to keep them safe. Hughes was blamed for her suicide, especially after Assia killed herself in 1969, taking their daughter Shura with her. Shortly before his death, Hughes published his collection *Birthday Letters* (1998) telling his side of the saga.

Plath's final three collections, edited by Hughes, were published posthumously: *Ariel* (1965), *Winter Trees* and *Crossing the Water* (1971). Her *Collected Poems* appeared in 1981. In 2004 her daughter Frieda Hughes published and introduced *Ariel: The Restored Edition* based on the book's original manuscript, with facsimile drafts.

The baby in 'Morning Song' is Frieda. Written in Devon, this ambivalent poem is both descriptive and mythic in its address. The mother feels connected by love as well as separate from her child. According to Edna Longley, 'when [Plath] speaks as a mother, she conveys the elemental rather than domestic meaning of that state. Further, maternity and poetry are entangled in her work. Sometimes this suggests creative fertility ('Metaphors'), sometimes the reverse ('Stillborn'), sometimes a chilling sense that motherhood and bodily life must be sacrificed for the sake of artistic "perfection" ('Edge').' [46]

DENISE LEVERTOV (1923–1997)

Living

The fire in leaf and grass
so green it seems
each summer the last summer.

The wind blowing, the leaves
shivering in the sun,
each day the last day.

A red salamander
so cold and so
easy to catch, dreamily

moves his delicate feet
and long tail. I hold
my hand open for him to go.

Each minute the last minute.

[*The Sorrow Dance*, 1967]

Denise Levertov was one of the 20th century's foremost American poets, born and raised in England, the daughter of a Russian Jewish scholar turned Anglican priest and a Welsh Congregationalist mother, both parents descended from mystics. She emigrated to the US in 1948, where she became involved with the Objectivist and Black Mountain schools of poetry, and was much influenced by the work of William Carlos Williams, a lifelong friend and correspondent. Her poetry is notable for its visionary approach to the natural world. 'Meditative and evocative, Levertov's poetry concerns itself with the search for meaning. She sees the poet's role as a priestly one; the poet is the mediator between ordinary people and the divine mysteries' (Susan J. Zevenbergen).[47]

GEOFFREY HILL (1932–2016)

September Song

born 19.6.32 – deported 24.9.42

Undesirable you may have been, untouchable
you were not. Not forgotten
or passed over at the proper time.

      As estimated, you died. Things marched,
sufficient, to that end.
Just so much Zyklon and leather, patented
terror, so many routine cries.

(I have made
an elegy for myself it
is true)

September fattens on vines. Roses
flake from the wall. The smoke
of harmless fires drifts to my eyes.

This is plenty. This is more than enough.

[First published in *Stand*, vol. 8 no.4 (1967); *King Log*, 1968]

Sir Geoffrey Hill was born in Bromsgrove, Worcestershire, the
son of a police constable. He taught at Leeds University from 1954
to 1980, and thereafter at Cambridge and Boston. He was Oxford
Professor of Poetry in 2010-15, and was knighted in 2012. He pub-
lished his *Collected Critical Writings* in 2008 and *Broken Hierarchies:
Poems 1952–2012* in 2013. A final collection, *The Book of Baruch
by the Gnostic Justin*, was published posthumously, in 2013.

Hill's densely allusive poetry earned him a reputation for 'diffi-
culty' which he defended as the poet's right in the face of cultural
disintegration, political opportunism and media-driven mediocrity,

arguing that to be difficult is to be democratic and equating the demand for simplicity with the demands of tyrants. His approach to 'difficulty' included subjecting his own lyricism to intense interrogation and self-questioning, as in 'September Song', an early poem written for an unknown child who died anonymously in one or other concentration camp. Throughout this oblique and understated poem, Hill writes with an acute awareness of how the Nazis perfected the art of misusing language to disguise the nature of their 'Final Solution', simultaneously masking and revealing the horror behind that phrase through painful irony, awful double-meanings and juxtapositions ('routine cries'), so that the meaning of each line changes, or shifts, with each unsettling line-break.

Brendan particularly wanted to include a poem by Geoffrey Hill in our book, having known him at a formative time in his life and work, the year he spent as a postgraduate studying under Dublin-born Yeats scholar A.N. (Derry) Jeffares at Leeds University in 1962-63. Jeffares nurtured a lively, international community of young poets and academics at the School of English which included Tony Harrison, Peter Redgrove, Jon Silkin, James Simmons, Ken Smith [332], Wole Soyinka, and Geoffrey Hill, whose debut collection, *For the Unfallen*, had been published in 1959. Readings by resident and visiting poets – including Brendan – were recorded by Hill and Peter Lewis in the Poetry Room set up by Jeffares and the British Council.

The introverted policeman's son and the mischievous Irishman were polar opposites but came to respect and learn from each other, with Hill becoming a stronger reader and Brendan writing with greater discernment. Brendan came to Leeds as a Trinity College graduate who'd latterly been working as a bus conductor in London. 'It was 1962 – the year of the Cuba crisis,' he told Michael Murphy. 'There was a fantastic political consciousness on the campus and I tried to capture that feeling in my second novel. I think I failed. I was too ardent, too earnest.' [48] His coming of age novel, *The Florentines* (1967), draws on his experiences in Leeds (Barfield in the book).

Brendan's immersion in a cultural milieu so different then from Dublin and Ireland was to have a profound impact on his life and work. His own influence on his Leeds contemporaries was also significant. Peter Lewis recalls many playful encounters between the two poets. On one occasion Brendan grabbed hold of Geoffrey Hill and lifted him up bodily, telling him: 'You're constipated, Hill. You need to free yourself up, open up your work.'

AUSTIN CLARKE (1894–1974)

The Redemptorist

'How many children have you?' asked
The big Redemptorist.
                        'Six, Father.'
                                        'The last,
When was it born?'
                        'Ten months ago.'
'I cannot absolve your mortal sin
Until you conceive again. Go home,
Obey your husband.'
                        She whimpered:
                                        'But
The doctor warned me...'
                                Shutter became
Her coffin lid. She twisted her thin hands
And left the box.
                        The missioner,
Red-bearded saint, had brought hell's flame
To frighten women on retreat:
Sent on his spiritual errand,
It rolled along the village street
Until Rathfarnham was housing smoke
That sooted the Jesuits in their Castle.
'No pregnancy. You'll die the next time,'
The Doctor had said.

                        Her tiredness obeyed
That Saturday night: her husband's weight
Digging her grave. So, in nine months, she
Sank in great agony on a Monday.
Her children wept in the Orphanage,
Huddled together in the annexe,
While, proud of the Black Cross on his badge,
The Liguorian, at Adam and Eve's,
Ascended the pulpit, sulphuring his sleeves
And setting fire to the holy text.

Born in Dublin, **Austin Clarke** came of age as a writer at the same time as the independent Irish state came into existence, dedicating his life to an imaginative excavation of personal, historical, political and spiritual repression, drawing on European literature as well as Irish mythology and English poetry and drama. His reading of European languages inspired the complex musicality of his early work. He described his method to Robert Frost as: 'I load myself with chains and try to get out of them.' After writing some of the most anguished and beautifully fashioned lyrics in the language, adapting techniques from Irish-language and classical poetry, he developed a more direct style to respond to day-to-day events in Ireland. His later sardonic style is distinguished by its intellectual rigour, its questioning of authority and its sexual frankness.

Brendan especially wanted Austin Clarke to be featured in this anthology. We wavered between candidates including 'The lost heifer' (1925) and 'Pilgrimage' (1929) among the early poems, the transitional poem 'Martha Blake' (1938), and a possible extract from the later autobiographical long poem, 'Mnemosyne lay in dust' (1966), but never settled on a final choice.

In the end the only commentary by Brendan on an Austin Clarke poem I could draw upon was his account of 'The Redemptorist', in his essay 'Poetry and Violence' in *Journey into Joy*.[49] This was adapted from the introduction to his *Penguin Book of Irish Verse* (Penguin Books, 1970; 1981) which appeared not long after Clarke's publication of the poem in his 1967 collection *Old-fashioned pilgrimage and other poems*. Including such a late poem by Clarke here presents him not as a key Irish poet of the inter-war years but as a poet of the 1960s, although – like Kavanagh – he was, of course, both. The references to abortion in Ireland in Brendan's narrative are of that time (and other times) and obviously predate changes in the law made in 2018. Given the remit of this anthology, the pairing of this commentary with Clarke's poem felt just right. Apart from the colonial yoke, there has been no heavier bear borne by Irish people than the Roman Catholic church.

BK ■ In Austin Clarke's poem, a woman goes to confession, to a Redemptorist priest, a missioner. She tells him it is ten months since the birth of her last child. The Redemptorist priest says this is a sin; and he cannot forgive her until she conceives again. She protests a little, but in vain. She goes home, her husband makes love to her that Saturday night, she conceives, she dies giving birth. It is a simple, frightening parable of the power of priests over women; of the violence done by an institution against a single, fragile, vulnerable woman. It is important to realise that the dialogue takes place in the extremely *quiet* privacy of the confessional. The reference in this poem to Adam and Eve's is to a church in Dublin.

This poem is also an excellent illustration of the kind of poem that Austin Clarke perfected – imagistic, anecdotal, making use of dialogue and brief, vivid, effective moments of characterisation. The poem is, in effect, a little drama, a small play in a confession-box as a result of which the woman dies and the priest goes on his proud, powerful way, self-inflated with rhetoric and images of hell-fire. One gets in this poem a sense of the male conspiracy between priest and husband which has always been strong in Ireland. It is the *woman* who suffers as a result of the violence implicit in the "morality" of the institution of which she is a member, and in the doctrines of which she, presumably, believes. The violence done to her, her actual death, is brought about by the very fact of her belief. One wonders how many women have died because of their sincerity.

What Austin Clarke gets at, in a ruthless, penetrating way, is the hypocrisy engendered by the violence of the institution of the Church, directed against its members, especially women. Some four thousand Irish girls go to England every year to have abortions there. This suits perfectly. There are, you see, no abortions in Ireland. That means we're pure. But you can have an abortion in England. Aren't the English terrible? As a race, we Irish are so casually hypocritical in such matters that it is almost unbelievable.

And yet, precisely because of this blend of tyranny, hypocrisy and oppression, Irish poets have always celebrated the integrity, energy and heroic common-sense of women.

W.S. GRAHAM (1918-1986)

The Beast in the Space

Shut up. Shut up. There's nobody here.
If you think you hear somebody knocking
On the other side of the words, pay
No attention. It will be only
The great creature that thumps its tail
On silence on the other side.
If you do not even hear that
I'll give the beast a quick skelp
And through Art you'll hear it yelp.

The beast that lives on silence takes
Its bite out of either side.
It pads and sniffs between us. Now
It comes and laps my meaning up.
Call it over. Call it across
This curious necessary space.
Get off, you terrible inhabiter
Of silence. I'll not have it. Get
Away to whoever it is will have you.

He's gone and if he's gone to you
That's fair enough. For on this side
Of the words it's late. The heavy moth
Bangs on the pane. The whole house
Is sleeping and I remember
I am not here, only the space
I sent the terrible beast across.
Watch. He bites. Listen gently
To any song he snorts or growls
And give him food. He means neither
Well or ill towards you. Above
All, shut up. Give him your love.

■ **W.S. Graham** was born in Greenock in 1918, but established himself as a poet in London before settling near St Ives in Cornwall in the company of the artists who influenced his later work. The West Coast of Scotland forms a background of loss to his impassioned speculative poetry. His first books were very much under the influence of Dylan Thomas – only the primacy given to the associative powers of language indicates the direction to be taken in *The White Threshold* (1949) and the brilliant long poem *The Nightfishing*, which cast its metaphysical nets in the same year (1955) as the Movement promulgated its very different agenda. As a result Graham vanished for 15 years. His two late books, *Malcolm Mooney's Land* (1970) and *Implements in Their Places* (1977) focussed on abstraction, on the space generated by a poem, between writer and reader, a space occupied by 'The beast that lives on silence'. The austerity of this, much admired by Harold Pinter, is coloured by the Cornish landscape and the directness of the voice: the reader is addressed as friend or lover, existentially remote but nonetheless cherished.

[W.N. Herbert & Matthew Hollis, *Strong Words: modern poets on modern poetry*, 2000]

(William) Sydney Graham left school at 14 to become an apprentice draughtsman in a Clydeside shipyard. After studying structural engineering, he took up a bursary to Newbattle Abbey College, in 1938, where he met his stalwart wife, Nessie Dunsmuir. He began publishing his poetry in the early 1940s, moving to Cornwall in 1943 where he could devote himself to his writing while living rent-free in a caravan. After a meeting with T.S. Eliot in London in 1948 Faber published his next two collections, but lost touch with him when he failed to submit anything after *The Nightfishing*. During the years when he was thought to have fallen silent – or prey to whisky – he was rethinking his poetry, fed by his engagement with the work and ideas of the abstract painters he knew in Cornwall (Roger Hilton, Peter Lanyon and Bryan Wynter, among others) which connected with his earlier interest as an engineer in structure and space. First published in the American journal, *Poetry*, in April 1967, 'The Beast in the Space' appeared in *Malcolm Mooney's Land* (1970), the first of the two collections of his later period, both concerned with difficulties of language and communication.

ADRIENNE RICH (1929-2012)

Diving into the Wreck

First having read the book of myths,
and loaded the camera,
and checked the edge of the knife-blade,
I put on
the body-armor of black rubber
the absurd flippers
the grave and awkward mask.
I am having to do this
not like Cousteau with his
assiduous team
aboard the sun-flooded schooner
but here alone.

There is a ladder.
The ladder is always there
hanging innocently
close to the side of the schooner.
We know what it is for,
we who have used it.
Otherwise
it's a piece of maritime floss
some sundry equipment.

I go down.
Rung after rung and still
the oxygen immerses me
the blue light
the clear atoms
of our human air.
I go down.
My flippers cripple me,
I crawl like an insect down the ladder

and there is no one
to tell me when the ocean
will begin.

First the air is blue and then
it is bluer and then green and then
black I am blacking out and yet
my mask is powerful
it pumps my blood with power
the sea is another story
the sea is not a question of power
I have to learn alone
to turn my body without force
in the deep element.

And now: it is easy to forget
what I came for
among so many who have always
lived here
swaying their crenellated fans
between the reefs
and besides
you breathe differently down here.

I came to explore the wreck.
The words are purposes.
The words are maps.
I came to see the damage that was done
and the treasures that prevail.
I stroke the beam of my lamp
slowly along the flank
of something more permanent
than fish or weed

the thing I came for:
the wreck and not the story of the wreck
the thing itself and not the myth

the drowned face always staring
toward the sun
the evidence of damage
worn by salt and sway into this threadbare beauty
the ribs of the disaster
curving their assertion
among the tentative haunters.

This is the place.
And I am here, the mermaid whose dark hair
streams black, the merman in his armored body.
We circle silently
about the wreck
we dive into the hold.
I am she: I am he

whose drowned face sleeps with open eyes
whose breasts still bear the stress
whose silver, copper, vermeil cargo lies
obscurely inside barrels
half-wedged and left to rot
we are the half-destroyed instruments
that once held to a course
the water-eaten log
the fouled compass

We are, I am, you are
by cowardice or courage
the one who find our way
back to this scene
carrying a knife, a camera
a book of myths
in which
our names do not appear.

1972 [*Diving into the Wreck*, 1973]

Adrienne Rich was born in Baltimore, elder daughter of Arnold Rich, a pathologist at Johns Hopkins Medical School. Her mother, Helen, was a pianist and composer. Her involvement with civil rights and the women's movement during the 1960s in New York saw a sea change in her work, and her collections published in the 1970s and 1980s became central texts for the second-wave feminist movement. Writing in *The New York Times Book Review*, Carol Muske-Dukes described Rich's progression 'in life (and in her poems) from young widow and disenchanted formalist, to spiritual and rhetorical convalescent, to feminist leader [...] and doyenne of a newly-defined female literature'.

Written in the early 70s, 'Diving into the Wreck' is a key poem in a pivotal collection reviewed by Margaret Atwood in 1973 (also in *The New York Times Book Review*): 'The wreck she is diving into, in the very strong title poem, is the wreck of obsolete myths, particularly myths about men and women. She is journeying to something that is already in the past, in order to discover for herself the reality behind the myth, "the wreck and not the story of the wreck / the thing itself and not the myth". What she finds is part treasure and part corpse, and she also finds that she herself is part of it, a "half-destroyed instrument". As explorer she is detached; she carries a knife to cut her way in, cut structures apart; a camera to record; and the book of myths itself, a book which has hitherto had no place for explorers like herself. [...] The truth, it seems, is not just what you find when you open a door: it is itself a door, which the poet is always on the verge of going through.'

The poem was later included in her highly influential compilation, *The Fact of a Doorframe: Poems Selected and New 1950–1984* (1984). In her foreword to the later expanded retrospective, *The Fact of a Doorframe: Selected Poems 1950–2001*, Rich wrote: 'To work in a medium which can be, has been, used as an instrument of trivialisation and deceit, not to mention colonisation and humiliation, is somewhat different from working a medium like stone, clay, paint, charcoal, even iron or steel. A poet cannot refuse language, choose another medium. But the poem can re-fuse the language given to him or her, bend and torque it into an instrument for connection instead of dominance and apartheid toward what Edouard Glissant has wonderfully called "the poetics of relation".'

MICHAEL LONGLEY (*b.* 1939)

Wounds

Here are two pictures from my father's head –
I have kept them like secrets until now:
First, the Ulster Division at the Somme
Going over the top with 'Fuck the Pope!'
'No Surrender!': a boy about to die,
Screaming 'Give 'em one for the Shankill!'
'Wilder than Gurkhas' were my father's words
Of admiration and bewilderment.
Next comes the London-Scottish padre
Resettling kilts with his swagger-stick,
With a stylish backhand and a prayer.
Over a landscape of dead buttocks
My father followed him for fifty years.
At last, a belated casualty,
He said – lead traces flaring till they hurt –
'I am dying for King and Country, slowly.'
I touched his hand, his thin head I touched.

Now, with military honours of a kind,
With his badges, his medals like rainbows,
His spinning compass, I bury beside him
Three teenage soldiers, bellies full of
Bullets and Irish beer, their flies undone.
A packet of Woodbines I throw in,
A lucifer, the Sacred Heart of Jesus
Paralysed as heavy guns put out
The night-light in a nursery for ever;
Also a bus-conductor's uniform –
He collapsed beside his carpet-slippers
Without a murmur, shot through the head
By a shivering boy who wandered in

Before they could turn the television down
Or tidy away the supper dishes.
To the children, to a bewildered wife,
I think 'Sorry Missus' was what he said.

May 1972 [Published in *An Exploded View*, 1973]

Michael Longley is an Irish poet of English parentage who has
spent most of his life in Belfast and at his coastal retreat at Carrig-
skeewan in Co. Mayo. A dedicated naturalist, he studied Classics
at Trinity College Dublin, and worked for the Arts Council of
Northern Ireland from 1970 to 1991. Longley's poetry is formally
inventive and precisely observed, spanning and blending love
poetry, war poetry, nature poetry, elegies, satires, verse epistles,
art and the art of poetry. He has extended the capacity of the lyric
to absorb dark matter: the Great War, the Holocaust, the Northern
Irish 'Troubles'; and his translations from classical poets speak to
contemporary issues. He co-edited *The Essential Brendan Kennelly:
Selected Poems* (2011) with Terence Brown.

I have extracted Brendan's commentary on Longley's poem
'Wounds' from his essay 'Poetry and Violence' (1988), reprinted in
Journey into Joy. This is preceded by some general remarks taken
from his review of Longley's 1991 collection, *Gorse Fires*, in the
journal *Fortnight*.

BK ■ Michael Longley is probably the most confident poet writing
in Ireland today. By that I mean he is the one who most successfully
resists the temptation to explain himself or his work. A Longley poem
is simply there, like a cat or a tree or a flower or a bench in a park.
His sense of wonder at the *thereness* of things, at the fact of the
facts of existence, is the source and substance of much of his poetry.

A fair amount of criticism has a kind of skilled vulgarity in this
matter of explaining things away, and quite a share of it comes
from poets themselves – including myself when I am trying to
"present" myself. But Longley has escaped this disease with a
certain submissive gaiety of mind, a smiling intellectual impish-
ness, right through the decades. The result is that his work is the

closest we have to what George Moore once called 'pure poetry'; or what, I believe, imagists such as Richard Aldington, 'HD' and the early Ezra Pound were trying to do – to release from language and from the poem to the reader, the trapped, abused, resonant, imagistic purity that is at once so fragile and so powerful. It takes great confidence, patience and skill, as well as a refusal to explain oneself, to do this. Longley has all these qualities and talents. [...]

Longley's elegies have a simplicity and nobility rare in our times. It doesn't matter whether he's remembering someone famous like Philip Larkin or somebody almost unknown these qualities persist. With Longley, memory is a shrine and a sanctuary.[50]

BK ■ Michael Longley looks at history, and sees wounds, the wounds of people, the wounds of history. Longley is a Northern Unionist; his father fought for the English, with the Ulster Division, at the Somme. His father survived that war, and died later when his wounds turned to cancer. Longley links his father's death and burial with the burial of three young English soldiers, and the death of a bus conductor, murdered by a youngster, a teenager, as the family prepared to watch television, after supper. I choose this poem, 'Wounds', because it depicts the consequences in a atmosphere of domestic normality. A boy, become the instrument of history's blind hatred, *kills*, because he himself is both victim and instrument. This poem is a striking example of the grotesque normality of that violence which is the consequence of previous violence which is itself the consequence of previous violence – and so on. What is appalling is the reader's realisation of something about the very nature of violence – that is, its fertility, its spawning, helpless fertility, endlessly begetting itself in infinite form, like a demented Proteus.

What is 'civilised' in us must condemn violence, as leaders of governments do with predictable clichés and platitudes. These do not diminish the sincerity of leaders; but they *do* emphasise the ready-to-hand slogan-like quality of their condemnations, as if leaders sensed something hollow in their own rhetoric of condemnation. If what is 'civilised' in us must condemn, what is exploratory and creative in us must enquire and ponder.

What *is* violence? [51]

DEREK MAHON   (1939-2020)

A Disused Shed in Co. Wexford

> Let them not forget us, the weak souls among the asphodels.
>
> SEFERIS, *Mythistorema*

(for J.G. Farrell)

Even now there are places where a thought might grow –
Peruvian mines, worked out and abandoned
To a slow clock of condensation,
An echo trapped for ever, and a flutter
Of wildflowers in the lift-shaft,
Indian compounds where the wind dances
And a door bangs with diminished confidence,
Lime crevices behind rippling rain barrels,
Dog corners for bone burials;
And in a disused shed in Co. Wexford,

Deep in the grounds of a burnt-out hotel,
Among the bathtubs and the washbasins
A thousand mushrooms crowd to a keyhole.
This is the one star in their firmament
Or frames a star within a star.
What should they do there but desire?
So many days beyond the rhododendrons
With the world waltzing in its bowl of cloud,
They have learnt patience and silence
Listening to the rooks querulous in the high wood.

They have been waiting for us in a foetor
Of vegetable sweat since civil war days,
Since the gravel-crunching, interminable departure
Of the expropriated mycologist.
He never came back, and light since then
Is a keyhole rusting gently after rain.
Spiders have spun, flies dusted to mildew
And once a day, perhaps, they have heard something –

A trickle of masonry, a shout from the blue
Or a lorry changing gear at the end of the lane.

There have been deaths, the pale flesh flaking
Into the earth that nourished it;
And nightmares, born of these and the grim
Dominion of stale air and rank moisture.
Those nearest the door grow strong –
'Elbow room! Elbow room!'
The rest, dim in a twilight of crumbling
Utensils and broken pitchers, groaning
For their deliverance, have been so long
Expectant that there is left only the posture.

A half century, without visitors, in the dark –
Poor preparation for the cracking lock
And creak of hinges; magi, moonmen,
Powdery prisoners of the old regime,
Web-throated, stalked like triffids, racked by drought
And insomnia, only the ghost of a scream
At the flash-bulb firing-squad we wake them with
Shows there is life yet in their feverish forms.
Grown beyond nature now, soft food for worms,
They lift frail heads in gravity and good faith.

They are begging us, you see, in their wordless way,
To do something, to speak on their behalf
Or at least not to close the door again.
Lost people of Treblinka and Pompeii!
'Save us, save us,' they seem to say,
'Let the god not abandon us
Who have come so far in darkness and in pain.
We too had our lives to live.
You with your light meter and relaxed itinerary,
Let not our naive labours have been in vain!'

[First published in *The Listener*, 17 September 1973; *The Snow Party*, 1975.]

Derek Mahon was the most formally accomplished Irish poet of a generation including Seamus Heaney and Michael Longley. His early influences included Yeats, MacNeice, Auden and Beckett along with the French poets and dramatists he continued to translate. Born in Belfast, he was educated at Trinity College Dublin, and lived in France, London and New York before returning to Ireland, to Kinsale in Co. Cork. His work for the theatre included versions of Molière, Racine, Rostand, Sophocles and Euripides, and his poetry translations include two editions of Philippe Jaccottet.

Mahon's 'A Disused Shed in Co. Wexford' is one of the great poems of the 20th century. The mushrooms in Mahon's 'disused shed' have been waiting in the dark 'since civil war days'. Their presence is symbolic, standing for all the marginalised people and mute victims of history. Charged with meaning and remembrance by the poem, this forgotten shed behind the rhododendrons is an imagined lost world ('one of those places where a thought might grow') remembered from *Troubles* (1970), a novel set just after the First World War in the decaying Majestic Hotel in rural Ireland by J.G. Farrell, to whom the poem is dedicated (Mahon's friend was a polio victim, and died in Ireland in a drowning accident not long after the poem was written).

Written during the Irish 'Troubles' in the 1970s, the poem is both timeless and timely, as Seamus Deane has pointed out: 'It is a poem that heartbreakingly dwells on and gives voice to all those peoples and civilisations that have been lost and/or destroyed. Since it is set in Ireland, with all the characteristics of an Irish "Big House" ruin, it speaks with a special sharpness to the present moment and the fear, rampant in Northern Ireland, of communities that fear they too might perish and be lost, with none to speak for them.' [52]

Mahon's poem achieves its remarkable effects through sound, beginning with a mellifluous evocation through consonance and assonance of fading sounds in the first stanza, through which the first sentence unspools to the metre like a rollcall, with a breathjump across the stanza gap at the end of line 10, not meeting the first full-stop until the end of the 13th line of the poem, at the light-giving keyhole. Edna Longley's close reading[53] of this poem shows how from this point 'rhythms expressive of the mushrooms crowding to the poem's keyhole, of growth and accumulation, answer those of diminuendo', and also how complementary rhythms trace the 'posture' of 'expectancy' and 'desire' asserted in the narrative. The ten-line stanzas which Mahon handles with such delicacy and consummate skill are "big houses" of his own building indebted to past models, to his formal masters W.B. Yeats and Louis MacNeice.

Brendan didn't write a commentary on 'A Disused Shed in Co. Wexford', but his responses to Mahon's work as a whole offer a wider context for a reading of the poem. The following paragraphs are excerpted from his essay 'Derek Mahon's Humane Perspective' (1989), published in *Journey into Joy*.[54]

BK ■ Probably the single most difficult problem for anyone seeking to get into Mahon's poetry is trying to define the quality of his voice, as it is indeed with most poetry. There are many elements in that voice. In his best poems all these elements are held in a calm and dignified balance. It is a quiet voice, not too dramatic. It is a consciously educated voice. It is learned but not pedantic. It is self aware and self mocking. It is perhaps too ironic to be noticeably passionate, and yet there is no doubt of its intensity. It is the kind of voice that craves an eloquent linguistic precision and often finds it. It is a voice of conscience, scrupulously examined, stylishly projected, rhythmically elaborated, a pleasure to hear, mysterious to think about. [...]

Mahon is a true wit. There is an element of cruelty in his perception and in his precision but there is no lack of compassion. It is a complex wit: sceptical, ironic, nostalgic, funny, philosophical, mickey-taking, impudent, lonely, relishing the absurd and the lyrical simultaneously. [...]

But one of the problems for this kind of writer, for an ironic, romantic, sceptical, witty, nostalgic humanist is what I shall call the problem of yourself. What are you to do with yourself? Where does 'self' stand in the poem? Where is Mahon in his poetry? I said he is a poet of the perimeter, meditating on the centre, with a mixture of amusement and pain. He is not, or he is very rarely, at the centre of his poems. He has a modesty, a kind of good manners of the imagination which nearly always prevents him from indulging in any form of Whitmanesque self-exhibitionism. So how then does he actually say things? How does the peripheral stance convey a central statement?

In different ways: and one of his principal ways is that of invoking the help of other poets, other poems. And he does this methodically and shamelessly. Immediately, therefore, we enter the indirect world. Yeats said that the poet 'never speaks directly as to somebody at the breakfast table – there is always a phantasmagoria'. I think that is debatable, but I can see the point of it. There is very direct poetry in Yeats and very indirect. I want to talk about the value of imaginative indirectness, about not being candid, not being totally direct to anyone. This is a vital aspect of Mahon's humanistic stance.

First of all, from the point of view of the writer, it removes the embarrassment of having to say I, I, I or me, me, me all the time. The helpless egotism of mere selfhood, mere identity is put at a remove. And in the space created between the centre that the self would occupy and the perimeter to which the self is shifted with dignity but firmness, there arises an altruistic world, peopled by others but still paradoxically controlled by the removed self. Indirectness involves control through a deliberate act of imaginative self-abnegation. In this self-abnegation there exists not only a new order of control but also new possibilities for exciting imaginative freedom. And also, it must be admitted, a certain capacity for cunning and effective manipulation is made possible, made available. In this situation, the shadow manipulates the various substances.

By removing the self from the centre of the poem, by opting for an indirect stance, by putting other poets and other poems at the centre, by seeming to substitute a sophisticated deference for an aggressive statement, a new control, freedom and cunning imaginative power are achieved. And things can be said with a certain calm altruistic dignity which previously could only be said with perhaps an obtrusive egotism, a limited, assertive sense of self. Self is freed from self so that self may become more comprehensively articulate.

ELIZABETH BISHOP (1914–1979)

One Art

The art of losing isn't hard to master;
so many things seem filled with the intent
to be lost that their loss is no disaster.

Lose something every day. Accept the fluster
of lost door keys, the hour badly spent.
The art of losing isn't hard to master.

Then practice losing farther, losing faster:
places, and names, and where it was you meant
to travel. None of these will bring disaster.

I lost my mother's watch. And look! my last, or
next-to-last, of three loved houses went.
The art of losing isn't hard to master.

I lost two cities, lovely ones. And, vaster,
some realms I owned, two rivers, a continent.
I miss them, but it wasn't a disaster.

– Even losing you (the joking voice, a gesture
I love) I shan't have lied. It's evident
the art of losing's not too hard to master
though it may look like (*Write* it!) like disaster.

October 1975 [First published in *The New Yorker*, 26 April 1976]

Elizabeth Bishop is now recognised as one of the greatest poets of
the 20th century. When she died in 1979, she had only published
four collections, yet had won virtually every major American
literary award. She maintained close friendships with poets such
as Marianne Moore and Robert Lowell, and was always highly

regarded by other writers, but her work has only come to eclipse that of her contemporaries in the years since her death. Her closely observed poetry mirrors the ambivalence she perceived in the world, 'the always-more-successful surrealism of everyday life', transforming the world through close observation as though seeing is believing.

Born in Worcester, Massachusetts, Elizabeth Bishop was a virtual orphan from an early age, brought up by sometimes abusive relatives in New England and Nova Scotia, following her father's death and her mother's committal to an asylum. The tragic circumstances of her life – from alcoholism to repeated experiences of loss in her relationships with women – nourished an outsider's poetry notable both for its reticence and tentativeness. Her greatest loss was that of her lover, architect Lota de Macedo Soares, with whom she lived for 15 years in Brazil, and who took an overdose after their break-up while staying with Bishop in New York. Her villanelle, 'One Art', is her response to that loss as well as to her estrangement at the time of writing from her later partner, the much younger Alice Methfessel, who had begun a relationship with a man.

Robert Frost wrote that 'Poetry provides the one permissible way of saying one thing and meaning another'. A perfect example of that would be Bishop's 'One Art', which claims 'The art of losing isn't hard to master', but the effect of its repeatedly rhymed assertions is to assert the opposite, with the parenthesised inter-jection ('Write it!') brilliantly disrupting the clinching last line. Indirection and understatement can often provide a stronger means of expressing and confronting a conflict between thought and feeling than open lament or direct description.

In her *New Yorker* essay on 'One Art', Megan Marshall chron-icles Bishop's writing of the poem through 17 drafts, detailing how she changed the poem from 'a prose-heavy first draft' to its final, more distanced response to 'the two great disasters of her adult life, leaving out Methfessel's blue eyes and selecting physical characteristics she'd loved in both Methfessel and Lota de Macedo Soares [...] By draft 15, the poem had acquired its title. Bishop had been practicing the art of losing since infancy; art had become her one means of mastery. "One Art" was the elegy she had wanted for so long to write.'[55] The one line which remained unchanged throughout, as the poem took its shape as a villanelle, was the first, 'The art of losing isn't hard to master'.

DEREK WALCOTT (1930–2017)

Love after Love

The time will come
when, with elation,
you will greet yourself arriving
at your own door, in your own mirror
and each will smile at the other's welcome,

and say, sit here. Eat.
You will love again the stranger who was your self.
Give wine. Give bread, Give back your heart
to itself, to the stranger who has loved you

all your life, whom you ignored
for another, who knows you by heart.
Take down the love letters from the bookshelf

the photographs, the desperate notes,
peel your own image from the mirror.
Sit. Feast on your life.

[*Sea Grapes*, 1976]

Sir Derek Walcott was born in St Lucia. He was not only the
foremost Caribbean poet of modern times (as well as a dramatist
and painter) but a major figure in world literature, recognised
with the award of the Nobel Prize in Literature in 1992 'for a
poetic *œuvre* of great luminosity, sustained by a historical vision,
the outcome of a multicultural commitment'. Most of his work
explores the Caribbean cultural experience, the history, landscape
and lives of its multiracial people, fusing folk culture and oral
tales with the classical, avant-garde and English literary tradition.

PHILIP LARKIN (1922–1985)

Aubade

I work all day, and get half-drunk at night.
Waking at four to soundless dark, I stare.
In time the curtain-edges will grow light.
Till then I see what's really always there:
Unresting death, a whole day nearer now,
Making all thought impossible but how
And where and when I shall myself die.
Arid interrogation: yet the dread
Of dying, and being dead,
Flashes afresh to hold and horrify.

The mind blanks at the glare. Not in remorse
– The good not done, the love not given, time
Torn off unused – nor wretchedly because
An only life can take so long to climb
Clear of its wrong beginnings, and may never;
But at the total emptiness for ever,
The sure extinction that we travel to
And shall be lost in always. Not to be here,
Not to be anywhere,
And soon; nothing more terrible, nothing more true.

This is a special way of being afraid
No trick dispels. Religion used to try,
That vast moth-eaten musical brocade
Created to pretend we never die,
And specious stuff that says *No rational being*
Can fear a thing it will not feel, not seeing
That this is what we fear – no sight, no sound,
No touch or taste or smell, nothing to think with,
Nothing to love or link with,
The anaesthetic from which none come round.

And so it stays just on the edge of vision,
A small unfocused blur, a standing chill
That slows each impulse down to indecision.
Most things may never happen: this one will,
And realisation of it rages out
In furnace-fear when we are caught without
People or drink. Courage is no good:
It means not scaring others. Being brave
Lets no one off the grave.
Death is no different whined at than withstood.

Slowly light strengthens, and the room takes shape.
It stands plain as a wardrobe, what we know,
Have always known, know that we can't escape,
Yet can't accept. One side will have to go.
Meanwhile telephones crouch, getting ready to ring
In locked-up offices, and all the uncaring
Intricate rented world begins to rouse.
The sky is white as clay, with no sun.
Work has to be done.
Postmen like doctors go from house to house.

29 November 1977 [First published in *The Times Literary Supplement*, 23 December 1977; *Collected Poems* (1988).]

Philip Larkin was an influential and popular English poet, the leading figure in the 'Movement' group whose plain-speaking, descriptive poetry using traditional forms was the dominant poetic mode in British poetry of the 1950s and early 60s. He was also a novelist and jazz critic. The main themes of his poetry are love, marriage, freedom, destiny, loss, ageing and death. Influenced by Yeats, Eliot, Auden and Hardy, Larkin was a late Romantic lyric poet who evolved a persona suited to his pessimistic postwar outlook on life: dry, sceptical, modest and unshowy, thinking aloud in an apparently commensensical fashion, yet also honest, emotional and capable of rich surprises of thought and imagery.

Born in Coventry, he worked in Hull in the university library for the last 30 years of his life.

As many have noted, including Seamus Heaney, the appearance of 'Aubade' in the *TLS* just before Christmas in 1977, came as quite a surprise to his readers. Apart from 'The Mower', it was the only significant poem Larkin wrote after his final collection, *High Windows* (1974). The poem's date is responsible for its seemingly anachronistic position in this anthology, with most of the other Larkin poems we considered being much earlier, including 'Church Going' (from 1954), 'Toads' (1954), 'Mr Bleaney' (1955) and 'The Whitsun Weddings' (1958). Even those dates seem incongruous with some poems (including the last two) not made available to readers in book form for several years. Larkin only published four collections in his lifetime. His Yeatsian debut, *The North Ship* (1945), reads now like the work of another poet.

In an essay on the late poetry of Yeats and Larkin (from his 1990 Oxford lectures),[56] Heaney calls Larkin's 'Aubade' 'the definitive post-Christian English poem, one that abolishes the soul's traditional pretension to immortality', yet an absence of life after death is as questionable as its presence. Larkin's poem copes with the eternal subject of death, said Czesław Miłosz, 'in a manner corresponding to the second half of the twentieth century', and yet it 'leaves me not only dissatisfied but indignant [...] poetry by its very essence has always been on the side of life. Faith in life everlasting has accompanied man in his wanderings through time, and it has always been larger and deeper than religious or philosophical creeds which expressed only one of its forms.' Heaney believed that in imagining death, poetry brings human existence into a fuller life.

ANNE STEVENSON (1933–2020)

Poem for a Daughter

'I think I'm going to have it,'
I said, joking between pains.
The midwife rolled competent
sleeves over corpulent milky arms.
'Dear, you never have it,
we deliver it.'
A judgement years proved true.
Certainly I've never had you

as you still have me, Caroline.
Why does a mother need a daughter?
Heart's needle, hostage to fortune,
freedom's end. Yet nothing's more perfect
than that bleating, razor-shaped cry
that delivers a mother to her baby.
The bloodcord snaps that held
their sphere together. The child,
tiny and alone, creates the mother.

A woman's life is her own
until it is taken away
by a first particular cry.
Then she is not alone
but part of the premises
of everything there is:
a time, a tribe, a war.
When we belong to the world
we become what we are.

24 June 1978 [*Minute by Glass Minute*, 1982]

Anne Stevenson was an American and British poet known for her thoughtful and richly musical lyric and narrative poetry, as well as for *Bitter Fame* (1989), her controversial biography of her near contemporary, Sylvia Plath.

Rooted in close observation of the world and acute psychological insight, Anne Stevenson's poems continually question how we see and think about the world. They are incisive as well as entertaining, marrying critical rigour with personal feeling, and a sharp wit with an original brand of serious humour.

Born in England of American parents, she grew up in New England and Michigan, but lived in Britain for most of her adult life, and was married four times. Her father was the philosopher C.L. Stevenson, who was studying at Cambridge with Wittgenstein and G.E. Moore at the time of her birth. With expectations of becoming a professional musician, she herself studied music, European literature and history at the University of Michigan, returning later to read English. After several transatlantic switches, she settled in Britain in 1964, living in Cambridge, Scotland, Oxford, the Welsh Borders, and latterly in North Wales and Durham.

She published the first critical study of Elizabeth Bishop, in 1966, drawing on her correspondence with Bishop in Brazil during the early 1960s. Bishop's meticulous style 'influenced her own poetry, which often focused on landscapes that soon became psychological and moral landscapes, symbolic in their resonances. [...] Although influenced by Robert Frost, Bishop, Wallace Stevens, her poems are recognisably her own, defiantly independent [...] training a critical eye on the world before her, which she illuminates and dissects with a distinctive shrewdness and affection' (Jay Parini).[57]

Her epistolary collection, *Correspondences, a Family History in Letters* (1974), chronicles the lives of a fictional New England family from 1879 to 1972. Part of the impetus for writing what she fondly called 'my 19th-century novel' was her buried grief at her mother's death from cancer, in 1963, along with the disintegration of her second marriage. It was also the poem with which she 'finally cut the umbilical cord to the America my parents taught me to believe in'.[58] 'Poem for a Daughter' was written for her daughter's birthday and originally titled 'To Caroline at Twenty-One'.

KEN SMITH (1938–2003)

Being the third song of Urias

Lives ago, years past generations
perhaps nowhere I dreamed it:
the foggy ploughland of wind
and hoofprints, my father
off in the mist topping beets.

Where I was eight, I knew nothing,
the world a cold winter light
on half a dozen fields, then
all the winking blether of stars.

Before like a fool I began
explaining the key in its lost locked box
adding words to the words to the sum
that never works out.

               Where I was
distracted again by the lapwing,
the damp morning air of my father's
gregarious plainchant cursing
all that his masters deserved
and had paid for.
            Sure I was
then for the world's mere being
in the white rime on weeds
among the wet hawthorn berries
at the field's edge darkened by frost,
and none of these damned words to say it.

I began trailing out there in voices,
friends, women, my children,
my father's tetherless anger, some

like him who are dead who are
part of the rain now.

[*What I'm Doing Now*, 1980]

Ken Smith was a northern English poet whose work and example
inspired a whole generation of younger poets. His poetry shifted
territory with time, from rural Yorkshire, America and London to
the war-ravaged Balkans and Eastern Europe (before and after
Communism). His early books span a transition from a preoccupation
with land and myth to his later engagement with urban Britain
and the politics of radical disaffection. Smith grew up in the North
Riding of Yorkshire, the son of an itinerant farm labourer, and
this poem is written from dual perspectives, evoking the boy back
in the raw landscape of his childhood as well as the grown-up man
looking back at his life, examining his feelings of separation from
the inarticulate, violent, often terrifying father he sought to under-
stand in this and other poems. The Urias of his title is a persona,
a wanderer-figure who appears in a number of his poems.

In an interview in 1997 with Colin Raw,[59] Smith recalled his
childhood as being 'one long battle', and how his haunted father
still haunted his own dreams decades later: 'He's still in my head.
Every now and again I write a poem in which I say goodbye, this
is it, get out of my head. But he always comes back. [...] Haunted,
but I don't know what by because he never talked about himself.
He never gave any details. I didn't even know where he was born
until he was dead and we got a birth certificate, which I'm still not
sure to this day is actually him. John Smith, right! Well I didn't
know that there was a Patrick between the John and the Smith.
Nor, indeed, that he was born in Donegal and shipped over to
England, aged 10, to an uncle, in inverted commas, who was just
a farmer who put him to work, at the age of 10, and that he had
spent his first years till then in an orphanage in Derry.'

Ken Smith's formative years as a poet coincided with Brendan
Kennelly's at Leeds University in the early 1960s, meeting, reading
and learning from other poets of the 'Leeds Renaissance' including
Geoffrey Hill [305], Jon Silkin and Tony Harrison in particular. The
two old friends met again in the 1980s and 90s when I arranged
for them to share the stage at readings in England and Berlin.

SEAMUS HEANEY (1939–2013)

from Sweeney Astray

Donal, son of Aodh, won the battle that day. A kinsman of Sweeney's called Aongus the Stout survived and came fleeing with a band of his people into Glen Arkin. They were wondering about Sweeney because they had not seen him alive after the fight and he had not been counted among the casualties. They were discussing this and deciding that Ronan's curse had something to do with it when Sweeney spoke out of the yew:

Soldiers, come here.
You are from Dal-Arie,
and the man you are looking for
roosts in his tree.

The life God grants me now
is bare and strait;
I am haggard, womanless,
and cut off from music.

So I am here at Ros Bearaigh.
Ronan has brought me low,
God has exiled me from myself –
soldiers, forget the man you knew.

[...]

The bushy leafy oak tree
is highest in the wood,
the forking shoots of hazel
hide sweet hazelnuts.

The alder is my darling,
all thornless in the gap,

some milk of human kindness
coursing in its sap.

The blackthorn is a jaggy creel
stippled with dark sloes;
green watercress in thatch on wells
where the drinking blackbird goes. [...]

The aspen pales
and whispers, hesitates:
a thousand frightened scuts
race in its leaves.

But what disturbs me most
in the leafy wood
is the to and fro and to and fro
of an oak rod.

[...]

Almighty God, I deserved this,
my cut feet, my drained face,
winnowed by a sheer wind
and miserable in my mind.

Last night I lay in Mourne
plastered in wet; cold rain poured.
Tonight, in torment, in Glasgally
I am crucified in the fork of a tree.

[...]

All this is hard to thole, Lord!
Still without bed or board,
crouching to graze on cress,
drinking cold water from rivers.

Alarmed out of the autumn wood,
whipped by whins, flecked with blood,
running wild among wolf-packs,
shying away with the red stag.

Son of God, have mercy on us!
Never to hear a human voice!
To sleep naked every night
up there in the highest thickets,

to have lost my proper shape and looks,
a mad scuttler on mountain peaks,
a derelict doomed to loneliness:
Son of God, have mercy on us!

[1983/1984]

Seamus Heaney was born into a Catholic farming family in Co.
Derry, left Northern Ireland in 1972, and lived in America, Wicklow
and Dublin. His concerns for the land, language and troubled
history of Ireland run through all his work. His early poetry is
notable for its sensory, lyrical evocations of nature and rural life,
and of childhood, which nurtured many of his most memorable
poems. He received the Nobel Prize in Literature in 1995.

We had intended to include Heaney's seminal poem 'Digging'
from his first collection *Death of a Naturalist*, which Brendan
reviewed when it was published in 1966, calling it 'a startlingly
good collection', but I've not been able to trace a copy of that
review. The only writing by Brendan on Seamus Heaney's work
I've been able to find is a review of *Sweeney Astray* (1983/1984) he
wrote for *The New York Times*.[60] I've prefaced this with those
sections of Heaney's translation which he discusses or quotes from
in the review.

In *Stepping Stones*, Heaney tells Dennis O'Driscoll that the last
time he saw Patrick Kavanagh was at a reading by Brendan Kennelly
in Hodges Figgis bookshop in Dublin.[61] He also mentions being a
guest at Brendan's wedding to Peggy O'Brien in 1969.

BK ■ One of the crucial signs of a genuine imagination is its ability to give new life to old myths, stories and legends. By that criterion, *Sweeney Astray*, a complete translation of the medieval Irish work *Buile Suibhne*, shows that Seamus Heaney's imagination is continuing to deepen in intensity and range.

Sweeney is cursed by a Christian cleric named Ronan whom he has insulted and humiliated. As a result, he becomes a mad outcast, a paranoid fugitive from life, a shifty victim of panic who lives on watercress and water and is driven to the tops of trees, from which vantage point he gazes down, terrified yet furiously articulate. From the heights of his mad agony, Sweeney makes sad, beautiful, thrilling poems. He is the voice of darkness and nightmare but also, in his naked and ravaged loneliness, the celebrant of the natural beauty of Ireland. This paranoid is a superb poet, and it takes a superb poet to capture, in translation from the Irish, the full range of pain and beauty in Sweeney's poetry. Seamus Heaney has produced an exhilarating version of this most unusual story poem.

And it is a story poem. Many poets, impatient with the sometimes irritating machinery of narrative, would have cut the story and gone for the climactic lyrical moments. In his introduction, Heaney admits he found himself faced with this temptation:

> My first impulse had been to forage for the best lyric moments and to present them as poetic orphans, out of the context of the story. These points of poetic intensity, rather than the overall organisation, establish the work's highest artistic level and offer the strongest invitations to the translator of verse. Yet I gradually felt I had to earn the right to do the high points by undertaking the whole thing: what I was dealing with, after all, is a major work in the canon of medieval literature.

That passage perfectly illustrates Heaney's patient sense of responsibility toward and respect for the original work. In the art of translation, this sense is vitally connected with the quality of the ultimate product – in this case, with a new, exciting creation that seems to grow into an original work. Some prose passages and even some of the poems are relatively flat, deliberately so. The original is also prose and poetry, but it is only as one reads and rereads Heaney's version that one realises that the counterpointing of prose with poetry intensifies the climactic lyric moments. To my mind, this is true of Irish literary works as far apart in time as the

Old Irish epic dominated by the hero Cuchulain, *Táin Bó Cúailnge*, and Joyce's *Ulysses*. Both have heavy, tedious moments, but also an ecstatic, soaring quality. We appreciate the moments of flight all the more deeply because we have been earthbound for a while.

Something similar happens in *Sweeney Astray*. A number of the prose passages have clarity and solid force; but they remain prose. These slow moments stress the poem's intensity, as in the opening part of our selection where Sweeney addresses the soldiers from the yew tree.

This balancing of slowness with speed, casualness with concentration, is not merely a linguistic technique or structural device; it reflects the very core of the poem. Sweeney is mad, in this world. His inspired frenzies occur on a familiar stage. To the other characters on that commonplace stage, he is a driven figure raving gibberish. Sweeney in his turn sees them as if he were a mad Adam driven alone through a lunatic Eden. The language of the poem reflects this gulf – between the 'civilised' and the outcast, the accepted and the accursed, agonised aimlessness and calm resoluteness, the man of pain and the men of purpose. Heaney, in his magical way, balances all these matters with a strong sense of drama and unfailing control.

I mentioned Sweeney as the man of pain apart from the men of purpose. *Sweeney Astray*, I believe, will come to be seen as a compelling poem of human pain – the vague yet vivid pain of the waking imagination, an almost unutterable loneliness. 'I am the bare figure of pain,' Sweeney cries:

> Almighty God, I deserved this,
> my cut feet, my drained face,
> winnowed by a sheer wind
> and miserable in my mind.
>
> Last night I lay in Mourne
> plastered in wet; cold rain poured.
> Tonight, in torment, in Glasgally
> I am crucified in the fork of a tree.

If the poem were kept at this pitch from beginning to end, it would become almost unendurable. Flann O'Brien, who used the figure of Sweeney in his comic novel, *At Swim-Two-Birds*, realised this, and so his Sweeney makes us laugh aloud even as we are touched with pity. This dual response enriches the novel. […] What Heaney offers as an alternative to Sweeney's pain is Heaney's own lyric gift, his inimitable music. If there is anything in this work that balances the poetry of pain, it is the poetry of praise. And what is praised most beautifully and convincingly is the landscape of Ireland, its fields, meadows, hills, rivers, mountains, glens, the sea's eternal caress and threat.

Sweeney, driven to live in the trees, praises them with a love and knowledge I find unforgettable. Yet even here the sense of beauty is shot through with loneliness and fear. Sweeney never escapes completely. Menace lives even at the heart of praise.

> But what disturbs me most
> in the leafy wood
> is the to and fro and to and fro
> of an oak rod.

In his poem, 'The Harvest Bow', Heaney says, 'The end of art is peace'. At the end of this work, Sweeney finds his own kind of peace. But what one remembers most about *Sweeney Astray* is the delicate, dramatic balance between pain and praise. The poem is a balanced statement about a tragically unbalanced mind. One feels that this balance, urbanely sustained, is the product of a long, imaginative bond between Heaney and Sweeney. This is quite literally true. Heaney says, 'When I began work on this version, I had just moved to Wicklow, not all that far from Sweeney's final resting ground at St Mullins. I was in a country of woods and hills and remembered that the green spirit of the hedges embodied in Sweeney had first been embodied for me in the persons of a family of tinkers, also called Sweeney, who used to camp in the ditchbacks along the road to the first school I attended. One way or another, he seemed to have been with me from the start.'

EAVAN BOLAND (1944–2020)

The Journey

(for Elizabeth Ryle)

> Immediately cries were heard. These were the loud wailing of
> infant souls weeping at the very entrance-way; never had they
> had their share of life's sweetness for the dark day had stolen
> them from their mothers' breasts and plunged them to a death
> before their time.
>
> VIRGIL, The Aeneid, BOOK VI

And then the dark fell and 'there has never'
I said 'been a poem to an antibiotic:
never a word to compare with the odes on
the flower of the raw sloe for fever

'or the devious Africa-seeking tern
or the protein treasures of the sea-bed.
Depend on it, somewhere a poet is wasting
his sweet uncluttered metres on the obvious

'emblem instead of the real thing.
Instead of sulpha we shall have hyssop dipped
in the wild blood of the unblemished lamb,
so every day the language gets less

'for the task and we are less with the language.'
I finished speaking and the anger faded
and dark fell and the book beside me
lay open at the page Aphrodite

comforts Sappho in her love's duress.
The poplars shifted their music in the garden,
a child startled in a dream,
my room was a mess –

the usual hardcovers, half-finished cups,
clothes piled up on an old chair –
and I was listening out but in my head was
a loosening and sweetening heaviness,

not sleep, but nearly sleep, not dreaming really
but as ready to believe and still
unfevered, calm and unsurprised
when she came and stood beside me

and I would have known her anywhere
and I would have gone with her anywhere
and she came wordlessly
and without a word I went with her

down down down without so much as
ever touching down but always, always
with a sense of mulch beneath us,
the way of stairs winding down to a river

and as we went on the light went on
failing and I looked sideways to be certain
it was she, misshapen, musical –
Sappho – the scholiast's nightingale

and down we went, again down
until we came to a sudden rest
beside a river in what seemed to be
an oppressive suburb of the dawn.

My eyes got slowly used to the bad light.
At first I saw shadows, only shadows.
Then I could make out women and children
and, in the way they were, the grace of love.

'Cholera, typhus, croup, diptheria'
she said, 'in those days they racketed
in every backstreet and alley of old Europe.
Behold the children of the plague.'

Then to my horror I could see to each
nipple some had clipped a limpet shape –
suckling darknesses – while others had their arms
weighed down, making terrible pietàs.

She took my sleeve and said to me, 'be careful.
Do not define these women by their work:
not as washerwomen trussed in dust and sweating,
muscling water into linen by the river's edge

'nor as court ladies brailled in silk
on wool and woven with an ivory unicorn
and hung, nor as laundresses tossing cotton,
brisking daylight with lavender and gossip.

'But these are women who went out like you
when dusk became a dark sweet with leaves,
recovering the day, stooping, picking up
teddy bears and rag dolls and tricycles and buckets –

'love's archaeology – and they too like you
stood boot deep in flowers once in summer
or saw winter come in with a single magpie
in a caul of haws, a solo harlequin.'

I stood fixed. I could not reach or speak to them.
Between us was the melancholy river,
the dream water, the narcotic crossing
and they had passed over it, its cold persuasions.

I whispered, 'let me be
let me at least be their witness,' but she said
'what you have seen is beyond speech,
beyond song, only not beyond love;

'remember it, you will remember it'
and I heard her say but she was fading fast
as we emerged under the stars of heaven,
'there are not many of us; you are dear

'and stand beside me as my own daughter.
I have brought you here so you will know forever
the silences in which are our beginnings,
in which we have an origin like water,'

and the wind shifted and the window clasp
opened, banged and I woke up to find
the poetry books stacked higgledy piggledy,
my skirt spread out where I had laid it –

nothing was changed; nothing was more clear
but it was wet and the year was late.
The rain was grief in arrears; my children
slept the last dark out safely and I wept.

[First published in *The Journey* (Deerfield Press, 1983); *The Journey and Other Poems* (Carcanet Press, 1987)]

Eavan Boland was born in Dublin, the daughter of Frederick Boland, Ireland's first ambassador to both Britain and the United Nations, and painter Frances J. Kelly, but lived outside Ireland from the age of six, the family moving with her father's postings to London and then New York. She returned to Ireland to complete her education, graduating from Trinity College Dublin in 1966. From 1996 she divided her time between Dublin and California where she was a Professor of English at Stanford University.

When we were discussing which Eavan Boland poem to include, Brendan sent me a sheaf of poems – many ticked – photocopied from her 1995 *Collected Poems*, and after much deliberation, we settled on what was then a quite recent poem, 'Time and Violence' from *In a Time of Violence* (1994). But with no commentary from him on that poem, I decided to include instead another of his favourite Eavan Boland poems, 'The Journey', the title-poem of *The Journey and Other Poems* (1987), together with his *Irish Times* review of that collection (6 December 1986).

BK ■ I first knew Eavan Boland in the early 60s when she studied English at Trinity College. She was brilliant and beautiful, with a mind fiercely her own, a gift for talking which I've rarely seen, or heard, equalled, a riotous sense of humour, an aggressive conviction that Dublin is the only *really* worthwhile spot on Earth, red hair as fiery as her temper, a genius for mimicry guaranteed to keep you in stitches, vehement opinions about history, art and politics, and a love of poetry as passionate as it was informed. She revelled in telling jokes and yarns that showed her theatrical flair in full comic flight.

She was a delight to know then; and from what I've seen of her and her work over the years, she has grown in grace as a person and strikingly increased in stature as a poet. Her recently published *The Journey and Other Poems* is a Choice of the Poetry Book Society. It seems to me to be the best single book of poems out of Ireland since Kavanagh's *Come Dance with Kitty Stobling*. It is a passionately felt, beautifully crafted collection, full of poems that startle you with their musical clarity and elegance, their calm, deep insights into many facets of human experience, their sweetly articulated respect for human dignity at a time when a person might be forgiven for thinking that such respect is a thing of the past.

By exploring her experience as a woman in her various roles as wife, mother, sister, daughter, friend, observer, thinker, she reveals, with an attractive blend of reticence and force, her rich, complex humanity. The title poem of *The Journey and Other Poems* is one of the most intensely visionary works I've read in years. It's one of those rare poems impossible to quote from because only one form of quotation will do it justice – the entire thing.

As I write that word 'quotation', I can see her saying one of her poems. In her late teens, she had an astonishing memory both for her own work and that of others. When speaking a poem, she would always remain standing, not unlike somebody on a Feis stage, her outstretched right hand moving in unison with the rhythm of her words. There was no faltering or fumbling, no tremulous hesitation, only a tense, hypnotic flow of language that carried listeners along in a musical momentum. I remember her speaking that fine dramatic poem 'New Territory' which is the title poem of her first significant collection. The ending is imprinted on my mind:

> Out of the dark man comes to life and into it
> He goes and loves and dies,

(His element being the dark and not the light of day)
So the ambitious wit
Of poets and exploring ships have been his eyes –
Riding the dark for joy –
And so Isaiah of the sacred text is eagle-eyed because
By peering down the unlit centuries
He glimpsed the holy boy.

No poem is fully alive until it is spoken with love, respect and precision. The human voice uniquely animates what the imagination creates. When critics speak of a poet 'finding his or her voice' they can be taken quite literally. Eavan found her voice early on. More than 20 years ago, it was sweet and low, dramatic and musical, measured and impassioned. Today, in her maturity, it has deepened in resonance and authority.

In those *New Territory* days, it was no trouble to Eavan to talk almost non-stop for eight or ten hours at a stretch. She loved to talk with the warmest possible humour about her family, especially her father, the late Dr Frederick Boland, and her mother, Judy [Frances J. Kelly], a fine artist who encouraged Eavan's early, intense interest in poetry. Because of her father's work as an Irish Ambassador at the Court of St James's in London, and also as Ireland's Permanent Representative to the United Nations in New York, she spent several years in schools in both these cities. She missed Ireland, especially Dublin, a great deal. Exile was a real pain to her. That early pain of exile has grown into a sympathetic, critical acceptance of life in Ireland today.

At one level, *The Journey and Other Poems* is a book about acceptance achieved through various kinds of pain. This may help to account for the relaxed, sensuous wisdom of the book. All the fiery talk of the early years has helped to bring the philosophic mind to this probing, vigilant writer. The trouble with philosophic minds is that the language they use or choose is too often aridly complex, its relentless dullness suffocating the act of attention. Eavan Boland's language is intelligent and warm and thrillingly precise.

She is married to Kevin Casey, the novelist, and has two daughters, Sarah and Eavan Frances. She is a happy woman. Not many people have succeeded in writing well about happiness; much poetry seems to grow out of various forms of unhappiness, or at least discontent or restlessness. The happiness of *The Journey and Other Poems* is the happiness of a highly sophisticated, alert and subtle consciousness, working intensely and deliberately within a given, familiar world that can suddenly turn magical and strange, but is always deeply experienced, acutely observed, and scrupulously recorded.

> They used to leave milk
> out once on these windowsills
> to ward away
> the child-stealing spirits. [...]
>
> You wake first thing
> and in your five-year-size
> striped nightie you are
> everywhere trying everything:
> the springs on the bed,
> the hinges on the window.
>
> You know your a's and b's
> but there's a limit now
> to what you'll believe.
>
> When dark comes I leave
> a superstitious feast
> of wheat biscuits, apples,
> orange juice out for you
> and wake to find it eaten.

('On Holiday')

I thought long and carefully before using that word 'happiness', since I haven't seen in the world I have experienced and observed much evidence of what I imagine the condition to be. I had always thought that if it were achieved, the achievement would need no comment, no chronicling, since the enjoyment of the thing itself would be enough. Such a reality would need no recording; its own existence would be its own purest celebration.

With Eavan, this happiness is a matter of self-definition, achieved through a flexible openness to experience. Certain poems in *The War Horse* (1975), *In Her Own Image* (1980) and *Night Feed* (1982) show this process of self-definition at work in ways that range from the gentle to the aggressive, the utterly calm to the frighteningly nightmarish, the self-doubting to the self-trusting. Over the years, she has conducted this deliberate experience in self-definiton with passionate intelligence and courage. This kind of courage usually means that the person who has it is going to be claimed and labelled because such courage is in short supply.

It would be a critical and human belittlement of Eavan's achievement to say that she is a feminist and to leave it at that. An intelligent, discriminating feminist is included in the full, poetic personality and spirit so richly present in *The Journey and Other Poems*. Because her feminism is placed in perspective, she is a more coherent and convincing feminist than most. The conscious happiness of her achieved self-definition, chiselled from circumstances and increasingly independent of them, has been won through pains that persist, doubts that linger, uncertainties closer than the nearest neighbours. Yet out of all that there emerges a clear-eyed, determined purpose:

> I am Chardin's woman
>
> edged in reflected light
> hardened by
> the need to be ordinary.

> ('Self-Portrait on a Summer Evening')

Self-definition is lucidly expressed in the following lines:

> What I have done I have done alone.
> What I have seen is unverified.
> I have the truth and I need the faith.
> In time I put my hand in her side.

> If she will not bless the ordinary,
> if she will not sanctify the common,
> then here I am and here I stay and then am I
> the most miserable of women.

> ('Envoi')

There is always a special pleasure in seeing a person reach confident and fruitful maturity. When that person is an artist and had been one's friend for many years, the pleasure seems deeper still. Eavan has reached the stage where her poems 'bless the ordinary' and 'sanctify the common'. It is this natural ability, consciously crafted, to scrutinise and celebrate the 'ordinary' that has helped to make her one of the most extraordinarily accomplished contemporary poets.

REFERENCES

Preface: The Making of the Heavy Bear

1. Brendan is quoting Yeats here: 'My conscience or my vanity appalled' from 'Vacillation'.

2. Brendan Kennelly, *Journey into Joy: Selected Prose*, ed. Åke Persson (Newcastle upon Tyne: Bloodaxe Books, 1994)..

3. Richard Pine (ed.), *Dark Fathers into Light: Brendan Kennelly*, Bloodaxe Critical Anthologies: 2 (Newcastle upon Tyne: Bloodaxe Books, 1994), 194-224.

4. Robyn Bolam (ed.), *Eliza's Babes: four centures of women's poetry in English*, c. *1500-1900* (Tarset: Bloodaxe Books, 2005).

5. W.N. Herbert & Matthew Hollis (eds.), *Strong Words: modern poets on modern poetry* (Tarset: Bloodaxe Books, 2000).

6. Edna Longley (ed.), *The Bloodaxe Book of 20th Century Poetry from Britain and Ireland* (Tarset: Bloodaxe Books, 2000).

7. Deryn Rees-Jones (ed.), *Modern Women Poets* (Tarset: Bloodaxe Books, 2000).

Delmore Schwartz

8. John Berryman, 'Dream Song #157, *The Dream Songs* (London: Faber & Faber, 1964), 176.

John Donne

9. T.S. Eliot, 'The Metaphysical Poets', in *Selected Essays* (London: Faber & Faber, 1932), 287.

Andrew Marvell

10. T.S. Eliot, 'Andrew Marvell', in *Selected Essays*, 295, 296.

William Cowper

11. Jonathan Bate, *The Song of the Earth* (Cambridge, MA: Harvard University Press; London: Picador Books, 2000), 9-11.

Oliver Goldsmith

12. Terry Gifford, *Green Voices: Understanding Nature Poetry* (Manchester: Manchester University Press, 1995), 56-58.

Lord Byron

13. Jonathan Bate, *The Song of the Earth*, 94-98.

John Clare

14. Jonathan Bate, *The Song of the Earth*, 164.

Gerard Manley Hopkins

15. Brendan Kennelly: 'Gerard Manley Hopkins: The Quest for Essence', RTÉ Television, *Telefís Scoile* (archive A30/899), 23 January 1975.

Edwin Arlington Robinson

16. Charles Cestre: *Introduction to Edwin Arlington Robinson* (New York, 1930), 60.

17. Ronald Moran: *CLQ*, VII (March 1967), 385-92.

18. Ronald E. McFarland: 'Robinson's "Luke Havergal", *Colby Quarterly*, series 10, no.6, June 1974, 366.

19. Denham Sutcliffe (ed.): *Untriangulated Stars* (Cambridge, MA, 1947), 226.

20. (14 December 1895). Ibid, 238.

21. Ibid, 7.

22. McFarland, 366

Robert Frost

23. Joseph Brodsky: 'On grief and reason', *The New Yorker*, 26 September 1994, collected in On Grief and Reason: Essays (Farrar, Straus & Giroux: New York, 1995).

24. Matthew Hollis: *All Roads Lead to France: The Last Years of Edward Thomas* (London: Faber & Faber, 2011), 233-34.

25. Robert Frost at Bread Loaf Conference, 23 August 1953, quoted in Lawrance Thompson, *Robert Frost: The Years of Triumph, 1915-1938* (New York: Holt, Rinehart and Winston, 1970), 546.

W.B. Yeats

26. Poetry and Violence, in Kennelly, *Journey into Joy*, 23-45.

27. 'Irish Poetry to Yeats', part I of 'A View of Irish Poetry', *Journey into Joy*, 46-54.

28. Brendan Kennelly, 'Late Yeats' in *Familiar Strangers: Selected Poems 1960-2004* (Tarset: Bloodaxe Books, 2004), 301.

29. 'Irish Poetry to Yeats', *Journey into Joy*, 53-54.

30. John Millington Synge, 'Preface' to *The Poems*. For example, Collected Works, Vol. 1, edited by Robin Skelton (London: Oxford University Press, 1962), p.xxxvi.

31. 'Poetry and Violence', *Journey into Joy*, 42-44.

Marianne Moore

32. Elizabeth Bishop, 'Efforts of Affection', in *The Collected Prose*, ed. Robert Giroux (New York: Farrar, Straus and Giroux, 1984), 144-45.

Wallace Stevens

33. Robert Pack: *From Wallace Stevens: An approach to his poetry and thought* (Rutgers University Press, New Brunswick, 1958)

34. Wallace Stevens: 'The Relations Between Poetry and Painting' in *The Necessary Angel: Essays on Reality and the Imagination* (Alfred A. Knopf, New York, 1951), 169:

Patrick Kavanagh

35. Brendan Kennelly, 'Late Yeats' in *Familiar Strangers: Selected Poems 1960-2004* (Tarset: Bloodaxe Books, 2004), 298.

36. 'Irish Poetry Since Yeats', part II of 'A View of Irish Poetry', *Journey into Joy*, 55-56.

37. Patrick Kavanagh, 'Signposts', *Collected Pruse* (London: Mac-Gibbon and Kee, 1964), 20-21

38. 'Patrick Kavanagh's Comic Vision', *Journey into Joy*, 111-13.

Ruth Pitter

39. Letter, Ruth Pitter to Andrew Nye, dated 18 May 1985.

40. Elizabeth Jennings in Ruth Pitter, *Collected Poems* (London: Enitharmon Press, 1990), pp. 16-17.

Elizabeth Daryush

41. Donald Davie. 'The Poetry of Elizabeth Daryush', *Poetry Nation* No.5 (1975), archived at http://poetrymagazines.org.uk/magazine/record2e6f.html?id=6381

42. Yvor Winters, 'Robert Bridges and Elizabeth Daryush', *Uncollected Essays and Reviews*, ed. & intr. Francis Murphy, Chicago: Swallow Press, 1973.

43. Donald Davie, ibid.

Louis MacNeice

44. 'Louis MacNeice: An Irish Outsider', *Journey into Joy*, my edits from 136, 137, 140, 142.

45. 'Derek Mahon's Humane Perspective', *Journey into Joy*, my edits from 128, 129.

Sylvia Plath

46. Edna Longley (ed.), *The Bloodaxe Book of 20th Century Poetry from Britain and Ireland* (Tarset: Bloodaxe Books, 2000), 247.

Denise Levertov

47. Susan J. Zevenbergen in *The Oxford Companion to Women's Writing in the United States*, ed. Cathy N. Davidson and Linda Wagner-Martin (New York: Oxford University Press, 1995).

Geoffrey Hill

48. Michael Murphy, 'Brendan's Voyage', interview in *Hot Press*, 1 February 1985.

Austin Clarke

49. 'Poetry and Violence', *Journey into Joy*, my edit from 37-38.

Michael Longley

50. Brendan Kennelly, 'Wonder and awe', review of *Gorse Fires* by Michael Longley in *Fortnight* (May 1991).

51. 'Poetry and Violence', *Journey into Joy*, my edits from 33-35.

Derek Mahon

52. Seamus Deane, in *Lifelines 4* (The Underground Press, Wesley College, Dublin, 1992; repr. Town House, Dublin, 1992).

53. Edna Longley, 'The Singing Line: Form in Derek Mahon's Poetry', *Poetry in the Wars* (Newcastle upon Tyne: Bloodaxe Books, 1986), 181-83.

54. 'Derek Mahon's Humane Perspective', *Journey into Joy*, my edits from 131, 133, 133-34.

Elizabeth Bishop

55. Megan Marshall: 'Elizabeth and Alice: The last love affair of Elizabeth Bishop, and the losses behind "One Art"', *The New Yorker*, 27 October 2016.

Philip Larkin

56. Seamus Heaney, 'Joy or Night: Last Things in the Poetry of W.B. Yeats and Philip Larkin', *Finders Keepers: Selected Prose 1971-2001* (London: Faber & Faber, 2002), 322-23

Anne Stevenson

57. Jay Parini, 'Anne Stevenson: Obituary', *The Guardian*, 18 September 2020.

58. Alfred Hickling, 'Border crossings', *The Guardian*, 2 October 2004.

Ken Smith

59. Colin Raw, 'The Godfather of the New Poetry', interview (29 December 1997) from *You Again: last poems & other words* (Bloodaxe Books, 2004).

Seamus Heaney

60. *New York Times*, 27 May 1984.

61. Dennis O'Driscoll: *Stepping Stones: interviews with Seamus Heaney* (London: Faber & Faber, 2008), 73.

ACKNOWLEDGEMENTS

The poems in this anthology are reprinted from the following books, all by permission of the publishers listed unless stated otherwise. Thanks are due to all the copyright holders cited below for their kind permission: **W.H. Auden:** *Collected Poems*, ed. Edward Mendelson (Faber, 1991), by permission of Curtis Brown, New York and Faber & Faber Ltd. **Elizabeth Bishop:** *Complete Poems 1927-1979* (Farrar, Straus and Giroux, 1983), copyright © 1979, 1983 by Alice Helen Methfessel, by permission of Farrar, Straus and Giroux, LLC. **Eavan Boland:** *New Collected Poems* (Carcanet Press, 2005). **Austin Clarke:** *Collected Poems*, ed. R. Dardis Clarke (Carcanet Press, 2008). **E.E. Cummings:** Complete Poems 1904-1962 (Liveright, 1994), by permission of W.W. Norton & Company, copyright © 1991 by the Trustees for the E.E. Cummings Trust and George James Firmage. **Elizabeth Daryush:** *Collected Poems* (Carcanet Press, 1976). **Walter de la Mare:** *The Complete Poems of Walter de la Mare* (Faber & Faber, 1973) by permission of the Literary Trustees of Walter de la Mare and the Society of Authors as their representative. **T.S. Eliot:** *The Complete Poems and Plays* (Faber & Faber, 1969). **W.S. Graham:** *New Collected Poems* (Faber & Faber, 2005), by permission of Michael and Margaret Snow. **Seamus Heaney:** *Sweeney Astray* (Faber & Faber, 1984). **Geoffrey Hill:** *Broken Hierarchies: Poems 1952-2012* (Oxford University Press, 2013). **Langston Hughes:** *The Collected Poems of Langston Hughes* (Alfred A. Knopf, Inc, 1994), by permission of David Higham Associates. **Ted Hughes:** *Collected Poems*, ed. Paul Keegan (Faber & Faber, 2003) and *Winter Pollen: Occasional Prose* (Faber & Faber, 1994). **Patrick Kavanagh:** *Selected Poems*, ed. Antoinette Quinn (Penguin, 1996), by permission of the Trustees of the Estate of the late Katherine B. Kavanagh, and through the Jonathan Williams Literary Agency. **Philip Larkin:** *Collected Poems*, ed. Anthony Thwaite (Faber & Faber, 2003). **Denise Levertov:** *New & Selected Poems* (Bloodaxe Books, 2003). **Michael Longley:** *Collected Poems* (Jonathan Cape, 2006), by permission of the Random House Group Ltd. **Louis MacNeice:** *Collected Poems*, ed. Peter McDonald (Faber, 2007), by permission of David Higham Associates Ltd. **Derek Mahon:** *New Collected Poems* (The Gallery Press, 2011). **Archibald MacLeish:** *Collected Poems 1917-1982* (Houghton Mifflin, USA, 1985). **Marianne Moore:** *The Poems of Marianne Moore*, ed. Grace Schulman (Faber & Faber, 2003). **Ruth Pitter:** *Collected Poems* (Enitharmon Press, 1990), by permission of the publisher and the Ruth Pitter Estate. **Sylvia Plath:** *Collected Poems*, ed. Ted Hughes (Faber, 1981), by permission of Faber & Faber Ltd. **Adrienne Rich:** *Collected Poems 1950-2012* (W.W. Norton and Company, 2012). **Siegfried Sassoon:** *Collected Poems* (Faber, 1984), by permission of Barbara Levy Literary Agency. **Delmore Schwartz:** *Summer Knowledge: Selected Poems* (New Directions, 1967), by permission of New Directions Publishing Corporation. **Ken Smith:** *Collected Poems* (Bloodaxe Books, 2018). **Stevie Smith:** *Collected Poems*, ed. James MacGibbon (Penguin, 1985), by permission of the James MacGibbon Estate. **Wallace Stevens:** *Collected Poems* (Faber & Faber, 1955). **Anne Stevenson:** *Poems 1955-2005* (Bloodaxe Books, 2005). **Dylan Thomas:** *Collected Poems* (J.M. Dent, 1988), by permission of David Higham Associates. **Derek Walcott:** *The Poetry of Derek Walcott, 1948-2013*, ed. Glyn Maxwell (Faber & Faber, 2014). **Sheila Wingfield:** *Collected Poems 1938-1983* (Enitharmon Press, 1983). Every effort has been made to trace copyright holders of the poems published in this book. We apologise if any material has been included without permission or without the appropriate acknowledgement, and would be glad to be told of anyone who has not been consulted.